The
Collected
Ghazals
of
Hafiz

# The Collected Ghazals of Hafiz

*With the Original Farsi Poems,*
*English Translation, Transliteration and Notes*

VOLUME ONE

JAMILUDDIN MORRIS ZAHURI
WITH MARYAM MOGHADAM

BEACON BOOKS

Published by Beacon Books and Media Ltd
Innospace
The Shed
Chester Street
Manchester
M1 5GD
UK

www.beaconbooks.net

| ISBN Volume 1 | 978-0-9954960-1-9 |
|---|---|
| ISBN Volume 2 | 978-0-9954960-2-6 |
| ISBN Volume 3 | 978-0-9954960-3-3 |
| ISBN Volume  3 | 978-0-9954960-4-0 |
| ISBN Full set | 978-0-9954960-0-2 |

A C.I.P. record for this book is available from the British Library

All artwork by the author

Cover design by Bipin Mistry

The present volume is the first of four volumes that (together with the appendix) contain the 573 poems of the entire collection of ghazals presented by Wilberforce-Clarke; of these 486 are in the main body of the four volumes and are accompanied by the original Farsi and a transliteration in 'roman' script. Some original verses by this writer are included in the introduction under the pen name *Zahuri*.

# About this book

The Khwaja Hafiz Shirazi Foundation was originated by Dr Zahurul Hasan Sharib of Ajmer (d.1996) with the publication of *'Hafiz and His Rubaiyat' (Sharib Press, Southampton, 1993)*, being translations of the quatrains in that style by Hafiz Saheb. This work is being carried forward by the present author with the intention of presenting to a wider English language audience the much more extensive ghazals. This volume is therefore the second publication, linked to the foundation, to be completed. The full ghazaliyat is to be found in three subsequent volumes.

---

This book is primarily a rendition in rhyming couplets of the collected ghazals from the Divan of Khwaja Hafiz Shirazi, from English sources, by Jamiluddin Morris Zahuri. It is edited with reference to the original Farsi by Maryam Moghhadam of Shiraz.

---

Biographical

Dr Zahurul Hassan Sharib (1914-96); born in Moradabad, India, but passed much of his later life in Ajmer, India, where his study overlooked the shrine of the great Sufi Saint Khwaja Muinuddin Hasan Chishti. He published well over 100 books in English and Urdu mostly on Sufi themes but also on rural reconstruction. He was fluent in several languages including Farsi. He led the Gudri Shahi Order of Sufis from 1973 till his demise in 1996.

---

Jamiluddin Morris Zahuri; born in Hastings, Sussex, England, in 1946. He was trained in the Sufi tradition of the Chishti Order for over twenty years, from 1976, by Dr Sharib. He later received the benefit of the company of Hazrat Nuri Baba of Konya and still regularly visits the shrines of Khwaja Muinuddin Hasan Chishti in Ajmer and Mevlana Jalaluddin Rumi in Konya.

Originally trained in fine art, Jamil has lived in Southampton, England for the past 30 years with his Indian wife Farhana. He is the founder of Sharib Press, which has produced a dozen books on Islamic Mysticism and Qur'an Commentary. He has provided the design and art work for the present volume.

Now retired from practice as a therapist he writes poetry with a mystical theme and guides a number of followers on the Sufi path. Since 1998 he has run the Zahuri Sufi Website for which he has written many articles and poems. (zahuri.org)

---

Maryam Moghadam (born 1982) is a native of Shiraz and a teacher of English there. She is a devotee of Hafiz Saheb and a regular visitor to the Hafizya where Hafiz Saheb's mortal remains are interred. Her home overlooks the shrine of Baba Kuhi. She is also a regular visitor to Mevlana Rumi's shrine in Konya, Turkey. She holds weekly Masnevi sessions in her home.

# Contents

Tomb of Hafiz in Shiraz, Iran

# Acknowledgements

The initial and continuing inspiration for undertaking this work derives from our beloved guide, Dr Zahurul Hassan Sharib Gudri Shah Baba (1914-96) of Ajmer, India. He has translated all the Rubaiyat of Hafiz direct from Farsi and written an excellent short introduction to what little is known about the life of Hafiz (The Rubaiyat of Hafiz; Sharib Press; Southampton 1993). In essence, anything of value in this present work can be rightly attributed to his influence and enthusiasm for Hafiz. Our special thanks go to the successor of Dr Zahurul Hassan Sharib, Hazrat Inam Hasan Gudri Shah Baba, for honouring us with a short foreword and thus giving our work his kind blessings.

Most importantly, I can never overstate the debt to my dear wife Farhana for her loving support whilst this work was in preparation, along with insightful comments from her knowledge of Urdu and Farsi poetry. Discussions with her on various aspects of Hafiz's verses greatly helped at the commencement of the work. May Hafiz reward her as she deserves.

In the timely fashion of the Saints, (that some will see as coincidence), we were given great help by some Iranian enthusiasts for Hafiz we happened to meet at the 'Urs of Mevlana Jalaluddin Rumi in Konya, shortly after we started the work.

Chiefly, of course, we cannot thank enough Maryam Moghadam from Shiraz for her patient labour in providing the transliterations and re-typing the original Farsi text, and particularly for her painstaking and detailed advice with regard to the original Farsi sources. This has been an essential contribution to the project. May the blessings of Hafiz Saheb descend on her for the many, many, many hours of tireless and enthusiastic work, almost daily over more than three years, that she has put into producing the final version of this book. We must also mention those who helped in proof reading the Farsi. Yasmin Arjomand of Kirman, Iran, gave many hours of unstinting labour, in this respect along with Mariya Javanmardi, Samira Shafiee, Fateme Karimi, Zahra Siroos, Saeede Sourghalik, Fateme Mehrjoo and Shahrbanoo Karimi.

Maryam Nazari, Mikail Ali Clarke, Riaz Sharif and Bahar Tadikonda all deserve my gratitude for their practical or moral support. May Hafiz Saheb reward them all suitably. We are indebted also to Mohammed Siraj of Holland for his helpful comments at the outset of the work.

The main translations we have used as the basis of our renditions are the works of H. Wilberforce-Clarke (Octagon Press 1974), Peter Avery (Archetype 2007) and Reza Saberi (UPA 2002), and at times, Paul Smith (New Humanity Books 1986). In addition we have referred to other translators such as Squires, Bicknell, Bell, and Alston. We are indebted to all these translators.

The main Farsi sources accessed by Maryam Moghadam to aid with translation were:

1) *Divani Hafez,* volume 1, with emendation and notes of Parviz Natel Khanlari, third published version (n.d.) (the second version's publication is 1983), Kharazmi Publication Company.

2) *Hafez be sa"ye saaye,* with emendation of Amir Hooshang Ebtehaj, Tehran, Karnaame publication company, 1994, ISBN 978-964-431-008-9.

No one is ever likely to claim to make a perfect presentation of Hafiz's wonderfully intricate and extraordinarily profound ghazals in another language. The faults in our presentation of these great masterpieces are our responsibility alone. For this we ask the forgiveness of Hafiz Saheb and the patient understanding of the reader.

*Jamiluddin Morris Zahuri*

*Southampton October 2016.*

# Technical Notes

This presentation of Hafiz's Divan does not pretend to be a work of scholarship in any sense, but is intended for the general reader with a genuine interest in mysticism and mystical poetry.

In Farsi it is possible to refer to the beloved without using a gender specific personal pronoun. We have avoided therefore the use of 'he' or 'she' in English unless it is clear it is only a man or woman being referred to. Both in Farsi and English it is possible to take any number of varying meanings from the verses.

We have not used capital letters to denote the 'beloved' or the 'friend' or 'you' or 'yours' as this would imply that the Divinity alone was being referred to and the ambiguity we believe to be important would be lost. Hafiz uses terms like 'beloved' or 'heart' in different ways even within the same ghazal. We did not use the older forms, 'Thou' or 'Thine' for reasons of modernity.

The individual verses included in various editions of the Divan in Farsi vary. In some cases we could not locate particular lines translated by Mr Wilberforce-Clarke (Octagon Press) and we have placed these in the appendix.

The numbering of the ghazals broadly follows Wilberforce-Clarke. Some ghazals are placed only in the appendix due to unavailability of Farsi texts in the modern Farsi editions. In some cases it is just because the verses seem of doubtful authenticity on grounds of style or content.

The Farsi used here we understand to be that used in present day Iran. We have referred to several Farsi sources but mostly that of Khanlari and our ordering of the individual verses in most ghazals follow his order, which is also used by Avery and Saberi.

We have placed footnotes in a separate commentary section. The glossary provides information on terms that might not be initially understood by those unfamiliar with this genre of poetry or with Islamic or Sufi references.

# Foreword

by Hazrat Inam Hasan Gudri Shah Baba

History bears evidence that Iran, erstwhile Persia, is well known around the world for its etiquette and culture.

Firdausi's *Shahnama*, Omar Khayyam's *Rubaiyat*, Sheikh Sadi's *Gulistan* and *Bustan* and Hafiz Shirazi's *Divan-i-Hafiz* are well liked, well known, well read and well heard of the world over due to their popularity and acceptance.

*Shahnama* charts the map of how *Mehfil* should be conducted and Khayyam's Rubaiyat is an archive of freethinking; Sadi's *Gulistan* and *Bustan* lays out the code of ethics and morality. In Hafiz's poetry we find divine inspiration and for this reason, *Divan-i-Hafiz* is viewed with great respect.

The sweetness of love is ingrained in the *Divan* and thus it is replete with mystical knowledge. It is also predictive of the future and is as such, considered a book of revelations. Today, one can find a copy of the *Divan* kept safely and respectfully in the library of almost every Sufi khanqah. The saints of the Gudri Shahi order always kept a copy of *Divan-i-Hafiz* with them and would benefit from its study from time to time.

In Persian poetry Hafiz's *Saqi-Nama* is matchless and incomparable. Hafiz has not only established as his own forte the lyrical poetic form of the *ghazal*, but he has also tried his hand masterfully at many other forms and styles like *makhmas, musaddis, Qata, masnavi, qasida, takeeb-band, tarjeh-band* and *rubaiyat*.

Jamil Uddin Morris Zahuri, who is a dear and close disciple of Dr. Zahurul Hassan Sharib, Gudri Shah Baba, has spent a long time studying the works of Hazrat Shamsuddin Hafiz Shirazi and with this rendition of the book into English, he has done a great favour to the readers of the English language. The rendition is very close to the authentic text and is in a simple and lucid style, which has further embellished the work and made it as likeable as is the original masterpiece.

Hazrat Inaam Hasan Gudri Shaha Baba  (Ajmer, India)

# Preface

*Scaling Mount Hafiz*

*When we were invited to climb this mountain, called 'impossible',*
*We found a love that made those rough, tough, tracts passable.*

*It seemed the mountain itself smiled, or so it seemed to me;*
*Or was it just drunk and happy to see our mad impetuosity!*

*Or maybe it just enjoyed the fact we had no kit with which to climb;*
*Only the gift of happy words, happy thoughts, and happy rhyme;*

*No pick to tickle that august mountain with, nor ropes to strangle it,*
*And soft boots, made of gratitude, which leave no rough print on it.*

*A wise and wonderful friend told me, 'The difficult is easy,*
*But the impossible takes a little longer' - how wise was he.*

*So in hope that the mountain's smile augers well for our trial,*
*We will continue, with God's help, to try to go the extra mile.*

*Zahuri*

The purpose of this presentation of Hafiz's poetry is to convey to today's English-knowing reader a flavour of the mystical qualities of his collected Ghazals (lyrical poems). What Hafiz refers to in the verses in this book are mystical states, stations and intuitions that are as available to the mystics of today as they were to Hafiz Saheb in his lifetime. To turn these mystical insights into an approachable form of rhyming verse in modern English we have cast our reliance primarily on the universal and continuing presence of Hafiz Saheb himself; living, as he still is, behind the veil of normal perception. This statement alone should establish our approach as essentially mystical rather than literary, historic, scholarly, or artistic. *'The heart that is alive with love, never dies'* Hafiz Saheb says, and we take this to be a simple statement of truth that applies to Hafiz himself.

That the wonderful words of the holy Qur'an can be sensed concealed beneath the courtly language of love and profligacy can hardly be surprising, given that Hafiz had clearly memorised the holy book by heart rather than by rote. This is evidenced in the quality of spiritual insight he demonstrates. The holy Qur'an is a manifestation of universal truth. The one who is truly imbued with its deeper implications cannot but speak of the same truth, though his language and style may be suited to a particular and a different time and circumstance. The 'mirror-like' quality, which is one aspect of the holy book, can be discerned in Hafiz's verses. The person who approaches it in a suitably respectful and insightful manner finds his or her own unconscious situation revealed.

In 'The Conference of the Birds' by Khwaja Fariduddin Attar, the birds who set out to reach the seat of the King of Birds (Divinity) discovers there, eventually, a mirror in which they see their own inner nature. All the translations we have come across seem to us to have actually presented the translator as much as Hafiz himself

Included is a transliteration of the verses into 'roman' script so that the person who does not know the original Farsi script can nevertheless *recite* the poems. The modern Farsi pronunciation is used rather than that used at the time of Hafiz Saheb. Recitation, irrespective of the meaning-content, carries a power of its own. We have not come across any publication that has done this before, and hope it will therefore be a distinct and unique contribution to the work of promoting awareness of the majestic mysticism of Hafiz in the English language world.

The musically-oriented traditional ghazal form does not pass easily into English poetry and we have generally, but with a number of exceptions, not attempted to capture it. Instead we have mostly used an archaic form of simple rhyming couplets, (as found for example in the Masnevi of Mevlana Rumi). We have also tried to avoid using Hafiz's verses as a mere springboard for any poetic inclinations we may have, or as a way of expressing some philosophy of our own. In short we have aspired only to making the mirror as clear as we can for the English reader. We have, so to speak, done our best to fit out Hafiz's 'beauty queens' (his verses), in practical, albeit far less elegant, apparel suited for the present day English speaking world.

Our earnest hope is that Hafiz Saheb accepts our little labours. If so the understanding reader may find, through his blessings, access to rare and perfect pearls beyond price.

*To be daily drunk on divine love, and in ecstasy,*
*In the tavern of Hafiz, the pearl of Shiraz, try to be.*

*To get light from sublime poetry, that purifies purity,*
*Or the key to unlock the door of your own destiny;*

*Beyond the seven heavens you will need to journey,*
*To where beauty dances daily in patterns of harmony.*

*Become nothing but just a silent empty wine cup,*
*That the generous Master, Hafiz, you pray, will fill up.*

*Zahuri*

Jamiluddin Morris Zahuri
Southampton, October 2016.

# Introduction

*This introduction is based partly on the introduction to the book 'Hafiz and His Rubaiyat' by Dr Zahurul Hassan Sharib (1914-96).*

We have chosen to ignore scholarly concerns or controversy in favour of presenting the reader who is new to this field with a brief outline of popularly accepted accounts of Hafiz Saheb's life. Dr Sharib was a practising Sufi master in the Qadri/Chishti tradition and this presentation of his introduction can be expected to provide the historical 'narrative' as understood by many modern Sufis. This in itself has a value irrespective of so-called historical fact. Sources for the material were not indicated by Dr Sharib.

Hafiz is the *takhallus* or 'nom-de-plume' of Khwaja Shemsuddin Muhammed-i-Hafiz Shirazi. 'Hafiz' means one who guards or preserves the holy Qur'an by committing it to memory. Hafiz Saheb himself says he was familiar with as many as fourteen different modes of Qur'an recital. This may mean he was able to recite it using different forms of 'qirat' – the melodious chanting forms in which the holy book is recited out loud. It may also mean he had insight into the many layers of meaning hidden in the holy book.

In the literature of the Muslim world this *takhallus* was usually built into to the last lines of a poem as is mostly the case with Hafiz himself.

'*Khwaja*', (also spelt Khawaja and Hoja) like 'Saheb' (Sahib) indicates a respected elder, though it can sometimes be used ironically.

## The Life of Hafiz

It is generally agreed that Hafiz was born in Shiraz, the capital city of Fars, a region in the south of modern day Iran, between 1320 AD and 1342 AD. He died 1389/90 AD. He remained in Shiraz, which was famed for its beauty and culture, for most of his life.

*If you love beauty, you mean you love the heart of Fars - that's Shiraz,*
*If you love that sweet city you mean of course you love Hafiz of Shiraz;*
*If the poetry of love on you casts a spell; that's the magic he weaves,*
*That doyen of intoxicated lovers, the eternal Saki, Hafiz of Shiraz.*

*Zahuri*

Hafiz came from a middle class family with a strong interest in spirituality and fond of learning and culture. His grandfather came from Sarkan, a small town near Isfahan, from whence he migrated to Shiraz. His father Bahauddin, a merchant, died before Hafiz reached his majority. This left the family in poor economic circumstances. Hafiz's two brothers were forced to seek employment elsewhere, leaving Hafiz to look after his mother. She appears to have been an important and beneficial influence, encouraging Hafiz to learn patience and contentment in difficult times.

Finally Hafiz was put in to service, to work for a cruel and difficult man, but after enduring this for some time he took up employment in a bakery. Near the bakery was a school, providing an Islamic education. This he was able to attend. It is often said that he gave one third of his income to his mother, one third to the school, and the remainder to charity.

During this time he committed the holy Qur'an to memory and thus earned the widely respected title of 'Hafiz' (Hafez). Later he studied under a learned theologian called Maulana Shemsuddin Muhammed Abdullah of Shiraz. From him he learned Tafsir (Qur'an commentary). Hafiz gained from him the name Shemsuddin (Shamsuddin).

From Syed Sharif Jargani he learned about metaphysics, Hadith (customs and sayings of the holy prophet Muhammad), and other traditional sciences. He became extremely proficient in Arabic and in the Persian literature of the time. He began to acquire some fame as a man of learning. He spent his working life as a teacher in a school owned by Hajji Qayyamuddin Taghahi, a minister of Abu Ishaq, the then ruler of Shiraz.

There are various opinions as to whether Hafiz Saheb was ever formally initiated into a Sufi order, but Dr Sharib says it appears he was the disciple of one of the perfect saints called Mahmud Attar. He acknowledges, however, that it has also been said Hafiz may have been directly inspired by the holy Prophet himself.

Hafiz married and had children. He wrote touching heartfelt verses grieving for the death of his wife, and also his son.

During his lifetime Hafiz saw the rise and fall of seven rulers. The political atmosphere of the time was difficult in the extreme, with multiple opposing factions in the royal court creating great uncertainty; and external political and military forces that added immensely to the general atmosphere of instability. Political assassinations were the order of the day rather than the exception.

As previously mentioned Hafiz had the respect of Hajji Qayyamuddin Taghahi who entrusted his school to Hafiz Saheb. Under Shah Shuja Hafiz gained the patronage of a minister called Khwaja Qayam who was later murdered. He found another admirer in Jalaluddin Turan Shah another of Shah Shuja's ministers.

Tamerlane was the most powerful ruler in the Islamic world of his time, conquering great swathes of territory from India to Syria. He was also a man with an interest in culture. He had heard of Hafiz's fame and upon conquering Shiraz sent for him. When Hafiz arrived at court Tamerlane caused one of the lines Hafiz had written to be recited;

> *If that Turk, the beauty of Shiraz, would take my heart in hand,*
>
> *For that one's dark mole I will give up Bokhara and Samarqand.*

Upon Hafiz confirming the line as his, Tamerlane ordered one of his courtiers to get ten thousand dinars from Hafiz. Hafiz smiled and said that he had not such an amount of money. Tamerlane then turned to Hafiz and said;

"We have devastated hundreds of cities for the purpose of acquiring these cities as our own, yet for a single mole you are ready to give them up. Now, when we ask for a paltry sum of money like this, you say you do not have it!"

Hafiz replied: "It is due to this and similar prodigality I have been placed in such a deplorable condition." Upon hearing this reply Tamerlane presented gifts to Hafiz.

Hafiz fame as a poet spread far and wide during his own lifetime. In an age and culture that held poetry in great esteem Hafiz became widely accepted as the perfect poet, both within and far beyond the boundaries of Persia.

He received various invitations from rulers from many countries but he rarely left his beloved Shiraz. He did, however, almost travel to the Deccan in India at the invitation of its ruler Sultan Shah Mahmud. Reaching Hormuz, with the intention of boarding a boat for the Deccan, Hafiz was apparently deterred from going by witnessing a violent storm.

## Hafiz: the Poet and the Saint

Hafiz's interest in poetry comes from his childhood. At the time of his birth the great poet Sheikh Saadi was the pre-eminent poet-philosopher of Shiraz and Hafiz must have felt his influence strongly in those formative years. As it happened he had an uncle of the same name, Saadi, and he was also a poet. One day his uncle had gone out before he could complete a certain poem. Hafiz took up the paper and completed the poem. On his return the uncle was surprised to see the verse completed, and on discovering it was the work of Hafiz became immensely pleased and got him to complete the entire poem. Upon reading it he made a prophecy that whoever read Hafiz's poetry would become intoxicated and absorbed, an effect Dr Sharib attests to even today.

To begin with Hafiz's poems lacked structure and even the necessary sublime thought. People did not appreciate them and would in fact ridicule them. Nevertheless Hafiz continued.

The turning point came when, from suffering so much criticism, Hafiz became despondent. He sought refuge at the shrine of Baba Kohi, a renowned Sufi saint whose tomb exists in Shiraz to this day. That night a dream came to him of a holy person putting some morsel of food in his mouth. That personage informed him that he need not be distressed and that the gate of Divine Knowledge had been opened to him. On inquiry he learned that he had been addressed by none other than Hazrat Ali, the fountainhead of the Sufis and known by them as the keeper of the Gate of Divine Knowledge.

On waking Hafiz found he was full of inner peace and joy. He had realised a deep power within that was to affect his life and his poetic ability deeply. The same day he completed a poem that described his experience. From that time onward his poems had a dimension to them that amazed the poetic aficionados of Shiraz – and were destined to astound the world of letters.

It is our view that Dr Sharib held Hafiz to be a saint-poet rather than a poet-saint. The respect Hafiz is held in, even in present day Iran where he remains household name, may have more to do with his poetry as high art or with its power of prognostication, but I suspect that, as always, with Hafiz there is an ambiguity: seek fine art in Hafiz – you find it; seek the spirituality of a saint - you find it; seek a prognostication - you find it. This can only come from inspiration that is of an entirely different order of magnitude from the flow of ideas we usually mean when speaking of inspiration.

*From the blessings of Hafiz, poetry gained sanctity,*
*His sainthood he did not get from writing poetry.*

*Those enchanted and enchanting images and rhymes,*
*But for Hafiz's perfect purity could be mere idolatry.*

*Ah, it's so easy to get caught by culture's hook,*
*But those succeed best who for another bait look.*
*Gain the ruby of a loving heart and pure white soul;*
*Find the source of all art, the Mother of the Book.*

*More than all the beauty of a good book,*
*Is found in your one, long, lingering, love-look.*
*The Mother of the book was seen in your heart,*
*When away the veil of indifference you took.*


*Zahuri*


## The Divan as Oracle

The Divan of Hafiz enjoys an extraordinary reputation as a means of prognostication (known as *'Fal'*) – both amongst sophisticated literary-minded people and 'the man in the street'. It has been used for centuries by people wishing to determine a course of action when uncertain. Hafiz Saheb is called the *'Lisan-ul-Ghaib'*; or 'Tongue of the Unseen', and *'Tarjuman-i-Israr'*; the Interpreter of Hidden Secrets. *'Fal'* implies framing a question and then opening the book, with or without ritual, and reading the verse or verses that present themselves to the reader.

The future Moghul Emperor of India, Jehangir, for example, opened the book and took counsel from the passage that it presented to him, when, as Prince Salim, he needed to decide if he should return to meet his father, the Emperor Akbar. At the time he was living apart from Akbar in a distant city and the politics of the court were complex and risky. The verses he found are given here:

*Why not think about going back to my own country,*
*Why not as dust at the feet of the friend prepare to be.*

*When the arrows of adversity and sorrow I cannot bear,*
*To my own country I go and the crown of king I wear.*

*I may become the confidant of the people of the canopy,*
*Amongst my master's slaves counted as one I may be.*

*It is better when there is no certainty about breath,*
*To be in the presence of the beloved on the day of death.*

*Of my dormant fortune and resource less working,*
*I complain; then my own secret I will be keeping.*

*Reckless loving has always been my profession,*
*Now I will seek to practise my chosen vocation.*

*Hafiz, perhaps the grace of God your guide will be,*
*If not, endless, surely this shame of yours will be.*

Upon receipt of this guidance, which fitted his situation perfectly, Prince Salim departed for the court of his father Akbar, was received warmly and appointed as successor. Akbar died shortly thereafter and he ascended the throne as Emperor Jahangir.

When Hafiz Saheb passed on there was apparently disagreement as to how he should be buried. Many of the orthodox Muslims objected to the content of his poems with their emphasis on love and drinking wine; references to human beauty; and his dislike of the hypocrisy of both the so-called pious (Zahids) and the so-called Sufis alike. People raised objection to his being buried as a Muslim. To resolve the conflict it was agreed they would use his Divan. The many poems were divided into separate verses and placed in a container. A young child was asked to pull one out at random. The verse that was pulled out is the last verse of ghazal number (W-C 60) in this edition.

*O from the shrouded corpse of Hafiz, pray do not walk away,*

*For all the sin he is wrapped in, yet he goes to paradise this day.*

To general agreement he was formally buried in the Islamic way as a Muslim.

## Hafiz, the Man

Based on his reading of Hafiz's poetry Dr Sharib has described Hafiz as a man who led a chaste and simple life and who enjoyed the wealth of contentment, showing remarkable patience at times of difficulty. From his poetry it is possible to deduce that he had involvement with the royal courts at various periods of his life. He emphasised the importance of service to Dervishes and unflinching love for the spiritual guide but hated hypocrisy in its various guises. His constant preoccupation was with the love of God. He faced opposition from many of a conservative and orthodox frame of mind but remained resolute against all odds. Amongst the issues that created dislike or even hatred from the orthodox were the references to wine drinking, music and human beloveds and profligacy.

The words of Khwaja Muinuddin Hasan Chishti clarify the mystic's understanding of wine: "The real wine in a clear heart is the sign and symbol of moving about in Allah, and refers to the virtues and qualities and to the way of life to be moulded according to the attributes of Allah. "[1]

With regard to love focussed on a human beloved, in his book *The Culture of the Sufis* Dr Sharib says;"Love is of two kinds, one is *Haqiqi* (real) love, and the other is *Majazi* (non-real love). *Haqiqi* love means and implies to love Allah with all His attributes and actions. The *majazi* love is of two kinds. The one is *nafsani* (pertaining to the self) and the other is *haywani* (relating to the brute in man). The former emphasises the identity and similarity in the self of the lover and the beloved. The latter emphasises sex and physical pleasure. To the Sufis this is lust pure and simple. In some cases the *majazi* love is a stepping stone to the end. The end being the attainment of the love of Allah..."

With regard to Hafiz's relation to love and wine Dr Sharib says; "In love, as in wine, one forgets one's own self... but in wine the intoxication is temporary, whereas silent and sincere love confers tranquillity, peace and concentration. Its intoxication is never diminished. Its end is its beginning and its beginning is its end. Such being the effect of non-real love what can be said of Real love. The wine of Hafiz is love, earthly or divine, real and none-real. The love of two women, one named Shak-i-Nabat and the other Farrukh, served as an aid and a stimulant to Hafiz to be lost in the love of God."

Though Dr Sharib does not discuss it, the use of music, poetry or art to stimulate spiritual effort may be considered in a similar way. It remains even today a point of disagreement between the orthodox Muslims and those inclined to the Sufi way.

*The essence of poetry must be this,*
*For us to taste the fine flavour of bliss:*
*This is what Hafiz meant by a kiss,*
*Or is this something your mind did miss?*

*The description of a fair one's charms,*
*Or of holding the beloved in one's arms,*

*Is intimacy with the divine ecstasy,*
*This all must clearly and surely see!*

*Though far beyond gender is this mystery,*
*A delicate heart by romance enlivened may be.*
*But for the gross mind, reading it mistakenly,*
*A poison it could surely turn out to be.*

*That there is a deeper secret, we are aware,*
*But with strangers this we do not seek to share;*
*And if inquisitively you should seek to guess,*
*'No step without a guide' says sublime Hafez.*

*Zahuri*

The term 'beloved' is used in many different ways, sometimes even within one ghazal. The 'heart' too may stand for many things - it can for example be a newborn child. "*Today I gave my heart away,*" (W-C 39) could refer to love for someone or for God but can also refer to a mother delivering a new born child. The term 'Saki' can also be understood in various ways. The Saki is traditionally a young boy who would serve wine at a party, but it can also be the spiritual guide who gives inspiration. Hazrat Abdul Qadir al-Jillani[2] mentions the holy Prophet saying –"I have seen my Lord in the shape of a most beautiful youth." He goes on to say: "As Allah is beyond all shape and form .... it is interpreted as the manifestation of the Lord's beautiful attributes reflected on the mirror of the pure soul.....this is called the child of the heart..... this reflected image is also a connection between the servant and his Lord."

The waist "*slender as a hair*" may be dismissed as a conventional poetic device by some, but actually can carry the connotation of "*Pul Sirat*", the extremely narrow bridge to paradise. It can also be a reference to the umbilical cord (Ghazal 35). The tall upright cypress may at times represent the erect posture of the mystic sitting in meditation as well as moral rectitude. The 'breeze' of dawn (Sabaa) can refer to mystical intuitions often received after Fajr prayers[3] or to the 'Breath of Mercy' (Nafas ar-Rehman) mentioned in Hadiths, or to the flow of spiritual energy that moves the mystic to dance.

## Hafiz Amongst the Stars

Hafiz is described by Dr Sharib as a poet of rare individuality who never dressed in the clothes of others. He says; "His rubaiyat, odes and sonnets are undoubtedly his own; expressing his inner feelings and his personal vision of the situation in which religion and mysticism were placed in his own lifetime.

Amongst near contemporaries one can look at Sheykh Saadi for his emphasis on a high moral tone with little of the mystical depth of Hafiz.

Fariduddin Attar made wide use of stories and wrote in a style 'characterised by lucidity and sweet idealism'. Mevlana Jalaluddin Rumi, author of the Masnevi, interwove high moral thinking and cautionary tales into fervent idealism and passionate love."

Dr Sharib describes Hazrat Jami as, aiming "to soothe and uplift the human soul." Hazrat Sarmad's works he says are full of pessimism and submissive sadness about the ways of the world.

About Omar Khayyam and Hafiz Dr Sharib says: "They resemble each other in as much as they were both persecuted and ridiculed, both hated hypocrisy, both denounced bigotry, orthodoxy and narrow mindedness... however whilst Omar Khayam is a philosopher and thinker, Hafiz is a mystic and a Sufi... to Omar Khayam mysticism is a way of escape; to Hafiz it is a way of life... to Khayam pleasure is the end (aim) of life, to Hafiz pleasure is a means to an end – the end being devotion to and service of the Beloved"

I have not found any better or more comprehensive summary of this great soul whose message is universal, true, and far beyond the reach of the analysis of his poetry as art.

## Conclusion

Emerson once wrote of Hafiz, "....such is the only man I wish to see or be;" and in doing so demonstrated his own insight. Goethe said, "Hafiz has no peer."

In Hafiz's poetry we find our own deeper nature for good or ill staring back at us. This is not on account of catering for all tastes, as it were – quite the reverse. Hafiz carries us into the Divine nature itself and that Nature has an incomprehensible ability to both absorb and reflect whatever approaches.

His poetry is a unique and invaluable combination of high art and direct mystical knowledge. It is an effective antidote to phony mystification, intellectual arrogance, and narrow minded orthodoxy.

Sufis tend to speak the 'language' of the culture they inhabit, not just in a linguistic sense. The Persian courtly culture of Hafiz's time was greatly enamoured of beauty, romance, passion, elegance, wit and grace; thus Hafiz spoke in that 'language' but beneath the cultural references Hafiz spoke the universal language of spiritual love, just as the message of the Qur'an was universal in application and not restricted to Arabs.

The poems of Hafiz can be used as a meditation, the various lines refer to inward states of various kinds and one can read them over and over until a deeper level of meaning presents itself.

To reach to the heart of Hafiz is not a journey that is without risk, and the seeker should be guided, but it is a destination that it is not possible to value sufficiently. If we say he is a living, palpable presence amongst the great souls who live forever, we do not mean this is some vague sense of living on only in his words or images; but that from the unseen he tangibly interacts with the physical world around us, as all the true saints do.

> *The spring of Shiraz Hafiz sends to the door,*
> *Of one like me, who in heart is one of the poor.*
> *His words bring sunshine, wine, and roses too,*
> *All the while my head is placed on his holy floor.*

*Zahuri*

[1] The Meditations of Khwaja Muinuddin Hasan Chishti (see bibliography under Sharib).

[2] "The Secret of Secrets" Hazrat Abdul Qadir al-Jillani (trans; Sheykh Tosun-al-Halveti (p 199; MMDI India))

[3] Khwaja Gharib Nawaz says; "one who (continues) to sit on the prayer carpet after dawn prayers, ...and (prays) after the sunrise will be admitted to heaven and if there are seventy people with him they will all find the gates of heaven open to them. (Khwaja Gharib Nawaz; Z. H. Sharib; Ahsraf Publications, India. 1991)

O server of love-wine, pass round and be offering the cup,
In the first place love looked easy, but problems came up,

In the hope the breeze might open a musk pod of that hair knot,
Lover's hearts, from that curl of hair, so much blood have got.

Colour the prayer mat with wine, if the Magian Pir[1] tells you to,
For knowledge he has of the Way and what you need to do.

At the beloved's sojourn, what ease or pleasure is there for me?
Momently the camel's bell[2] says, "Pack up your things, be ready!"

Fearful indeed is the wave and whirlpool in that dark night;
Those lightly burdened shore-huggers know what of our plight?

By doing things for my fulfilment, only notoriety I got;
What can remain secret when gatherings talk such a lot.

Hafiz, if 'presence' you want, from the beloved don't be absent,
When you get your desire, on its way the world should be sent.

---

[1]  "...Magian Pir..." See glossary at the end of this volume. Here it probably can be taken to mean the spiritual guide.
[2]  "...the camel's bell..." This is an indication the caravan is due to depart.

Allaa yaa ayyohas saaghi ader ka-san vanaa velhaa
Ke eshgh aasaan nomood avval vali oftaad moshkelhaa

الا يا ايّها السّاقي ادر كاسا و ناولها
كه عشق آسان نمود اوّل ولي افتاد مشكلها

Be booye naafe ei kaakher sabaa zaan torre bogshaayad
Ze taabe zolfe moshkinash che khoon oftaad dar delhaa

به بوي نافه اي كآخر صبا زان طرّه بگشايد
ز تاب زلف مشكينش چه خون افتاد در دلها

Bemey saajjade rangin kon garat pire moghaan gooyad
Ke saalek bi khabar nabvad ze raaho rasme manzelhaa

به مي سجّاده رنگين كن گرت پير مغان گويد
كه سالك بي خبر نبود ز راه و رسم منزلها

Maraa dar manzele jaanaan che amne eysh chon hardam
Jaras faryaad midaarad ke bar bandid mahmelhaa

مرا در منزل جانان چه امن عيش چون هر دم
جرس فرياد مي دارد كه بربنديد محملها

Shabe taariko bime mowjo gerdaabi chonin haael
Kojaa daanand haale maa sabokbaaraane saahelhaa

شب تاريك و بيم موج و گردابي چنين هائل
كجا دانند حال ما سبكباران ساحلها

Hame kaaram ze khod kaami be bad naami keshid aari
Nahaan key maanad aan raazi kaz aan saazand mahfelhaa

همه كارم ز خود كامي به بدنامي كشيد آري
نهان كي ماند آن رازي كزآن سازند محفلها

Hozoori gar hami khahi azou ghaayeb masho Hafez
Mataa maa talgha man tahvaa daeddonyaa va ahmelhaa

حضوري گر همي خواهي از او غايب مشو حافظ
متي ما تلق من تهوي دع الدّنيا و اهملها

From your face's light the moon's beauty shines true,
From the dimple in your chin beauty gets all its virtue.

O Lord, when will our ever-present desire attain to its realisation,
And in our gathered heart[1] be your hair's scattered profusion?

My life has reached my lip on its way out, but wants to see you;
Should it go out or stay in? I need you to say what I should do.

Draw back your robe from our dust and blood, when you pass by,
For there are many victims sacrificed to you, that on this way lie.

My heart is engaged in wrecking; better let its owner know,
Truly my friends, by my soul and yours, I tell you it is so.

From the revolving of your narcissus-eye[2] no one got an easy ride,
No point to sell concealment, those drunk on you cannot hide.

Our sleepy fortune may become more eager and alert, I daresay,
Because a drop, from your glistening cheek, into its eye did stray.

Along with the breeze send me, from your cheek, roses in a posy,
Your fragrance, from the rose-garden's dust, may then come to me.

Wine servers of the feast of Jam - long life and what you wish for, to you,
What though our cup is not filled with wine, as your rounds you do!

Hafiz makes a short prayer; hear it, and say, 'So may it be!"
"Let your sugar-sprinkling lip our daily food portion be."

O breeze, to the people of Yazd[4] convey our message with verve;
May truth deniers' heads[4] be the balls in your chaugan's[5] curve.

We may not be near but on the plain of nearness is our ardour,
The slave of your king we are, so we also praise your splendour.

O king of kings and star on high, for God's sake, a boon;
So this star may kiss the dust of your heavenly palace soon.

**(W-C 2) The radif here is "Yours".**

[1] "...gathered hearts..." The gathering of diversity into unity within the heart is a meditation of the Sufis.
[2] "...narcissus-eye..." The Narcissus flower with its golden/orange cup surrounded by the white petals can appear to be like an eye. Here it may be signifying the perception of God as W-C suggests.
[3] "...Yazd..." This is city to which Hafiz may have wished to go in order to gain some favour from the ruler (See Avery pp. 37). At another level this may stand for people of the Unseen dimension. Hafiz, as ever, finds the divine in the mundane. Here there is a political context i.e. Hafiz's relation with kings and princes. External life events, however, are divinely inspired Hafiz shows us how to seek their inner implication.
[4] "...truth deniers heads..." At the political level Hafiz may be talking about some people of Shiraz who were antagonistic to him.
[5] "...chaugan's curve..." See glossary at the end of this volume.

Ey forooghe maahe hosn az rooye rakhshaane shomaa
Aaberooye khoobi az chaahe zanakhdaane shomaa

ای فروغ ماه حسن از روی رخشان شما
آب روی خوبی از چاه زنخدان شما

Key dahad dast in gharaz yaarab ke hamdastaan shavand
Khaatere majmooe maa zolfe parishaane shomaa

کی دهد دست این غرض یا رب که همدستان شوند
خاطر مجموع ما زلف پریشان شما

Azme didaare to darad jaane bar lab aamade
Baaz gardad yaa bar aayad chist farmaane shomaa

عزم دیدار تو دارد جان بر لب آمده
بازگردد یا برآید چیست فرمان شما

Door daar az khaako khoon daaman cho bar maa bogzari
Kandarin rah koshte besyaarand ghorbaane shomaa

دور دار از خاک و خون دامن چو بر ما بگذری
کاندر این ره کشته بسیارند قربان شما

Del kharaabi mikonad deldaar raa aagah konid
Zinahar ey doostaan jaane mano jaane shomaa

دل خرابی می‌کند دلدار را آگه کنید
زینهار ای دوستان جان من و جان شما

Kas be dovre nargesat tarfi nabast az aafiyat
Beh ke nafrooshand mastoori be mastaane shomaa

کس به دور نرگست طرفی نبست از عافیت
به که نفروشند مستوری به مستان شما

Bakhte khaab aaloode maa bidaar khaahad shod magar
Zaanke zad bar dide aabe rooye rakhshaane shomaa

بخت خواب آلود ما بیدار خواهد شد مگر
زان که زد بر دیده آب روی رخشان شما

Baa sabaa hamraah befrest az rokhat goldastei
Boo ke booee beshnavam az khaake bostaane shomaa

با صبا همراه بفرست از رخت گلدسته‌ای
بو که بوئی بشنوم از خاک بستان شما

Omretaan baad o moraad ey saaghiaane bazme jam
Garche jaame maa nashod por mey be dovraane shomaa

عمرتان باد و مراد ای ساقیان بزم جم
گر چه جام ما نشد پر می به دوران شما

Mikonad Hafez doaaee beshno aamini begoo
Rooziye maa baad la-le shekkar afshaane shomaa

می‌کند حافظ دعائی بشنو آمینی بگو
روزی ما باد لعل شکرافشان شما

Ey saba baa saakenaane shahre yazd az maa begoo
Key sare hagh naashenaasaan gooye chovgaane shomaa

ای صبا با ساکنان شهر یزد از ما بگو
کای سر حق ناشناسان گوی چوگان شما

Garche doorim az basaate ghorb hemmat door nist
Bandeye shaahe shomaaeemo sanaa khaane shomaa

گر چه دوریم از بساط قرب همّت دور نیست
بنده شاه شمائیم و ثناخوان شما

Ey shahanshaahe boland akhtar khodaa raa hemmati
Taa beboosam hamcho gardoon khaake eyvaane shomaa

ای شهنشاه بلنداختر خدا را همّتی
تا ببوسم همچو گردون خاک ایوان شما

O Saki[1], light up this cup of ours with that wine of yours,
O maestro, sing of how we are tuned to fortune's course.

Reflected in the wine, it was the true beloved's face we did see,
You who know not what joy in our wine-drinking there can be!

Those sly glances and alluring forms, charm; but are nothing,
When that cypress-shape, swaying like a pine, comes strolling.

One whose heart is alive with love does not die ever;[2]
It is written on the universal tablet that we live forever.

I doubt that the cleric's lawful bread on the *Day of Awakening*,
Will be of more benefit than the forbidden wine we're drinking.

In the sight of the beloved our intoxication is pleasing,
So into drunken hands our heart's reins they are giving.

Kind wind, if you pass by the loved one's garden,
Be sure that to the beloved this message is given.

Say, "Why do you forget our name so deliberately,
Anyway one day time will wipe it from your memory."

O Hafiz; let your copious tears flow all night long,
Maybe the bird of union will be ensnared before long.

The sphere's vast, green, celestial ocean and the crescent shaped -
Ship of the moon, in the blessing Hajji Qavam gave, both drowned[3].

**(W-C 3) The radif here is "Ours".**
[1] *"...Saki..." This term usually refers to the youth who serves wine at a party. It may also refer to the spiritual guide.*
*Hazrat Abdul Qadir al-Jillani mentions the holy Prophet saying –"I have seen my Lord in the shape of a most beautiful youth." He goes on to say: "As Allah is beyond all shape and form ... it is interpreted as the manifestation of the Lord's beautiful attributes reflected on the mirror of the pure soul....this is called the child of the heart.....this reflected image is also a connection between the servant and his Lord."*
[2] *".. heart is alive with love..." The Sufis concentrated not on this world or the rewards of the next, but only on the love of Allah – the Eternal Divinity. Shah Wali Ullah amongst others tells us that after death the soul remains alive in the next world until its good deeds are exhausted. Thereafter it sleeps till Judgement Day. The soul who has love of God rather than concerns with paradise and rewards in the next world continues alive in the Unseen fed directly by Allah.*
[3] *Acc. to W-C, on being given a cup of wine the reflection of sky and crescent moon appeared in it and inspired this line.*

Saaghi be noore baade barafrooz jaame maa
ساقی به نور باده برافروز جام ما

Motreb begoo ke kaare jahaan shod be kaame maa
مطرب بگو که کار جهان شد به کام ما

Maa dar piyaale akse rokhe yaar dideem
ما در پیاله عکس رخ یار دیده‌ایم

Ey bikhabar ze lazzate shorbe modaame maa
ای بی‌خبر ز لذّت شرب مدام ما

Chandaan bovad kereshmevo naaze sahi ghadaan
چندان بود کرشمه و ناز سهی قدان

Kaayad be jelve sarve senovbar kharaame maa
کاید به جلوه سرو صنوبرخرام ما

Hargez namirad aanke delash zende shod be eshgh
هرگز نمیرد آن که دلش زنده شد به عشق

Sabt ast bar jarideye aalam davaame maa
ثبت است بر جریده عالم دوام ما

Tarsam ke sarfei nabarad rooze baaz khaast
ترسم که صرفه‌ای نبرد روز بازخواست

Naane halaale sheikh ze aabe haraame maa
نان حلال شیخ ز آب حرام ما

Masti be chashme shaahede delbande maa khosh ast
مستی به چشم شاهد دلبند ما خوش است

Zaanroo sepordeand be masti zamaame maa
زان رو سپرده‌اند به مستی زمام ما

Ey baad agar be golshane ahbaab bogzari
ای باد اگر به گلشن احباب بگذری

Zenhaar arze deh bare jaanaan payaame maa
زنهار عرضه ده بر جانان پیام ما

Goo naame maa ze yaad be amdaa che mibari
گو نام ما ز یاد به عمدا چه می‌بری

Khod aayad aanke yaad nabaashad ze naame maa
خود آید آن که یاد نباشد ز نام ما

Hafez ze dide daaneye ashki hami feshaan
حافظ ز دیده دانه اشکی همی فشان

Baashad ke morghe vasl konad ghasde daame maa
باشد که مرغ وصل کند قصد دام ما

Daryaaye akhzare falak o kashtiye helaal
دریای اخضر فلک و کشتی هلال

Hastand gharghe namate haaji ghavaame maa
هستند غرق نعمت حاجی قوام ما

Come, Sufi, the mirror of the cup shines brightly;
So it is possible to see the ruby colour clearly.

The secret within the veil, from the drunken rends[1] seek,
For, of this state the eminent Sufi is not able to speak.

The Anka[2] is not a prey that anyone can ensnare;
Withdraw your net, you will find only wind there.

Try to drink the bliss of the present moment,[3] for when it's gone,
As Adam had to leave the garden asylum – you too must move on.

At time's feast a jar or two will do, and then let it be,
Don't be greedy, perpetual union there won't be.

Youth passed O heart, no rose of joy you gathered,
In maturity, acquiring wisdom should be preferred.

Only to serve do your servants wait at your entrance;
O Khwaja[4] from pity spare your slave a second glance.

Of the wine cup Hafiz is the disciple, so convey O breeze,
This morning's salaam, to that Sheykh of *Jam*[5], please.

---

**(W-C 4)**

[1] *"..rends..."* This term is often translated as 'profligates' and it is extensively used by Hafiz. We have used both the original Farsi term and its translation in different ghazals.

[2] *"..Anka..."* This is sometimes spelt 'Anqa'. See the glossary in this volume.

[3] *"..drink the bliss of the present moment..."* This does not mean indulging in transient sensory pleasures, but in finding the Eternal in the present, rather than seeing joy as something to be postponed till after physical death.

[4] *"..Khwaja..."* This term means a venerated elder. It is used for great Saints as in the case of Khwaja Muinuddin Hasan Chishti – who is often referred to simply as Khwaja Saheb.

[5] *"..that Shaikh of Jam..."* This may refer to a specific person as suggested by W-C (pp.27) but Jam also carries the connotation of a wine cup and here may be shorthand for the wine cup in which the world and the seven heavens could be seen. Essentially this is the 'eye of the heart', so Hafiz may be saying "give my salaams (greetings) to a master who sees through the eye of the gathered heart".

Soofi biyaa ke aayene saafist jaam raa

Taa bengari safaaye meye lal faam raa

صوفی بیا که آینه صافیست جام را

تا بنگری صفای می لعل فام را

Raaza daroone parde ze rendaane mast pors

Kin haal nist soofiye aali maghaam raa

راز درون پرده ز رندان مست پرس

کاین حال نیست صوفی عالی مقام را

Anghaa shekaar mi nashavad daam baaz chin

Kinjaa hamishe baad be dast ast daam raa

عنقا شکار می نشود دام باز چین

کاینجا همیشه باد به دست است دام را

Dar eyshe naghd koosh ke chon aabkhor namaand

Aadam behesht rovzeye darossalaam raa

در عیش نقد کوش که چون آبخور نماند

آدم بهشت روضه دارالسّلام را

Dar bazme dovr yek do ghadah darkesho boro

Yani tama madaar vesaale davaam raa

در بزم دور یک دو قدح درکش و برو

یعنی طمع مدار وصال دوام را

Ey del shabaab rafto nachidi goli ze eysh

Piraane sar bekon honari nango naam raa

ای دل شباب رفت و نچیدی گلی ز عیش

پیرانه سر بکن هنری ننگ و نام را

Maa raa bar aastaane to bas haghghe khedmat ast

Ey khaaje baaz bin be tarahhom gholaam raa

ما را بر آستان تو بس حقّ خدمت است

ای خواجه باز بین به ترحّم غلام را

Hafez moride jaame meyast ey sabaa boro

Vaz bande bandegi beresaan sheikhe jaam raa

حافظ مرید جام می است ای صبا برو

وز بنده بندگی برسان شیخ جام را

Bestir yourself, and bring out the wine cup, O Saki,
The misery of this time, as dust make it to be.

Place on my palm the cup; then from my chest,
This patched blue robe I will be able to wrest.

The 'wise' think that all we have gained is notoriety,
But we never sought fame, nor yet sought infamy.

Enough! Give wine! This wind of pride is annoying;
Pour dust on the low-desiring soul's futile conniving.

From my heart's fire a pall of smoke is rising[1],
Like a sigh; and these sad raw ones it is burning.

No friend of my distraught heart's secret I see,
Not amongst the elect, nor folk more ordinary.

Now only that lovely one can really please,
Who all at once had robbed my heart of its ease.

One who, on the green, has seen that silver-limbed cypress,
No cypress of the common or the woods can ever impress.

Day and night have patience, O Hafiz, with adversity,
So that what your heart seeks may one day come to be.

---

**(W-C 5)**

[1] "...a pall of smoke is rising..." The 'Secret' according to Shah Wali Ullah in "Alt-ul Quds" (The Sacred Knowledge – see bibliography), is a state of the heart that has undergone many purifications. Mystics may experience, at one point in their development, the rise of inner smoke that has no apparent source. There is no specific solution to this but patience. This should be enough to remind us from what a deep spiritual perspective Hafiz's verses speak.

Saaghiyaa barkhizo dar deh jaam raa

ساقیا برخیزودرده جام را

Khaak bar sar kon ghame ayyam raa

خاک برسرکن غم ایّام را

Saaghare mey bar kafam neh taa ze bar

ساغر می بر کفم نه تا ز بر

Bar kasham in dalghe azragh faam raa

برکشم این دلق ازرق فام را

Garche bad naamist nazde aaghelaan

گر چه بدنامیست نزد عاقلان

Maa nemikhaahim nango naam raa

ما نمی‌خواهیم ننگ و نام را

Baade dar deh chand azin baade ghoroor

باده درده چند از این باد غرور

Khaak bar sar nafse naa farjaam raa

خاک بر سر نفس نافرجام را

Doode aahe sineye naalaane man

دود آه سینه نالان من

Sookht in afsordegaane khaam raa

سوخت این افسردگان خام را

Mahrame raaze dele sheidaaye khod

محرم راز دل شیدای خود

Kas nemibinam ze khaaso aam raa

کس نمی‌بینم ز خاص و عام را

Baa delaaraami maraa khaater khosh ast

با دلارامی مرا خاطر خوش است

Kaz delam yekbaare bord aaraam raa

کز دلم یکباره برد آرام را

Nangarad digar be sarv andar chaman

ننگرد دیگر به سرو اندر چمن

Har ke did aan sarve simandaam raa

هر که دید آن سرو سیم اندام را

Sabr kon Hafez be sakhti roozo shab

صبر کن حافظ به سختی روز و شب

Aaghebat roozi biyaabi kaam raa

عاقبت روزی بیابی کام را

My heart is slipping away from my control, O men of the Way,
For God sake help! What pain if love's secret it should betray.

Our boat is becalmed; O fair wind, you we require;
To see again the face of our intimate friend we desire.

For ten short days the illusory favours of the sphere beguile,
Friend, acts of kindness to friends take as a boon meanwhile.[1]

Last night, in the rose's company, the bulbul sang happily of wine,
Saying, "O give a drink to wake these drunken friends of mine."

See the secret of Alexander's mirror in the wine cup,
Showing all that on earth is going on, or will come up.

O owner of wonders, in gratitude for your own situation,
Show sympathy to the poor Dervishes without any ration.

Ease in the two worlds[2] is contained in two words only;
Affection (shown to friends); courtesy (to the enemy).

I have no access to the street of honour and reputation;
If this has not your approval, then change our situation.

The bitter wine is called 'The Mother of Woes', by the Sufi,
But to us, even in a virgin's kiss nothing sweeter can there be.

In hard times to make merry with wine and what pleases us,
Is the elixir that makes a seeming beggar of a Croesus[3].

Breathing new life into us are the lovely Farsi speakers,
O Saki, pass this news to older pious Persian revellers.

Not of his own will did Hafiz don this wine-soaked dress,
Spotless pure Sheykh we may need you to make our excuses.

**(W-C 6)**
[1] "...acts of kindness to friends..." There are times in the spiritual life when the seeker finds he is becalmed. During such times Hafiz's excellent advice is to focus attention on what the holy Qur'an calls 'neighbourly needs'.
[2] "...the two worlds..." This refers to this world, the present life, and the life after death. Neither are the concern of the mystic – they seek only eternal union with Allah.
[3] "...Croesus..." In the original text Karun or Korah is referred to. He was one of the tribe of Israel who departed from Egypt with prophet Musa (Moses). His wealth was fabulous but he was eventually swallowed by the earth. See Qur'an 28; 76 and notes in W-C pp 30. Since here the reference is primarily to his wealth we have used a name more familiar to a western audience.

Del miravad ze dastam saahebdelaan khodaa raa
Dardaa ke raaze penhaan khaahad shod aashkaaraa

دل می رود ز دستم صاحبدلان خدا را
دردا که راز پنهان خواهد شد آشکارا

Kashti shekastegaanim ey baade shorte barkhiz
Baashad ke baaz binim aan yaare aashnaa raa

کشتی شکستگانیم ای باد شرطه برخیز
باشد که باز بینیم آن یار آشنا را

Dah rooze mehre gadroon afsaane asto afsoon
Niki be jaaye yaaraan forsat shomaar yaaraa

ده روز مهر گردون افسانه است و افسون
نیکی به جای یاران فرصت شمار یارا

Dar halgheye golo mol khosh khaand doosh bolbol
Haate saboeh hobboo yaa ayohas sokaaraa

در حلقه گل و مل خوش خواند دوش بلبل
هات الصّبوح هبّوا یا ایّها السّکارا

Aaeeneye sekandar jaame mey ast bengar
Taa bar to arze daarad ahvaale molke daaraa

آینه سکندر جام می است بنگر
تا بر تو عرضه دارد احوال ملک دارا

Ey saahebe karaamat shokraaneye salaamat
Roozi tafaghoddi kon darvishe bi navaa raa

ای صاحب کرامت شکرانه سلامت
روزی تفقّدی کن درویش بینوا را

Aasaayeshe do giti tafsire in do harf ast
Baa doostaan morovat baa doshmanaan modaaraa

آسایش دو گیتی تفسیر این دو حرف است
با دوستان مروّت با دشمنان مدارا

Dar kooye nik naami maa raa gozar nadaadand
Gar to nemipasandi taghyeer kon ghazaa raa

در کوی نیکنامی ما را گذر ندادند
گر تو نمی پسندی تغییر کن قضا را

Bentol enab ke zaahed ommol khabaaesash khaand
Ash-haa lanaa va ahlaa men ghoblatel ezaaraa

بنت العنب که زاهد امّ الخبائثش خواند
اشهی لنا و احلی من قبله العذارا

Hengaame tangdasti dar eysh koosho masti
Kin kimiaaye hasti gharoon konad gedaa raa

هنگام تنگدستی در عیش کوش و مستی
کاین کیمیای هستی قارون کند گدا را

Khoobaane paarsi goo bakhshandegaane omrand
Saaghi bede beshaarat piraane paarsaa raa

خوبان پارسی گو بخشندگان عمرند
ساقی بده بشارت پیران پارسا را

Hafez be khod napooshid in khergheye mey aalood
Ey sheikhe paak daaman mazoor daar maa raa

حافظ به خود نپوشید این خرقه می آلود
ای شیخ پاکدامن معذور دار ما را

The shine of youthfulness to the garden once more has come,
To the sweet-voiced bulbul[1], good news of the rose has come.

O breeze, to the young in the meadow, if you pass that way,
Our respects, to the cypress, the rose and the sweet basil pay.

If, in the Magian Pir's wine-selling child[2], such brightness I discern,
Gladly with my eye-lashes I will sweep the entrance of the tavern.

You who draw across the moon the chaugan[3] of pure amber,
Don't make my head go round in this bewildering manner.

This tribe sneering at the lovers who drink wine's dregs,
I fear for them, that their own faith may lose its legs.

Be a friend of the friends of God, for in Noah's great ship,[4]
Is dust that wouldn't buy the flood, not even a single drip.

Of him whose last resting place is a small mound of dust,
Ask why one would want towers that toward the sky thrust.

Get out of this house, the sphere; don't look for bread,
In the end from this mean bowl all you get is – dead.

My moon of Canaan[5], the throne of Egypt awaits you;
Farewells to the time of captivity are long overdue.

Hafiz drink wine! Be profligate, and find joy in it too,
But don't use the Qur'an to deceive, as some try to do.

*(W-C 7)*
[1] *"...Bulbul..." See glossary at the end of this volume.*
[2] *...'The Magian Pir's... child..." This could be the Saki as described in the commentary on (W-C 3) above.*
[3] *"...chaugan..." See glossary.*
[4] *"...Noah's great ship..." This is often a symbol for the true religion.*
[5] *"...moon of Canaan..." Prophet Yusuf (Joseph). Here, following the references to dying in previous verses, the implication would appear to be to be the heavenly status given the soul as a reward after death, which is the escape from the prison of the body.*

Rovnaghe ahde shabaabast degar bostaan raa

رونق عهد شبابست دگر بستان را

Miresad mojdeye gol bolbole khosh alhaan raa

می‌رسد مژده گل بلبل خوش الحان را

Ey sabaa gar be javaanaane chaman baaz rasi

ای صبا گر به جوانان چمن بازرسی

Khedmate maa beresaan sarvo golo reyhaan raa

خدمت ما برسان سرو و گل و ریحان را

Gar chonin jelve konad moghbacheye baade foroosh

گر چنین جلوه کند مغبچه باده فروش

Khaak roobe dare meikhaane konam mojgaan raa

خاکروب در میخانه کنم مژگان را

Ey ke bar mah keshi az ambare saaraa chovgaan

ای که بر مه کشی از عنبر سارا چوگان

Moztarebhaal magardaan mane sargardaan raa

مضطرب حال مگردان من سرگردان را

Tarsam aan ghovm ke bar dord keshaan mikhandand

ترسم آن قوم که بر دردکشان می‌خندند

Dar sare kaare kharaabaat konand imaan raa

در سر کار خرابات کنند ایمان را

Yaare mardaane khodaa baash ke dar kashtiye nooh

یار مردان خدا باش که در کشتی نوح

Hast khaki ke be aabi nakharad toofaan raa

هست خاکی که به آبی نخرد طوفان را

Harkeraa khaabgaah aakher na ke moshti khaak ast

هر کرا خوابگه آخرنه که مشتی خاک است

Goo che hajat ke bar aari be falak eyvaan raa

گو چه حاجت که برآری به فلک ایوان را

Boro az khaaneye gadroon be daro naan matalab

برو از خانه گردون بدرونان مطلب

Kin siyah kaase dar aakhar bekoshad mehmaan raa

کاین سیه کاسه در آخر بکشد مهمان را

Maahe kan-aaniye man masnade mesr aane to shod

ماه کنعانی من مسند مصر آن تو شد

Gaahe aan ast ke bedrood koni zendaan raa

گاه آنست که بدرود کنی زندان را

Hafezaa mey khoro rendi kono khosh bash vali

حافظا می خور و رندی کن و خوش باش ولی

Daame tazvir makon chon degaraan ghoraan raa

دام تزویر مکن چون دگران قرآن را

If that Turk[1], the beauty of Shiraz, would take my heart in hand,
For that one's Hindu mole I will give up Bokhara and Samarqand[2].

Yes! Saki, give what remains of wine! For paradise has not,
Musalla's glades[3]; nor the stream of Ruknabad[4] has it got.

Oh dear, those sweet, city-tormenting saucepots and their flirting!
They stole the heart's patience; the way Turks do their plundering.

That beloved one doesn't need our feeble, fumbling, infatuation;
Does the beautiful face need any make up, mole, or colouration?

Talk of musician and wine and less of this sphere's mystery,
None can unravel by reason the enigma of this world's destiny.

Yusuf's blooming beauty was more manifest day by day;
I knew love must lift the veil of Zuleika's chastity one day.[5]

You spoke ill of me - I am content. Mercy Lord! You spoke nicely,
A bitter reply is so well suited to those sugar-supplying lips of ruby.

Youth, listen to good advice because the happy consider,
More precious than life the words of the wise old master.

Hafiz! In this ghazal perfect pearls you have threaded. Sing it -
So the heavens will sprinkle that cluster of seven-sisters[6] on it.

---

**(W-C 8)**

[1] "...Turk..." See glossary. There are detailed notes by W-C (pp. 40) and Avery (pp.22-23).
[2] Here Bokhara and Samarqand (two cities) may represent this world and the next. Hafiz prefers the mole;
the single point of Divine Unity.
[3] "...Musalla's glade..." This refers to a grassy gathering place near Shiraz.
[4] "...Ruknabad..." This refers to a stream flowing through Shiraz.
[5] "...Yusuf..." This refers to Prophet Joseph who is renowned, amongst other things, for his overwhelming
physical beauty.
One account of Hafiz receiving his gift of poetic inspiration is that he had wanted to marry a beautiful
woman of high station. Hearing that if one spent forty sleepless nights at the tomb of Baba Kuhi, one
would obtain whatever one desired, he decided to undertake that ordeal. When, however, he reached the
final night he realised the lowness of his ambition and was given a night of power in which amongst other
blessings he received his power of poetic inspiration.
It is conceivable that in the poem Hafiz is alluding to this. If we take the line referring to Prophet Yusuf as in fact
referring to his own growing spiritual beauty as he fasted nightly at the tomb of Baba Kuhi then Zuleika may
refer to the beautiful woman, Shaks-i-Nabat, (branch of sugar') who was his inspiration, but who had been
refusing him and perhaps speaking badly to him. In this case Bokhara and Samarqand that he forsook can

Agar aan torke shirazi be dast aarad dele maa raa
Be khaale hendooyash bakhsham samarghando bokharaa raa

اگر آن ترک شیرازی به دست آرد دل ما را
به خال هندویش بخشم سمرقند و بخارا را

Bede saaghi meye baaghi ke dar jannat nakhaahi yaaft
Kenaare aabe roknaabaado golgashte mosallaa raa

بده ساقی می باقی که در جنّت نخواهی یافت
کنار آب رکناباد و گلگشت مصلّی را

Faghaan kin looliyaane shookhe shirin kaare shahr aashoob
Chonaan bordand sabr az del ke torkaan khaane yaghmaa raa

فغان کاین لولیان شوخ شیرین کار شهر آشوب
چنان بردند صبر از دل که ترکان خوان یغما را

Ze eshghe naa tamaame maa jamaale yaar mostaghnist
Be aabo rango khaalo khat che haajat rooye zibaa raa

ز عشق ناتمام ما جمال یار مستغنی است
به آب و رنگ و خال و خط چه حاجت روی زیبا را

Hadis az motrebo mey goovo raaza dahr kamtar joo
Ke kas nagshoodo nagshaayad be hekmat in moammaa raa

حدیث از مطرب و می گو و راز دهر کمتر جو
که کس نگشود و نگشاید به حکمت این معمّا را

Man az aan hosne rooz afzoon ke yoosof daasht daanestam
Ke eshgh az pardeye esmat boroon aarad zoleikhaa raa

من از آن حسن روز افزون که یوسف داشت دانستم
که عشق از پرده عصمت برون آرد زلیخا را

Badam goftiyyo khorsandam afaakallah nekoo gofti
Javaabe talkh mizibad labe la-le shekar khaa raa

بدم گفتیّ و خرسندم عفاک الله نکو گفتی
جواب تلخ می زیبد لب لعل شکرخا را

Nasihat goosh kon jaanaa ke az jaan doost tar daarand
Javaanaane sa-aadatmand pande pire daanaa raa

نصیحت گوش کن جانا که ازجان دوستتردارند
جوانان سعادتمند پند پیر دانا را

Ghazal goftiyo dor softi biaavo khosh bekhaan Hafez
Ke bar nazme to afshaanad falak eghde sorayya raa

غزل گفتیّ و در سفتی بیا و خوش بخوان حافظ
که بر نظم تو افشاند فلک عقد ثریّا را

---

refer to him giving up sleep and food, and the Turk – the beauty of Shiraz – would then refer to Shaks-i-Nabat.
It is also possible the lifting of the veil by Zuleika refers to the enlightenment he received.
Verses three four and five may represent his giving up of other attractions such as the attractions of
beautiful women and also philosophy, along with sleep and food.
He then advises youths to prefer the wisdom of the spiritual master to a human beloved, just as he did in the
end.
One must stress that this is but a single possible reading of the ghazal and it can be read in other ways. The
ordering of verses in the ghazal is not, I understand, an exact science devoid of disputations.
6 "...seven-sisters..." The Pleiades star cluster. It could conceivably stand for the 'seven-oft repeated verses'
(al-Fatiha) which opens the holy Qur'an. The general sense is clear; that combining singing with poetry
(frowned on by the very orthodox) can cause the ghazal to be endowed with blessings from on high.

O soft breeze, to that gracious gazelle, gently speak;
Say, "Mountain and desert, you have made us seek!"

I say, "Long live the sugar-seller",[1] but I just wonder why,
There is no asking after the parrot that eats that supply?

Is it from pride in beauty the rose seems not inclined,
To inquire about the lovelorn bulbul's state of mind?

Only a benign temperament captivates the clear sighted,
For the wise bird cannot by guile, or by net, be defeated.

O, when with the beloved you sit, sweet wine sipping,
Consider frantic lovers, vainly at the wind snatching.

Tall, slender, cypress-like, dark-eyed moons; paragons of beauty,
I don't know why they have not the colour of easy familiarity.

One cannot find fault with the perfection of that beauty,
But in that lovely face there appears no signs of fidelity.

If in the heavens the words of Hafiz, Venus should sing,
Would it surprise if the Messiah is inspired to dancing.

**(W-C 9)**

[1] *"...sugar-seller..." See also the commentary to the previous ghazal. Given that the name of the woman who inspired some of Hafiz's verse means 'branch of sugar' one might be inclined to think that this is a reference to her, a metaphor, so to speak, for the divine beloved. The parrot would be Hafiz of course. In the next verse he uses another metaphor to the same end – the rose as the beloved and the nightingale (the bulbul) as the lover.*

Sabaa be lotf begoo aan ghazaale ranaa raa
Ke sar be kooho biyaabaaan to daadei maa raa

Shekar foroosh ke omrash deraaz baad cheraa
Tafaghoddi nakonad tootiye shekar khaa raa

Ghoroore hosn ejaazat magar nadaad ey gol
Ke porseshi bekoni andalibe sheidaa raa

Be kholgho lotf tavaan kard seide ahle nazar
Be bando daam nagirand morghe daanaa raa

Cho baa habib neshiniyo baade peimaaee
Be yaad daar mohebbane baad peimaa raa

Nadaanam az che sabab range aashenaaee nist
Sahi ghadaane siyah chashme maah simaa raa

Joz in ghadar natavaan goft dar jamaale to eyb
Ke vaze mehro vafaa nist rooye zibaa raa

Dar aasemaan na ajab gar be gofteye Hafez
Samaae zohre be raghs aavarad masihaa raa

صبا به لطف بگو آن غزال رعنا را
که سر به کوه و بیابان تو داده‌ای ما را

شکرفروش که عمرش دراز باد چرا
تفقّدی نکند طوطی شکرخا را

غرور حسن اجازت مگر نداد ای گل
که پرسشی بکنی عندلیب شیدا را

به خلق و لطف توان کرد صید اهل نظر
به بند و دام نگیرند مرغ دانا را

چو با حبیب نشینی و باده پیمایی
به یاد دار محبّان بادپیما را

ندانم از چه سبب رنگ آشنایی نیست
سهی قدان سیه چشم ماه سیما را

جز این قدر نتوان گفت در جمال تو عیب
که وضع مهر و وفا نیست روی زیبا را

در آسمان نه عجب گر به گفته حافظ
سماع زهره به رقص آورد مسیحا را

Last night, our master from mosque to tavern[1] headed;
What of us followers now? On what plan are we decided?

Well the Magian's tavern must be our place of sojourn;
This destiny surely was writ even before time was born.

How should we now face towards the Qibla of piety,
When our guide's gaze is towards the tavern only.

Some night, will these sighs and supplications do something,
To that stony heart? Our tears igniting and our heart burning.

If reason knew the heart's happiness in the locks of that one's hair,
Reasonable men would go quite wild just to be chained up there.

The wind ruffled your hair, now in the world only blackness I see,
This passion for your hair is the only benefit conferred on me.

Our falcon-heart had scarce caught collectedness[2] as its prey,
When you released your locks, startled it, and it flew away!

Your face's beauty unveiled a sign of great graciousness,
Since then our explanations[3] have only grace and goodness.

From this sphere passed the arrow of our sigh. Hafiz, silent be!
Have compassion for your soul, and our arrow avoid adroitly.


**(W-C 10)**

[1] "...to the tavern..." "The real tavern is in the heart; but without the guidance of the perfect spiritual guide the absorbed traveller on the way cannot understand it." (Khwaja Muinuddin Hasan Chishti. See; The Meditations of Khwaja Muinuddin Hasan Chishti in the bibliography). Individual verses in the holy Qur'an are known as 'signs', though the term is also used to describe every aspect of creation since their existence indicates a Creator and the nature of phenomena reflect the nature of the Noumena. Here surely Hafiz is speaking of having been given the inner knowledge of the holy Qur'an.
[2] "...collectedness..." This is a state of the heart experienced by mystics.
[3] "...Explanations..." This could refer to commentaries (Tafsir) on the holy Qur'an.

Doosh az masjed sooye meikhaane aamad pire maa
Chist yaaraane tarighat bad az in tadbire maa

دوش از مسجد سوی میخانه آمد پیر ما
چیست یاران طریقت بعد از این تدبیر ما

Dar kharaabaate moghaan maa niz ham manzel shavim
Kin chonin raftast dar ahde azal taghdire maa

در خرابات مغان ما نیز هم منزل شویم
کاین چنین رفته است در عهد ازل تقدیر ما

Maa moridaan rooy sooye kabe chon aarim chon
Rooy sooye khaaneye khammaar daarad pire maa

ما مریدان روی سوی کعبه چون آریم چون
روی سوی خانه خمّار دارد پیر ما

Baa dele sanginat aayaa hich dar girad shabi
Aahe aatashbaaro o sooze naaleye shabgire maa

با دل سنگینت آیا هیچ درگیرد شبی
آه آتش بار و سوز ناله شبگیر ما

Aghl agar daanad ke del dar bande zolfash chon khosh ast
Aaghelaan divaane gardand az peye zanjire maa

عقل اگر داند که دل در بند زلفش چون خوش است
عاقلان دیوانه گردند از پی زنجیر ما

Baad bar zolfe to aamad shod jahaan bar man siyaah
Nist az sovdaaye zolfat bish az in tovfire maa

باد بر زلف تو آمد شد جهان بر من سیاه
نیست از سودای زلفت بیش از این توفیر ما

Morghe del raa seide jam-iyyat be daam oftaade bood
Zolf bogshaadi ze shaste maa beshod nakhjire maa

مرغ دل را صید جمعیّت به دام افتاده بود
زلف بگشادیّ و باز از دست شد نخجیر ما

Rooye khoobat aayati az lotf bar maa kashf kard
Zaan sabab joz lotfo khoobi nist dar tafsire maa

روی خوبت آیتی از لطف بر ما کشف کرد
زان سبب جز لطف و خوبی نیست در تفسیر ما

Tire aahe maa ze gadroon bogzarad Hafez khamoosh
Rahm kon bar jaane khod parhiz kon az tire maa

تیر آه ما ز گردون بگذرد حافظ خموش
رحم کن بر جان خود پرهیز کن از تیر ما

To the attendants of the Sultan, who will carry this prayer?
"In gratitude for your power, do not drive away the beggar".

From the slinking whisperer[1] in our nature, I take refuge with God,
Maybe that bright light will give some help, for the sake of God.

If that dark eye-lash of yours is targeting our blood directly,
Consider the implications; and so don't fall into error easily.

When your face lights up, a world's heart burns fiercely;
What benefit do you get out of behaving so unkindly?

All-night long I hope that the dawn breeze the carrier may be,
Conveying from familiar friends, affectionate salaams to me.

Beloved, when you appear, what wild confusion in lovers there is,
Show your cheek; for your face[2] our heart and life a sacrifice is.

For the sake of God, a drink for Hafiz! The dawn-rising lover!
In this may his early morning prayers be your mover.

**(W-C 11)**
  [1] 'Slinking Whisperer' Shaitan (Satan) or else the promptings of the lower, nature - the nafs al-amarah.
  [2] "…cheek…face…" See glossary 1 in this volume under "The Body".

Be molaazemaane soltaan ke resaanad in doaa raa
Ke be shokre paad shaahi ze nazar maraan gedaa raa

به ملازمان سلطان که رساند این دعا را
که به شکر پادشاهی ز نظر مران گدا را

Ze raghibe div sirat be khodaaye khod panaaham
Magar aan shahaabe saagheb madadi dahad khodaa raa

ز رقیب دیوسیرت به خدای خود پناهم
مگر آن شهاب ثاقب مددی دهد خدا را

Mojeye siyaahat ar kard be khoone maa eshaarat
Ze faribe ou biandisho ghalat makon negaaraa

مژه سیاهت ار کرد به خون ما اشارت
ز فریب او بیندیش و غلط مکن نگارا

Dele aalami besoozi cho ezaar bar foroozi
To az in che sood daari ke nemikoni modaaraa

دل عالمی بسوزی چو عذار برفروزی
تو از این چه سود داری که نمی کنی مدارا

Hame shab dar in omidam ke nasime sobhgaahi
Be payaame aashenaayaan benavaazad aashenaa raa

همه شب درین امیدم که نسیم صبحگاهی
به پیام آشنایان بنوازد آشنا را

Che ghiamat ast jaanaa ke be aasheghaan nomoodi
Delo jaan fadaaye rooyat benamaa ezaar maar aa

چه قیامت است جانا که به عاشقان نمودی
دل و جان فدای رویت بنما عذار ما را

Bekhodaa ke joreei de to be Hafeze saharkhiz
Ke doaaye sobhgaahi asari konad shomaa raa

به خدا که جرعه‌ای ده تو به حافظ سحرخیز
که دعای صبحگاهی اثری کند شما را

Righteous work is where? Where is my ruined state[1]?
See how far it is, the way from one to the other state.

What connection can piety possibly have with this profligacy?
Where are vapid sermons? Where the string's striking melody?

Of prayer place and hypocrisy's patched cloak my heart had its fill,
Where is the Magian's[2] abode? Where can pure wine be had still?

 That one has gone – may our union remain pleasant in the memory.
Where has that kind glance gone? Where the look to rebuke me?

What can the black-hearted from the face of the Friend anticipate?
Where is the snuffed out lamp? Where that candle, the sun, so great?

The apple of the chin's dimple is a pit! Don't be looking there!
Where are you going O heart? Where are you rushing to? Where?

The dust of your doorstep is eye-balm, so that better our eyes will see.
Where are we to go? Give the command! Where should we be?

Friend! Neither ease, nor patience seek from Hafiz!
What of ease? What of patience? Say where sleep is!

---

**(W-C 12)  The radif here is "Where?"**
  [1] "...ruined state..." The state of run is sought by the mystics since the Treasure, God, is hidden beneath ruins.
  Outward ruin conceals the inward glory of the true mystic.
  [2] "..the Magian' abode..." See glossary in this volume.

Salaahe kaar kojaavo mane kharaab kojaa
Bebin taafavote rah kaz kojaast taa be kojaa

Che nesbat ast be rendi salaaho taghvaa raa
Samaae vaz kojaa naghmeye robaab kojaa

Delam ze sovme-e begrefto khergheye saaloos
Kojaast deire moghaano sharaabe naab kojaa

Beshod ke yaad khoshash baad roozegaare vesaal
Khod aan kereshme kojaa rafto aan etaab kojaa

Ze rooye doost dele doshmanaan che daryaabad
Cheraaghe morde kojaa sha-me aaftaab kojaa

Mabin be sibe zanakhdaan ke chaah dar raah ast
Kojaa hami ravi ey del bedin shetaab kojaa

Cho kohle bineshe maa khaake aastaane shomaast
Kojaa ravim befarmaa az in jenaab kojaa

Gharaaro khaab ze Hafez tama madaar ey doost
Gharaar chist saboori kodaam khaab kodaam

صلاح کار کجا و من خراب کجا
ببین تفاوت ره کز کجاست تا به کجا

چه نسبتست به رندی صلاح و تقوی را
سماع وعظ کجا نغمه رباب کجا

دلم ز صومعه بگرفت و خرقه سالوس
کجاست دیر مغان و شراب ناب کجا

بشد که یاد خوشش باد روزگار وصال
خود آن کرشمه کجا رفت و آن عتاب کجا

ز روی دوست دل دشمنان چه دریابد
چراغ مرده کجا شمع آفتاب کجا

مبین به سیب زنخدان که چاه در راه است
کجا همی روی ای دل بدین شتاب کجا

چو کحل بینش ما خاک آستان شماست
کجا رویم بفرما ازین جناب کجا

قرار و خواب ز حافظ طمع مدار ای دوست
قرار چیست صبوری کدام خواب کجا

I asked that sovereign of lovely ones to take pity on a stranger,
I was told that in the desires of the heart, lost, is the stranger.

I said, "Please stay awhile", but received just an excuse in reply,
"I am raised with home comforts; of a stranger's grief, what care I?"

One gently raised to sleep in royal ermine cannot feel the pain,
Of the stranger's bed of thorns, or stone on which his head has lain.

O you! In the chain of your curling locks so many lovers stay,
Strange the musky mole matches your complexion that way.

Your moon-like face blushes with red wine's reflection,
Strangely like a red bud's petal on a white rose's complexion.

Strange, too, the downy hair, parading like ants around your face,
In the portrait gallery musky shadings[1], like this, are common place.

I said, "Your midnight-black hair is dark as the 'Night of the Stranger[2]'."
Take care, at dawn a groan of grief may come from this stranger."

Said, "Hafiz, even friends are in bewilderment[3] - astounded!
Is it any wonder a stranger should be confused - confounded?"

---

**(W-C 16) The radif here is "Strange (or Stranger)"**

[1] "...the portrait gallery musky shadings ..." In portraits of the period a kind of stippling effect was used as shading to bring a three dimensional quality to the face. In that respect it can refer to either the male or females face. It is usually associated with the first growth of beard in a young boy. Down has spiritual connotations also – Avery (pp. 40) quotes Shabistari as calling it "the verdant field of the world of spirits". We relate it to the famous prayer of the holy Prophet asking to be shown "the reality of things as they really are".
[2] "...Night of Strangers..." See glossary under 'Ashura'
[3] "...Bewilderment..." This is a state of mind experienced by the mystic preceding advancement to a higher stage.

Goftam ey soltaane khoobaan rahm kon bar in gharib
گفتم ای سلطان خوبان رحم کن بر این غریب

Goft dar dombaale del rah gom konad meskin gharib
گفت در دنبال دل ره گم کند مسکین غریب

Goftamash magzar zamaani goft mazooram bedaar
گفتمش مگذرزمانی گفت معذورم بدار

Khaane parvardi che taab aarad ghame chandin gharib
خانه پروردی چه تاب آرد غم چندین غریب

Khofte bar sanjaabe shaahi nazanini raa che gham
خفته بر سنجاب شاهی نازنینی را چه غم

Gar ze khaaro khaare saazad bastaro baalin gharib
گر ز خار و خاره سازد بستر و بالین غریب

Ey ke dar zanjire zolfat jaane chandin aashenaast
ای که در زنجیر زلفت جان چندین آشناست

Khosh fetaad aan khaale meshkin bar rokhe rangin gharib
خوش فتاد آن خال مشکین بر رخ رنگین غریب

Minomaayad akse mey dar range rooye mahvashat
می‌نماید عکس می در رنگ روی مهوشت

Hamcho barge arghavaan bar safheye nasrin gharib
همچو برگ ارغوان بر صفحه نسرین غریب

Bas gharib oftaade ast aan moore khattat gerde rokh
بس غریب افتاده است آن مور خطّت گرد رخ

Garche nabvad dar negaarestaan khate meshkin gharib
گر چه نبود در نگارستان خط مشکین غریب

Goftam ey shaame ghariibaan torreye shabrange to
گفتم ای شام غریبان طرّه شبرنگ تو

Dar sahargaahaan hazar kon chon benaalad in gharib
در سحرگاهان حذر کن چون بنالد این غریب

Goft Hafez aashenaayaan dar maghaame heiratand
گفت حافظ آشنایان در مقام حیرتند

Door nabvad gar neshinad khastevo ghamgin Gharib
دور نبود گر نشیند خسته و غمگین غریب

Dawn arrives; with a veil, the cloud covers it up,
O my friends; the morning cup, the morning cup!

Dew drops are constantly freezing on the tulip's red face,
O my dear friends, the wine, the wine embrace!

From the green field the breeze of paradise is coming,
So keep on drinking wine; wine keep on, drinking!

In that field, the emerald throne of the rose see;
Go and seek there the wine that's fiery like the ruby!

Again the tavern's door they have shut tightly,
Oh, "Opener of doors"[1], their opener please be.

At a time like this it is really quite extraordinary,
They closed the tavern door with such alacrity.

**(W-C 17)**

[1] "..."Opener" of doors..." The opener of doors could here refer to Hazrat Ali (or see Avery pp. 58 for an alternative explanation). There were times when various rulers would operate a stricter code about actual taverns than was normal.

Midamad sobho kelle bast sahaab
Asabooh asabooh yaa as-haab

می دمد صبح و کلّه بست سحاب
الصّبوح الصّبوح یا اصحاب

Michekad jaale bar rokhe laale
Almodaam almodaam yaa ahbaab

می چکد ژاله بر رخ لاله
المدام المدام یا احباب

Mivazad az chaman nasime behesht
Bas benooshid daaeman meye nab

می وزد از چمن نسیم بهشت
بس بنوشید دایما می ناب

Takhte zomorrod zadast gol be chaman
Raahe chon la-le aatashin daryaab

تخت زمرّد زده ست گل به چمن
راح چون لعل آتشین دریاب

Dare meikhaane basteand degar
Eftateh yaa mofattehal abvaab

در میخانه بسته اند دگر
اقتتح یا مفتّح الابواب

Dar chonin movsemi ajab baashad
Ke bebastand meikade be shetaab

در چنین موسمی عجب باشد
که ببستند میکده به شتاب

The morn of fortune dawned and the sun-like bowl is where?
Bring the bowl of wine! What more opportune time is there?

A peaceful house, a friendly Saki, a subtle master of song,
It's the time of youth, of celebration and passing the bowl along.

The time for opening within, to enjoy the jewel of joy and beauty,
Happy mixture! The golden bowl receives the dissolving ruby.

From seeing the grace hid within wine, nature's bride-dresser,
Was secreting in the heart of the rose petal, the rosewater.

Musician and beloved, hand-waving[1]; the love-drunk dancers;
The Saki's glance[2] has driven sleep from wine-worshippers.

When, from Hafiz, that moon is purchasing his pearls so eagerly,
Up to Venus' ear the sound of the rebab is ever rising joyfully.

**(W-C 18)**
  [1] *"...hand waving..."* During the Sufi dancing at the time of music concerts or Zikr the spiritually drunk Sufi
  may indulge in waving his hands about from ecstasy.
  [2] *"...the Saki's glance..."* As well as carrying the meaning of the youth serving wine, the glance referred to can
  also be the look of attention from the Pir living in this world or the Unseen.

Sobhe dovlat midamad koo jaame hamchon aaftaab

Forsati zin beh kojaa baashad bede jaame sharaab

صبح دولت می دمد کو جام همچون آفتاب

فرصتی زین به کجا باشد بده جام شراب

Khaane bi tashvish o saaghi yaar o motreb nokte gooy

Movseme eish ast o dovre saaghar o ahde shabaab

خانه بی تشویش و ساقی یار و مطرب نکته گوی

موسم عیش است و دور ساغر و عهد شباب

Az peye tafrihe tab-o zivare hosn o tarab

Khosh bovad tarkibe zarrin jaam baa la-le mozaab

از پی تفریح طبع و زیور حسن و طرب

خوش بود ترکیب زرّین جام با لعل مذاب

Az khiaale lotfe mey mashaateye chaalaake tab

Dar zamire barge gol khosh mikonad penhaan golaab

از خیال لطف می مشاطه چالاک طبع

در ضمیر برگ گل خوش می کند پنهان گلاب

Shaahed o motreb be dast afshaan o mastaan paay koob

Ghamzeye saaghi ze chashme meyparastaan borde khaab

شاهد ومطرب به دست افشان ومستان پای کوب

غمزه ساقی ز چشم می پرستان برده خواب

Baashad aan mah moshtari dorhaaye Hafez raa agar

Miresad har dam be gooshe zohre golbaange robaab

باشد آن مه مشتری درهای حافظ را اگر

می رسد هردم به گوش زهره گلبانگ رباب

By the soul of Khwaja, by ancient right and by sacred covenant,
At dawn's early breath, prayer I befriend; your welfare our intent.

Though greater in extent than the flood of Noah, are my tears,
They didn't remove the image of your love, that in my heart appears.

Here's a real bargain! A genuine shattered heart is my offer;
In this state its worth more than myriad intact hearts most proffer.

Do not complain of my madness! From the beginning,
The guide, love, consigned me to the tavern and wine drinking.

The tongue of the ant harangued even Asaf [1]- quite rightly;
For he sought not the seal of Solomon he lost so carelessly.

Let not your heart lose hope, the friend's kindness is infinite,
When it boasts of love go 'all in', throw your head in with it.

You handed to me craziness in mountain and in plain,
But you have not pity enough to loosen the belt's chain.

Don't get het up nor expect shelter from heart stealers, Hafiz,
If this plant doesn't flourish does it mean the garden's fault it is?

*(W-C 20)*

[1] *"...Asaf..." He was the Vizier (prime-minister) of Prophet Solomon. He was inadvertently implicated in the seal ring of Solomon's authority being handed to a Jinni, but he did not seek it out (see Avery pp 53). For a while Solomon wandered without dignity but was eventually restored to the throne of authority.*

Be jaane khaajevo haghghe ghadimo ahde dorost
Ke moonese dame sobham doaaye dovlate tost

به جان خواجه و حقّ قدیم و عهد درست
که مونس دم صبحم دعای دولت توست

Sereshke man ke ze toofaane nooh dast bebord
Ze lovhe sine nayarast naghshe mehre to shost

سرشک من که ز طوفان نوح دست ببرد
ز لوح سینه نیارست نقش مهر تو شست

Bekon moamelei vin dele shekaste bekhar
Ke baa shekastegi arzad be sad hezaar dorost

بکن معامله‌ای وین دل شکسته بخر
که با شکستگی ارزد به صد هزاردرست

Malaamatam be kharaabi makon ke morshede eshgh
Havaalatam be kharaabaat kard rooze nokhost

ملامتم به خرابی مکن که مرشد عشق
حوالتم به خرابات کرد روز نخست

Zabaane moor be aasaf deraaz gashto ravaast
Ke khaaje khaatame jam yaave kardo baaz najost

زبان مور به آصف دراز گشت و رواست
که خواجه خاتم جم یاوه کرد و بازنجست

Delaa tama mabor az lotfe binahaayate doost
Cho laafe eshgh zadi sar bebaaz chaaboko chost

دلا طمع مبر از لطف بی‌نهایت دوست
چو لاف عشق زدی سر بباز چابک و چست

Shodam ze daste to sheidaaye kooho dashto hanooz
Nemikoni be tarrahom netaaghe selsele sost

شدم ز دست تو شیدای کوه و دشت و هنوز
نمی‌کنی به ترحّم نطاق سلسله سست

Maranj Hafezo az delbaraan hefaaz majooy
Gonaahe baagh che bashad cho in derakht narost

مرنج حافظ و از دلبران حفاظ مجوی
گناه باغ چه باشد چو این درخت نرست

My eye's sight is the vestibule of the house in which you live;
O be so kind as to drop by and a visit to your own house give!

Your mole and line of down[1] catch the heart of the knowing Sufi;
Beneath the grain[2] and trap many a fine subtlety waits quietly

O bulbul[3], may you enjoy happily your union with the rose;
Only your love song is heard and throughout the garden goes.

In the art of your lip place the remedy for our sick hearts,
In your treasury, that ruby medicine most excitement imparts.

My body is inadequate to give the service your worth deserves,
But my soul's very essence as the dust of your doorstep serves.

I am not the kind who gives the gold of the heart to just anybody,
Signed and sealed with your mark, is the door to the treasury.

What a masterful rider! You just have to show the whip,
magically that wild horse, the sphere, responds to your grip.

What of me? You amaze even that artful juggler, the sky,
With the store of magical tricks you employ on the sly.

Now the music from your gathering has heaven reeling,
Because the sweet verses of our Hafiz you are singing.

**(W-C 21)**
  1 *"...Line of down..." See comment to (W-C 16)*
  2 *"...grain..." In Muslim belief it was a grain of wheat rather than an apple that was the bait used in the seduction of Adam.*
  3 *"...bulbul..." This refers to the nightingale; symbolising the lover.*

Ravaaghe manzare chashme man aastaaneye tost
Karam namaayo forroodd aa ke khaane khaaneye tost

رواق منظر چشم من آستانه تست
کرم نمای و فرود آ که خانه خانه تست

Be lotfe khaalo khat az aarefaan roboodi del
Latifehaaye ajab zire daamo daaneye tost

به لطف خال و خط از عارفان ربودی دل
لطیفه‌های عجب زیر دام و دانه تست

Delat be vasle gol ey bolbole sahar khosh baad
Ke dar chaman hame golbaange aasheghaaneye tost

دلت به وصل گل ای بلبل سحرخوش باد
که در چمن همه گلبانگ عاشقانه تست

Alaaje zafe dele maa be lab havaalat kon
Ke aan mofarrahe yaghoot dar khazaaneye tost

علاج ضعف دل ما به لب حوالت کن
که آن مفرّح یاقوت در خزانه تست

Be tan moghasseram az dovlate molaazematat
Vali kholaaseye jaan khaake aastaaneye tost

به تن مقصّرم از دولت ملازمتت
ولی خلاصه جان خاک آستانه تست

Man aan niyam ke daham naghde del be har shookhi
Dare khazaane be mohre tovo neshaaneye tost

من آن نیم که دهم نقد دل به هر شوخی
در خزانه به مهر تو و نشانه تست

To khod che lo-bati ey shahsavaare shirin kaar
Ke tovsani cho falak raame taaziaaneye tost

تو خود چه لعبتی ای شهسوار شیرین کار
که توسنی چو فلک رام تازیانه تست

Che jaaye man ke belaghzad sepehre shobade baaz
Az in hiyal ke dar ambaaneye bahaaneye tost

چه جای من که بلغزد سپهر شعبده باز
از این حیل که در انبانه بهانه تست

Soroode majlesat aknoon falak be raghs aarad
Ke shere Hafeze shirin sokhan taraaneye tost

سرود مجلست اکنون فلک به رقص آرد
که شعر حافظ شیرین سخن ترانه تست

Of the beloved's love, the heart is the chamber;
Of the beloved's form, the eye is a mirror holder.

To neither of the two worlds[1] do I in anyway defer,
The weight of that one's grace, on my neck I prefer.

To you, the tall Tuba tree[2]; for me, the beloved's height!
Everyone is happy about reaching their aspiration's height.

If my garments happen to be soiled, what's the difference?
The whole world bears witness to the beloved's innocence.

This place is a sanctified palace, guarded by the breeze,
How should I expect to gain entrance to the beloved with ease.

The time of Majnun[3] has passed and our turn is now,
Everyone, for just five days, gets their time somehow.

The wide kingdom of love, and the treasure of joy,
Is from the grace and favour of the beloved that I enjoy.

Don't regard the apparent poverty of Hafiz,
His heart the great treasure trove of love is.

---

**(W-C 22) The radif here is "His".**
[1] *"...the two worlds..." This means this life and the life in the hereafter. The mystic does not care for either his goal
   is only the Beloved (God).*
[2] *"...tall Tuba tree..." See the glossary in this volume.
   The mystic cares not for the next world or this, but for the Beloved. This is true and eternal wealth.*
[3] *"...Majnun..." See the glossary in this volume.*

Del saraapardeye mahabbate oost
Dide aaeenedaare tal-ate oost

دل سراپرده محبّت اوست
دیده آیینه دار طلعت اوست

Man ke sar dar nayavaram be do kovn
Gardanam zire baare mennate oost

من که سر درنیاورم به دو کون
گردنم زیر بار منّت اوست

Tovo Toobaavo mavo ghaamate yaar
Fekre har kas be ghadre hemmate oost

تو و طوبی و ما و قامت یار
فکر هر کس به قدر هّمت اوست

Gar man aaloode daamanam che ziyaan
Hame aalam gavaahe esmate oost

گر من آلوده دامنم چه زیان
همه عالم گواه عصمت اوست

Man ke baasham dar aan haram ke sabaa
Pardedaare harime hormate oost

من که باشم در آن حرم که صبا
پرده دار حریم حرمت اوست

Dovre Majnoon gozasht o novbate maast
Har kasi panj rooz novbate oost

دور مجنون گذشت و نوبت ماست
هر کسی پنج روز نوبت اوست

Molkate aasheghiyyo ganje tarab
Harche daaram ze yomne dovlate oost

ملکت عاشقیّ و گنج طرب
هر چه دارم ز یمن دولت اوست

Faghre zaaher mabin ke Hafez raa
Sine ganjineye mahabbate oost

فقر ظاهر مبین که حافظ را
سینه گنجینه محبّت اوست

My head is willingly united with the doorstep of the friend[1],
Whatever goes over our head must be willed by the friend.

To my friend's face nothing compares; what though,
The sun and the moon as mirrors to that face I show.

O what can the breeze have to say of our heart's sad plight?
That, like the petals of the rosebud, is folded up so tight.[2]

In this reveller-burning tavern I am not alone in wine drinking;
In this workshop many a head is dust for wine-bowl making.

Did you comb your hair so that the ambergris fell from it?
The breeze became civit-like[3]; the dust was perfumed by it.

Sacrificed to your face each rose petal in the meadow is;
Sacrificed to your height every tall river-bank cypress is.

Your face entered my heart, so my desire I am attaining,
Following the happy omen, the happy state one is gaining.

It's not due to illusory time Hafiz's heart is in the fire of desiring;
Before time came into being[4] it received the wild tulip's marking.

Talk of longing makes foolish what the tongue inside is saying,
What hope for the gobbledygook the speechless pen is writing.

**(W-C 23)**
[1] "...my head...with the doorstep of the friend..." Submission to the Divine Will is symbolised here by the head on the doorstep of the Friend.
[2] "...the rosebud, is folded up so tight..." The heart like a rosebud is tight until it opens in the same way that a rose blooms.
[3] "...civit..." A lithe rather fox-like mammal associated with the smell of musk.
[4] "...Before time..." This refers to the Day in pre-eternity in which the pure souls have their existence, and which determines the events of this life. See in the glossary under "Alast"

Sare eraadate maavo aastaane hazrate doost

Ke harche bar sare maa miravad eraadate oost
سر ارادت ما و آستان حضرت دوست

که هر چه بر سر ما می‌رود ارادت اوست

Nazire doost nadidam agarche az maho mehr

Nahaadam aayenehaa raa moghaabele rokhe doost
نظیر دوست ندیدم اگر چه از مه و مهر

نهادم آینه‌ها را مقابل رخ دوست

Sabaa ze haale dele tange maa che sharh dahad

Ke chon shekange varaghhaaye ghonche too bar toost
صبا ز حال دل تنگ ما چه شرح دهد

که چون شکنج ورق‌های غنچه تو بر توست

Na man saboo keshe in deire rendsoozamo bas

Basaa saraa ke dar in kaarkhaane khaake saboost
نه من سبوکش این دیر رندسوزم و بس

بسا سرا که در این کارخانه خاک سبوست

Magar to shaane zadi zolfe ambarafshaan raa

Ke baad ghaaliye saayasto khaak ambar boost
مگر تو شانه زدی زلف عنبرافشان را

که باد غالیه سای است و خاک عنبربوست

Nesaare rooye to har barge gol ke dar chaman ast

Fadaaye ghadde to har sarv bon ke bar labe joost
نثار روی تو هر برگ گل که در چمن است

فدای قدّ تو هر سروبن که بر لب جوست

Rokhe to dar delam aamad moraad khaaham yaaft

Cheraa ke haale nekoo dar ghafaaye faale nekoost
رخ تو در دلم آمد مراد خواهم یافت

چرا که حال نکو در قفای فال نکوست

Na in zamaan dele Hafez dar aatashe havas ast

Ke daaghdaare azal hamcho laaleye khodroost
نه این زمان دل حافظ در آتش هوس است

که داغدار ازل همچو لاله خودروست

Zabaane naateghe dar vasfe shovghe maa laalast

Che jaaye kelke boride zabaane bihode goost
زبان ناطقه در وصف شوق ما لال است

چه جای کلک بریده زبان بیهده گوست

All the world's sweetness is in the black hue of that beautiful one[1],
The bright eye, laughing lip and joyful cheek; all are with that one.

Although those other sweet-spoken ones also have royalty,
He is the Solomon of the age, for his is the seal of sovereignty.

The dark, musky mole that sits on that fair wheat-coloured face,
Contains the secret of the grain[2] that robbed Adam of his place.

That heart-conqueror went on a journey! Friends, for God's sake,
What of my poor wounded heart? That one left and the cure did take!

He is fair skinned, perfect in skill, and robed in purity,
The spirits of the pure ones is with him of a certainty.

O who can we talk to about being killed by a stony-hearted one?
When all along that one has the breath of Jesus, Maryam's son.

Hafiz is a true believer; in your good regard hold him.
For the forgiving look of many a noble soul is on him.

**(W-C 24)**

[1] *"...black hue..." Hafiz uses blackness as a symbol of beauty. Amongst Sufis black is the colour of one who has gone beyond colours (beyond differentiation). Perhaps it is an allusion to the eternal blackness in which is found the Light; or to non-existence. Here the reference may be to the holy Prophet Muhammed the seal of prophecy who concludes the line of Prophecy that commenced chronologically with Adam. Other prophets are mentioned or perhaps just hinted at. Perhaps the tenor of the ghazal is that the prophets are one and in a sense within Prophet Muhammed who is the final manifestation of Prophecy viewed as a single manifestation of Divine Mercy; the Nur-i-Muhammed of Islamic theology.*
[2] *"...grain ...of wheat..." In Muslim belief it was a grain of wheat rather than an apple that was the bait used in the seduction of Adam.*

Aan siyah chorde ke shiriniye aalam baa oust
Chashme meigoon labe khandaan rokhe khorram baa oust

آن سیه چرده که شیرینی عالم با اوست
چشم میگون لب خندان رخ خرّم با اوست

Garche shirin dahanaan paadshahaanand vali
Ou soleimaane zaman ast ke khaatam baaa oust

گرچه شیرین دهنان پادشهانند ولی
او سلیمان زمان است که خاتم با اوست

Khaale shirin ke baraan aareze gandom goon ast
Serre aan daane ke shod rahzane aadam baa oust

خال شیرین که بران عارض گندم گون است
سرّ آن دانه که شد رهزن آدم با اوست

Delbaram azme safar kard khodaa raa yaaraan
Che konam baa dele majrooh ke marham baa oust

دلبرم عزم سفر کرد خدا را یاران
چه کنم با دل مجروح که مرهم با اوست

Rooy khoob asto kamaale honaro daaman paak
Laa jaram hemmate paakaane do aalam ba oust

روی خوب است و کمال هنر و دامن پاک
لاجرم همّت پاکان دو عالم با اوست

Baa ke in nokte tavaan goft ke aan sangin del
Kosht maa raavo dame isiye maryam baa oust

با که این نکته توان گفت که آن سنگین دل
کشت ما را و دم عیسی مریم با اوست

Hafez az motaghedaan ast geraami daarash
Zaanke bakhshaayeshe bas roohe mokarram baa oust

حافظ از معتقدان است گرامی دارش
زانکه بخشایش بس روح مکرّم با اوست

A great favour I am hoping for, from the threshold of the Friend,
A great sin I have done; my hope is that a pardon He will send.

So extensive was my weeping that every passerby who saw it,
Wondering at the stream of pearly tears, said, 'What river is it?'

I know that the Friend will overlook and not punish that sin I committed.
Vengeful like the Pari[1]? Yes, but to angelic mercy that one is committed.

At the top of your street, our head became a ball in play[2],
No one knows, "Which is the ball, which the street?" they say.

Without a single word your hair fatally draws my heart to it,
Your heart-catching hair! Who is there worthy to speak to it?

Your mouth - I can barely detect any trace of it, it's so small,
Your waist is thin as a hair[3]; I don't know what that hair is at all?

It's a lifetime since I got the scent of those curling locks of hair,
Yet in my heart the perfume of their perfume has a place there.

I wonder how it is that the image of you I see does not disappear;
Though my eye is washing it again, and again, with many a tear.

O Hafiz, in such a distracted and sorry state you are, this I can see,
But it's good, for from remembering the friend's hair it came to be.

**(W-C 25)  The radif here is "Is".**
[1] "...Pari..." See glossary under 'Jinn'.
[2] "...ball in play..." The mystic becomes like a ball that moves as it is thrown with no will of its own. The mystic aspires to this kind of dependence on God. It can also refer to moving with the invisible currents of the Spirit.
[3] "...waist is thin as a hair..." This ghazal's theme would appear to be 'Fana'. The references throughout are to things that are so fine they barely seem to exist at all. The individuality in Fana merges with a greater Reality so as to virtually (but not entirely) disappear in it. People can barely distinguish between the head and the street etc. That little which remains is in effect the foundation of the state that the Sufis call 'Baqa'. See also notes in the glossary.

Daaram omide aatefati az jenaabe doost

Kardam jenaayatiyyo omidam be afve oust

دارم امید عاطفتی از جناب دوست

کردم جنایتیّ و امیدم به عفو اوست

Chandaan gereistim ke har kas ke bar gozasht

Dor ashke maa cho did ravaan goft kin che joost

چندان گریستیم که هر کس که برگذشت

در اشک ما چو دید روان گفت کاین چه جوست

Daanam ke bogzarad ze sare jorme man ke ou

Garche parivash ast valiken fereshte khoost

دانم که بگذرد ز سر جرم من که او

گرچه پری وش است ولیکن فرشته خوست

Sarhaa cho gooy dar sare kooye to baakhtim

Vaaghef nashod kasi ke che gooy asto in che koost

سرها چو گوی در سر کوی تو باختیم

واقف نشد کسی که چه گوی است و این چه کوست

Bi gofto gooy zolfe to del raa hami kashad

Baa zolfe delkashe to keraa rooye gofto goost

بی گفت و گوی زلف تو دل را همی کشد

با زلف دلکش تو که را روی گفت و گوست

Hich ast aan dahaan ke nabinim az ou neshaan

Mooeest aan miaano nadaanam ke aan che moost

هیچ است آن دهان که نبینیم از او نشان

مویست آن میان و ندانم که آن چه موست

Omrist taa ze zolfe to booee shanideim

Zaan booy dar mashaame dele man hanooz boost

عمریست تا ز زلف تو بوئی شنیده‌ام

زان بوی در مشام دل من هنوز بوست

Daaram ajab ze naghshe khiaalash ke chon naraft

Az dideam ke dam be damash kaar shosto shoost

دارم عجب ز نقش خیالش که چون نرفت

از دیده‌ام که دم به دمش کار شست و شوست

Hafez bad ast haale parishaane to vali

Bar booye zolfe doost parishaaniat nekoost

حافظ بد است حال پریشان تو ولی

بر بوی زلف دوست پریشانیت نکوست

The reclusive brethren say, 'The Night of Power'[1] is tonight.
O Lord! What auspicious star brought this fortunate night?

To ensure no unworthy hand to your curling locks may attain,
In each ringlet every heart is saying "O Lord!" Again and again![2]

For your chin's dimple my life is given, for when I look fully,
In the collar beneath, the necks of myriad bulbuls' souls I see.

A mirror-case for the face of my royal knight-rider, the moon is,
Mere dust raised by his horse's hooves, the high sun's crown is.

On the beloved's cheek, reflecting the speeding sun's hot face, sweat see,
Whilst it is up, each day, the sun burns to unite with that sweat ardently.[3]

I will never give up the ruby lip of the beloved, nor the cup of wine,
O men of piety excuse me, for this religion I have taken as mine.

That beloved whose eye in a flash discharges a swift dart at me,
By the hint of a smile from that lip, Hafiz's life sustained will be.

The water of life leaks out from this so eloquent beak of mine,
In God's Name; a great drinker is the black crow; this pen of mine!

---

**(W-C 26) The radif here is "Is".**

[1] "...The Night of Power..." This is a night referred to in the holy Qur'an as a special blessed one in which a continuous flow of blessings descend on the fortunate recipient and there is peace in the soul till the dawn. Muslims generally regard this as being one of the holy nights towards the end of the fasting month of Ramadan. Some mystics say it can be any night. There are also possible references in the ghazal to the Night journey of the holy Prophet (Miraj) on a horse-like creature.

[2] "...again and again..." In other words they are reciting verbal zikr i.e. repeating many times one of the names of God collectively or individually – with voice or silently in the heart. It is possible the reference to ringlets may be intended to remind of the holy Prophet (see Avery pp. 61). It may also imply that state in which every cell of the Sufi is reciting the divine name without specific effort.

[3] "...to unite with that sweat ardently..." Whilst it is possible, as Avery says (pp 61), to link this and the previous verse to praise for a royal patron of Hafiz, at another level the image of multiple drops of sweat reflecting the sun can also be taken as a perfect metaphor for the simultaneous transcendence and immanence of God.

Aan shabe ghadri ke guyand ahle khalvat emshab ast
Ya rab in ta-sire dovlat dar kodaamin kovkab ast

Taa be gisooye to daste naasezaayan kam rasad
Har deli az halghei dar zekre yaa rab yaa rab ast

Koshteye chaahe zanakhdaane toam kaz har taraf
Sad hazarash gardane jaan zire tovghe ghabghab ast

Shahsavaare man ke mah aaeenedaare rooye oust
Taaje khorshide bolandash khaake na-le markab ast

Taabe khey bar aarezash bin kaaftaabe garmroo
Dar havaaye aan aragh ta hast har roozash tab ast

Man nakhaaham kard tarke la-le yaaro jaame mey
Zaahedaan mazoor daaridam ke inam mazhab ast

Anke naavak bar dele man zir chashmi mizanad
Ghoote jaane Hafezash dar khandeye zire lab ast

Abe heivanash ze menghaare balaaghat michekad
Zaaghe kelke man benaam izad che aali mashrab ast

آن شب قدری که گویند اهل خلوت امشب است
یا رب این تأثیر دولت در کدامین کوکب است

تا به گیسوی تو دست ناسزایان کم رسد
هر دلی از حلقه‌ای در ذکر یارب یارب است

کشته چاه زنخدان توام کز هر طرف
صد هزارش گردن جان زیر طوق غبغب است

شهسوار من که مه آیینه دار روی اوست
تاج خورشید بلندش خاک نعل مرکب است

تاب خوی بر عارضش بین کآفتاب گرم رو
در هوای آن عرق تا هست هر روزش تب است

من نخواهم کرد ترک لعل یار و جام می
زاهدان معذور داریدم که اینم مذهب است

آن که ناوک بر دل من زیر چشمی می‌زند
قوت جان حافظش در خنده زیر لب است

آب حیوانش ز منقار بلاغت می‌چکد
زاغ کلک من بنامیزد چه عالی مشرب است

Don't expect from my drunken state, ritual, promise, or piety,
For before time was[1], my wine drinking was famous, quite rightly.

Completing wudhu[2] in the fount of love, from all that's dead I went,
So made four invocations of 'Allahu Akbar'[3] on all things existent.

Give me wine so that I may give you news of destiny's mystery,
And tell you whose face and perfume made a drunken lover of me.

Here the mountain's waist is slenderer even than an ant's is,
So wine-worshipper, despair not; God's door of Mercy there is.

Except the intoxicated eye (may it be safe from the eye of malice),
Under the sky-blue of the dome no one always and ever happy is.

Ransom is my life for your mouth, for in the eye's garden know,
That the world's Gardener no sweeter rosebud than this did grow.

From the good fortune of love for you, Hafiz a Solomon became,
That is, out of union with you, into his hand the wind[4] alone came.

**(W-C 27)**

[1] *"..before time was..." The 'day' outside of time and space in which the souls exist/ed.*

[2] *"..Wudhu..." This refers to the ablutions before ritual prayer.*

[3] *"..four invocations of 'Allahu Akbar'..." During special funeral prayers the invocation of 'Greatness belongs to God', Allahu Akbar, is recited four times - rather than the two times it is recited during normal prayer. Here the implication is that to love is tantamount to being alive. Everything not enlivened by love is dead and the protagonist prays over every such thing as to him it is dead.*

[4] *"..a Solomon became..." Amongst other things Solomon had control over the wind and held conversation with an ant.*

Matalab taa-ato peimaano salaah az mane mast
Ke be peimaane keshi shohre shodam rooze alast

Man haman dam ke vozoo saakhtam az cheshmeye eshgh
Chaar takbir zadam yeksare bar harche ke hast

Mey bede taa dahamat aagahi az serre ghazaa
Ke be rooye ke shodam aashegho az booye ke mast

Kamare kooh kam ast az kamare moor aanja
Naaomid az dare rahmat masho ey baade parast

Bejoz an nargese mastaane ke chashmash maresaad
Zire in taarame firooze kasi khosh naneshast

Jaan fadaaye dahanat baad ke dar baaghe nazar
Chaman aaraaye jahaan khosh tar az in ghonche nabast

Hafez az dovlate eshghe to soleimaani shod
Yani az vasle toash nist bejoz baad be dast

مطلب طاعت و پیمان و صلاح از من مست
که به پیمانه کشی شهره شدم روز الست

من همان دم که وضو ساختم از چشمه عشق
چارتکبیر زدم یک سره بر هر چه که هست

می بده تا دهمت آگهی از سرّ قضا
که به روی که شدم عاشق و از بوی که مست

کمر کوه کم است از کمر مور آنجا
ناامید از در رحمت مشو ای باده پرست

بجز آن نرگس مستانه که چشمش مرساد
زیر این طارم فیروزه کسی خوش ننشست

جان فدای دهنت باد که در باغ نظر
چمن آرای جهان خوشتر از این غنچه نبست

حافظ از دولت عشق تو سلیمانی شد
یعنی از وصل تواش نیست بجز باد به دست

The pious form worshipper! No knowledge of our state has he!
So in whatever he says about us, no cause for hatred do I see.[1]

Tariqat is the stage of - 'Best is, whatever comes our way.'
Hey ho heart! On this straight way no one goes astray.

To show how the game goes I will move a pawn, just to see,
King and rook (warrior) have no power on the board of profligacy.

What is this smooth sky - a high ceiling with so many images?
In this world none comprehends this enigma, no such Sage there is.

What's this about having no need; and wisdom's power, O Lord?
There are many internal wounds and no time to sigh do you afford.

Maybe the minister forgot the time that will settle every score,
For in the royal signature, "For God's sake" appears no more.

Say, 'Come' and 'Speak,' to whosoever wishes, without regard;
In this court there's no arrogance, coquetry, chamberlain or guard.

Whenever something does not fit, it is due to our own form,
The honour robe is not short, but to its size one may not conform.

To reach the tavern door is for the ones of our (spiritual) colour,
There's no way to the wine-seller's street for any self-server.

I am the slave of the tavern's Pir, who shows constant generosity,
Not of a pious pretender who bestows and withholds favour fickly.

Hafiz's aspiration is high! If he doesn't sit in the 'high' place of dignity!
It's because the dreg-drinking wine-lover is not slave to rank or property.

**(W-C 28) The radif here is "Is none".**
[1] *The first four verses here are a succinct summary of four levels known to the mystics. Khwaja Muinuddin Hasan Chishti describes them thus; "The gnosis of the world of nasut is the shariat, the revealed law. The gnosis of the world of malakut is the tariqat, the path of purification. The gnosis of the world of jabarut is the haqiqat, the state of reality. The gnosis of the world of lahut is absorption into timeless unity." Hafiz has no argument with those who follow only the Shariat (form) and do not know the deeper implications of it. He accurately sums up Tariqat as "Whatever come my way is best". The reference to a chess game in describing the implications of Haqiqat in the next verse may seem obscure but a mystic familiar with Haqiqat would find it precise. Lahut or 'ma'rifat' is an enigma beyond description or understanding.*

Zaahede zaaher parast az haale maa aagaah nist
Dar haghe maa harche gooyad jaaye hich ekraah nist

زاهد ظاهرپرست از حال ما آگاه نیست
در حق ما هر چه گوید جای هیچ اکراه نیست

Dar tarighat harche pishe saalek aayad kheire oust
Bar seraate mostaghim ey del kasi gomraah nist

در طریقت هر چه پیش سالک آید خیر اوست
برصراط مستقیم ای دل کسی گمراه نیست

Taa che baazi rokh namayad beidaghi khaahim raand
Arseye shatranje rendaan ra majaale shaah nist

تا چه بازی رخ نماید بیدقی خواهیم راند
عرصه شطرنج رندان را مجال شاه نیست

Chist in saghfe bolande saadeye besyaar naghsh
Zin moamma hich daanaa dar jahaan aagaah nist

چیست این سقف بلند ساده بسیارنقش
زین معمّا هیچ دانا در جهان آگاه نیست

In che esteghnaast ya rab vin che ghaader haakem ast
Kin hame zakhme nahaan hasto majaale aah nist

این چه استغناست یا رب وین چه قادر حاکم است
کاین همه زخم نهان هست و مجال آه نیست

Saahebe divaane ma gooee nemidaanad hesaab
Kandarin toghraa neshaane "hasbatan lellah" nist

صاحب دیوان ما گویی نمی‌داند حساب
کاندر این طغرا نشان حسبه لله نیست

Harke khaahad goo biaavo harche khaahad goo begoo
Kebro naazo haajebo darbaan darin dargaah nist

هر که خواهد گو بیا و هر چه خواهد گو بگو
کبر و ناز و حاجب و دربان درین درگاه نیست

Harche hast az ghaamate naasaze bi andaame maast
Varna tashrife to bar baalaaye kas kootaah nist

هر چه هست از قامت ناساز بی اندام ماست
ور نه تشریف تو بر بالای کس کوتاه نیست

Bar dare meikhaane raftan kaare yekrangaan bovad
Khod forooshaan ra be kooye mey forooshaan raah nist

بر در میخانه رفتن کار یکرنگان بود
خودفروشان را به کوی می فروشان راه نیست

Bandeye pire kharaabaatam ke lotfash daaem ast
Varna lotfe sheikho vaaez gaah hasto gaah nist

بنده پیر خراباتم که لطفش دائم است
ور نه لطف شیخ و واعظ گاه هست و گاه نیست

Hafez ar bar sadr nanshinad ze aali hemmatist
Aasheghe dordi kesh andar bande maalo jaah nist

حافظ ار بر صدر ننشیند ز عالی همّتیست
عاشق دردی کش اندربند مال و جاه نیست

This messenger, who visited us from the land of the friend,
With the amulet of life from the musky writing[1] of the friend,

Happily showed us a sign of the Glory and Beauty of the friend;
So that in its seeking the heart gains hope from the friend.

For this good news I gave him my heart, but I felt bad,
That coin of so little worth I had to lay before the friend.

Praise belongs to God that with fortune's friendly favour,
In accord with my behaviour are the demands of the friend.

By what power is the sphere orbiting and moon turning?
They are moving this way by the command of the friend.

Even if the two worlds were to collide due to the wind of calamity,
We, our eye's light, and the path will be in expectation of the friend.

O breeze of the dawn bring kohl[2] that from pure pearl is ground,
From blessed dust, that can be found only where treads the friend.

If the enemy should speak of designs against the life of Hafiz,
Why fear! Thanks God, for me, there is no shame before the friend.

---

**(W-C 29) The radif here is "The friend". We have used this in the translation.**
  [1] One can read this ghazal as referring to the holy Qur'an and therefore the friend as referring to the holy
  Prophet Muhammed or to God.
  [2] "...kohl..." See glossary in this volume.

In peike naamvar ke resid az diyaare doost

Vavard herze jaan ze khate moshkbaare doost
اين پيک نامور که رسيد از ديار دوست
واورد حرز جان ز خط مشکبار دوست

Khosh midahad neshaane jamaalo jalaale yaar

Taa dar talab shaved dele ommidvaare doost
خوش می‌دهد نشان جمال و جلال يار
تا در طلب شود دل اميدوار دوست

Del daadamash be mojdeo khejlat hami baram

Zin naghde ghalbe khish ke kardam nesaare doost
دل دادمش به مژده و خجلت همی‌برم
زين نقد قلب خويش که کردم نثار دوست

Shokre khodaa ke az madade bakhte kaarsaaz

Bar hasbe aarezoost hame kaaro bare doost
شکر خدا که از مدد بخت کارساز
بر حسب آرزوست همه کار و بار دوست

Seire sepehro dovre ghamar raa che ekhtiaar

Dar gardeshand bar hasabe ekhtiaare doost
سير سپهر و دور قمر را چه اختيار
در گردشند بر حسب اختيار دوست

Gar baade fetne har do jahaan raa be ham zanad

Maavo cheraaghe chashmo rahe entezaare doost
گر باد فتنه هر دو جهان را به هم زند
ما و چراغ چشم و ره انتظار دوست

Kohlol javaaheri be man aar ey nasime sobh

Zaan khaake nikbakht ke shod rahgozaare doost
کحل الجواهری به من آر ای نسيم صبح
زان خاک نيکبخت که شد رهگذار دوست

Doshman be ghasde Hafez agar dam zanad che baak

Mennat khodaay raa ke niyam sharmsaare doost
دشمن به قصد حافظ اگر دم زند چه باک
منّت خدای را که نيم شرمسار دوست

Welcome, messenger of the longing ones! Give word of the friend,
So that, in blissful desire, I may sacrifice my very life, for that friend.

Weeping and wailing ever I am, as the bulbul in a cage would be;
A parrot's nature gave me love for the sugar and almonds of the friend.

My beloved's hair is a snare; that mole is grain, a bait to catch me.
From desire for that bait, I fell into the trap set for me by the friend.

Till the Morning of Assembly[1], from drunkenness never departed,
 One like me who before time began[2] drank from the cup of the friend.

I say very little regarding my own desire, because,
I don't want to be the cause of a headache for the friend.

If it comes to my hand, on my eye the collyrium I will put,
Of the dust of the blessed path where treads foot of the friend.

My wish is for union, but, preferring separation is the friend,
So I gave up my desire in favour of the desire of the friend.

Hafiz, continue to grieve; accept that there can be no cure,
For the restless pain has no remedy except the calm of the friend.

---

*(W-C 30) The radif here is "The friend". We have used this in the translation.*
  [1] *"...the Morning of Assembly..." This means the Day of Judgement.*
  [2] *"...Before time began..." This may be the 'Day of Alast' or the dimension outside of time and space where the eternal souls known as Pirs dwell.*

Marhabaa ey peike moshtaaghaan bede peighaame doost

مرحبا ای پیک مشتاقان بده پیغام دوست

Taa konam jaan az sare reghbat fadaaye naame doost

تا کنم جان از سر رغبت فدای نام دوست

Vaale o sheidaast daaem hamcho bolbol dar ghafas

واله و شیداست دایم همچو بلبل در قفس

Tootiye tab-am ze eshghe shekkaro baadaame doost

طوطی طبعم ز عشق شکر و بادام دوست

Zolfe ou daam asto khaalash daaneye aan daamo man

زلف او دام است و خالش دانه آن دام و من

Bar omide daanei otaadeam dar daame doost

بر امید دانه‌ای افتاده‌ام در دام دوست

Sar ze masti bar nagirad taa be sobhe rooze hashr

سر ز مستی برنگیرد تا به صبح روز حشر

Harke chon man dar azal yek jor-e khord az jaame doost

هر که چون من در ازل یک جرعه خورد از جام دوست

Mi begoftam shammei az sharhe shovghe khod vali

می بگفتم شمّه‌ای از شرح شوق خود ولی

Man nemikhaaham nemoodan bish az in ebraame doost

من نمی خواهم نمودن بیش از این ابرام دوست

Gar dahad dastam kesham dar dide hamchon tootiaa

گر دهد دستم کشم در دیده همچون توتیا

Khaake raahi kaan mosharraf gardad az aghdaame doost

خاک راهی کان مشرّف گردد از اقدام دوست

Meile man sooye vesaalo ghasde ou sooye feraagh

میل من سوی وصال و قصد او سوی فراق

Tarke kaame khod gereftam taa bar aayad kaame doost

ترک کام خود گرفتم تا برآید کام دوست

Hafez andar darde ou misoozo bi darmaan besaaz

حافظ اندر درد او می‌سوز و بی‌درمان بساز

Zaanke daaraami nadaarad dard bi aaraame doost

زان که درمانی ندارد درد بی‌آرام دوست

O breeze, from the land of the friend, if you happen by there,
From the musk-laden hair of the friend bring fragrance filled air.

I would gratefully give my life for you; on that one's life I say it!
If you would bring the friend's message, and to me deliver it.

If you can't pass through the door to see the friend personally,
Bring some dust from that doorstep as an eye salve for me.

A beggar such as I, in desire of union with the friend - really!
How to see the friend's fair form manifest? In sleep maybe?

My pine-cone shaped heart, like the willow is trembling,[1]
The pine-like, shapely tallness of the friend, it is desiring.

The friend wouldn't give a nickel to buy us, this we know:
For the world we won't sell a single hair of the friend though.

What does it matter if his heart's bondage to sorrow should end,
Since Hafiz is the bond slave and the servant of the friend?

---

**(W-C 31) The radif here is "The friend".**
[1] W-C talks about the trembling of the pine-cone shaped heart as part of the practice of zikr in which the
name Allah is forced into the heart. Whether or not this is true it is very likely that the ghazals of Hafiz often
refer to meditation practices. Here 'passing through the door' could refer to entering the spiritual heart.
Similarly the breeze (verse one) could conceivably refer here to the wave of bliss that floods the head or body
of the mystic engaged in zikr or meditation.

Sabaa agar gozari oftadat be keshvare doost
Biyaar nafhei az gisooye moambare doost

Be jaane ou ke be shokraane jaan bar afshaanam
Agar be sooye man aari payaami az bare doost

Agar chenaan ke dar aan hazratat nabaashad baar
Bedin do dide biyaavar ghobaari az dare doost

Mane gedaavo tamannaye vasle ou heihaat
Kojaa be chashm bebinam khiyaale manzare doost

Dele senovbariam hamcho bid larzaan ast
Ze hasrate ghado baalaaye chon senovbare doost

Agarche doost be chizi nemikharad maa raa
Be aalami naforooshim moee az sare doost

Che baashad ar shaved az bande gham delash aazaad
Cho hast Hafeze khosh khaan gholaamo chaakere doost

صبا اگر گذری افتدت به کشور دوست
بیار نفحه‌ای از گیسوی معنبر دوست

به جان او که به شکرانه جان برافشانم
اگر به سوی من آری پیامی از بر دوست

اگر چنان که در آن حضرتت نباشد بار
بدین دو دیده بیاور غباری از در دوست

من گدا و تمنّای وصل او هیهات
کجا به چشم ببینم خیال منظر دوست

دل صنوبریم همچو بید لرزان است
ز حسرت قد و بالای چون صنوبر دوست

اگر چه دوست به چیزی نمی‌خرد ما را
به عالمی نفروشیم موئی از سر دوست

چه باشد ار شود از بند غم دلش آزاد
چو هست حافظ خوشخوان غلام و چاکر دوست

Come, for the palace of Hope, on unsound foundation is standing,
Give the wine cup! Even life's foundation in the wind is blowing.

Under the sky-blue dome[1] I am the slave of that one's firm resolve,
To be free; who attachment to all shades and hues does dissolve.

What should I tell you about what happened in the tavern last night?
Dead drunk I was, but an immortal spirit gave me good news alright:

Saying; "Far-seeing falcon, your nest is in paradise's Sidhra[2] tree,
Not nesting in a dark corner of this sad and sorry city, should you be.

From the heavenly battlements on high[3], they are calling you;
I wonder what happened in this place of traps to ensnare you."

A piece of wise advice I give you – remember, and follow it too,
For it comes from the Pir, who very well the way of Tariqat[3] knew.

"No fidelity is found in this shifting world; an old hag;
A bride, who with a thousand lovers will happily shag".

Don't grieve for this old world – remember what I say clearly,
For a traveller in God's Way spoke these words sincerely.

Be content with what God gives and stop your brow's creasing,
For you and me the door of choice will not be opening.

In the smile of the rose you will not find agreement to fidelity,
Dear bulbul, rose-lover, cry! This is the place of tears you see.

O half-hearted verse-mongers, Hafiz why should you envy,
In heartfelt acceptance and graceful words, God's gift see.

**(W-C 32)**
[1] "...sky blue dome..." Whilst this is at one level a reference to the sky or the heavens, one might consider Hafiz's reference to Ma'rifat as the lofty sky in ghazal 28 above.
[2] "...Sidhra tree..." See the glossary in this volume.
[3] "...the heavenly battlements on high..." This could be a reference to the ninth heaven.

Biyaa ke ghasre amal sakht sost bonyaad ast    بیا که قصر امل سخت سست بنیادست
Biaar baade ke bonyaade omr bar baad ast    بیار باده که بنیاد عمر بر بادست

Gholaame hemmate aanam ke zire charkhe kabood    غلام همّت آنم که ز زیر چرخ کبود
Ze harche range ta-allogh pazirad aazaad ast    ز هر چه رنگ تعلّق پذیرد آزادست

Che guyamat ke be meykhaane doosh masto kharaab    چه گویمت که به میخانه دوش مست و خراب
Soroushe aalame gheibam che mojdehaa daadast    سروش عالم غیبم چه مژده‌ها دادست

Ke ey boland nazar shaahbaaze sedre neshin    که ای بلندنظر شاهباز سدره نشین
Neshimane to na in konje mehnat aabaad ast    نشیمن تو نه این کنج محنت آبادست

To raa ze kongereye arsh mizanand safir    تو را ز کنگره عرش می‌زنند صفیر
Nadanamat ke dar in daamgah che oftaadast    ندانمت که در این دامگه چه افتادست

Nasihati konamat yaad giro dar amal aar    نصیحتی کنمت یاد گیر و در عمل آر
Ke in hadis ze pire tarighatam yad ast    که این حدیث ز پیر طریقتم یادست

Majoo dorostiye ahd az jahaane sost nahaad    مجو درستی عهد از جهان سست نهاد
Ke in ajooze aroose hezaar daamaad ast    که این عجوزه عروس هزاردامادست

Ghame jahan makhoro pande man mabar az yaad    غم جهان مخور و پند من مبر از یاد
Ke in latifeye eshgham ze rahroee yaad ast    که این لطیفه عشقم ز رهروی یادست

Reza be daade bede vaz jabin gereh bogshaay    رضا به داده بده وز جبین گره بگشای
Ke bar mano to dare ekhtiyaar nagshaadast    که بر من و تو در اختیار نگشادست

Neshaane ahdo vafaa nist dar tabasome gol    نشان عهد و وفا نیست در تبسّم گل
Benaal bolbole aashegh ke jaaye faryaad ast    بنال بلبل عاشق که جای فریادست

Hasad che mibari ey sost nazm bar Hafez    حسد چه می‌بری ای سست نظم بر حافظ
Ghaboole khaatero lotfe sokhan khodaadaad ast    قبول خاطر و لطف سخن خدادادست

When the tip of your hair, the power of the breeze was feeling,
My passionate heart fell and broke in two, from deep yearning.

In the pre-dawn darkness your eye's eloquence is the magic sought;
But any imitation one tries turns out ill, in fact will fall far short.

Wonder what that mole is, framed by the curl of that hair?
It's the ink dot in the curve of letter Jeem[1] that just fell there.

What is that musk-scented hair in the garden of your cheek, there?
It is a peacock in the garden of your paradise that just fell there.

O friend of my soul! My heart your face was so much desiring,
It became road dust and into the power of the breeze was falling.

Like dust this body of dust by itself cannot rise at all;
So severely from the top of your street did it fall.

You of Jesus breath![2] Your cypress form, that me is shading,
Is like the reflection of a soul that on dried up bone is falling.

One whose only address was Kaaba[3], on recalling your lip, I saw,
He had fallen into addressing himself only to the tavern door.

O dearly beloved! Hafiz fell into a covenant with grief for you,
A covenant of friendship, established outside of time, is his too.

*(W-C 33) The radif here is "Fell".*
[1] *"...Jeem..." This refers to the hook shaped letter J, which in Farsi has a nukta (dot) within the curve.*
[2] *"...You of Jesus breath..." Jesus breath refers to the healing power of Jesus but perhaps also to the fact his birth was the result of the Divine breath of the Spirit or of Angel Gabriel.*
[3] *"...Kaaba..." Probably a reference to the story of the mystic Sheikh San'an who deserted the religion of Islam for love of a beautiful Christian girl – as told in the "The Conference of the Birds" by Fariduddin Attar. See Avery pp.70.*

Taa sare zolfe to dar daste nasim oftaadast

Dele sovdaa zade az ghosse do nim oftaadast

Chashme jaadooye to khod eyne savaade sehr ast

Likan in hast ke in noskhe saghim oftaadast

Dar khame zolfe to aan khaale siah daani chist

Noghteye doode ke dar halgheye jim oftaadast

Zolfe moshkine to dar golshane ferdovse ezaar

Chist taavoos ke dar baaghe naeem oftaadast

Dele man az havase rooye to ey moonese jaan

Khaake raahist ke dar paaye nasim oftaadast

Hamcho gard in tane khaaki natavaanad barkhaast

Az sare kooye to zaan roo ke azim oftaadast

Saayeye sarve to bar ghaalebam ey isaa dam

Akse roohast ke bar azme ramim oftaadast

Aanke joz ka-be maghaamash nabod az yaade labat

Bar dare meikade didam ke moghim oftaadast

Hafeze gomshode raa baa ghamat ey jaane aziz

Ettehaadist ke dar ahde ghadim oftaadast

تا سر زلف تو در دست نسیم افتادست

دل سودازده از غصّه دو نیم افتادست

چشم جادوی تو خود عین سواد سحر است

لیکن این هست که این نسخه سقیم افتادست

در خم زلف تو آن خال سیه دانی چیست

نقطه دوده که در حلقه جیم افتادست

زلف مشکین تو در گلشن فردوس عذار

چیست طاووس که در باغ نعیم افتادست

دل من از هوس روی تو ای مونس جان

خاک راهیست که دریای نسیم افتادست

همچو گرد این تن خاکی نتواند برخاست

از سر کوی تو زان رو که عظیم افتادست

سایه سرو تو بر قالبم ای عیسی دم

عکس روح است که بر عظم رمیم افتادست

آنکه جز کعبه مقامش نبد از یاد لبت

بر در میکده دیدم که مقیم افتادست

حافظ گمشده را با غمت ای جان عزیز

اتّحادیست که در عهد قدیم افتادست

In the breast a rose, wine in hand, and a beauty, all mine!
On such a day the ruler of the world is a slave of mine.

O don't bring a candle to this get-together tonight,
For our party, that friend's moon-face will be full and bright.

For the creed that we follow the wine will be lawful fare,
But unlawful if your slender cypress in rose-form is not there.

At our party the making of perfume is not our goal,
That hair tip's scent each moment perfumes our soul.

With the melody of string and reed-pipe's voice, my ears I fill,
With ruby lip and wine-cup passing round, my eyes I fill.

The sweetness of sugar-candy – don't mention that.
The sweetness of your ruby lip - my desire is that!

The treasure of grief for you dwelt in this ruined heart,
Since then from the corner of this tavern I don't depart.

Don't speak badly of shame, from shame came my fame,
Don't speak of my fame, from my fame came my shame.

Drunken rends, head spinning, glance-giving are we!
Is there anyone in this city who like us may not be?

To tell the guardian of morals of my crime no need there is,
Because like us in search of such a continuing bliss he also is.

Hafiz let no moment pass without wine and the lovely one,
The time of rose and jasmine and Eid partying has begun.

**(W-C 34)**
  *Though Hafiz's verses are sometimes deemed to extol worldly pleasure nothing could be further from the
  truth. Here he says the wine is lawful but only if the beloved (the pure heart filled with light) is present. Again
  he says it is not the sweetness of candy but the beloved's ruby lip (spiritual tasting) that is sought. The party
  he refers to would most likely in actuality be a serious zikr or musical gathering and the delights referred to
  be delights experienced in the heart.*

Gol dar baro mey dar kafo mashooghe be kaam ast         گل در بر و می در کف و معشوقه به کام است

Soltaane jahaanam be chonin rooz gholaam ast         سلطان جهانم به چنین روز غلام است

Goo sham mayaarid dar in jam ke emshab         گو شمع میارید در این جمع که امشب

Dar majlese maa maahe rokhe doost tamaam ast         در مجلس ما ماه رخ دوست تمام است

Dar mazhabe maa baade halaal ast valiken         در مذهب ما باده حلال است ولیکن

Bi rooye to ey sarve golandaam haraam ast         بی روی تو ای سرو گل اندام حرام است

Dar majlese maa atr mayamiz ke maa raa         در مجلس ما عطر میامیز که ما را

Har lahze ze gisooye to khoshbooy mashaam ast         هر لحظه ز گیسوی تو خوشبوی مشام است

Goosham hame bar ghovle neyo naghmeye chang ast         گوشم همه بر قول نی و نغمه چنگ است

Chashmam hame bar la-le labo gardeshe jaam ast         چشمم همه بر لعل لب و گردش جام است

Az chaashniye ghand magoo hicho ze shekkar         از چاشنی قند مگو هیچ و ز شکّر

Zaan roo ke maraa dar labe shirine to kaam ast         زان رو که مرا در لب شیرین تو کام است

Ta ganje ghamat dar dele viraane moghim ast         تا گنج غمت در دل ویرانه مقیم است

Hamvaare maraa konje kharaabaat moghaam ast         همواره مرا کنج خرابات مقام است

Az nang che gooee ke ma ra naam ze nang ast         از ننگ چه گویی که مرا نام ز ننگ است

Vaz naam che porsi ke maraa nang ze naam ast         وز نام چه پرسی که مرا ننگ ز نام است

Meikhaarevo sargashtevo rendimo nazar baaz         میخواره و سرگشته و رندیم و نظرباز

Vaan kas ke cho maa nist dar in shahr kodaam ast         وان کس که چو ما نیست در این شهر کدام است

Baa mohtasebam eyb magooeed ke ou niz         با محتسبم عیب مگویید که او نیز

Peyvaste cho maa dar talabe eyshe modaam ast         پیوسته چو ما در طلب عیش مدام است

Hafez maneshin bi meyo mashooghe zamaani         حافظ منشین بی می و معشوقه زمانی

Kayyaame golo yaasamano eide siyaam ast         کایّام گل و یاسمن و عید صیام است

What need has my garden of the fir tree and cypress?
The box tree, grown in the shade, how is it any less?

What religion have you espoused O my fair young beauty,
That my blood, licit as mother's milk, for you seems to be.

Since you envisage grief on the horizon - drink wine[1],
This diagnosis is correct and the cure is in the wine.

To take my head from the Magian Pir's doorstep - what for?
Fortune is in his house, and opening is in this door.

Yesterday, wine-fuelled promises from a wine filled head!
Today what will happen - what will come from that head?

Only broken hearts are purchased in this, our Way;
The market place for pretenders is some distance away.

Love's story is one and the same, what a wonderful tale,
But every lover will tell it quite differently, without fail.

Speak no ill of Shiraz; Ruknabad's water and a pleasant breeze it's got;
Of all the seven kingdoms it is the most pleasing beauty spot.

The water of life and Khizr[2], concealed in darkness, is very far,
Long is the journey to our water whose fountain is 'Allah ho Akbar'[3]

We won't detract from the honour of contentment and poverty,
So tell the king whatever we receive is on account of our destiny.

Hafiz, how marvellous your reed pen! Yes a sweet branch[4] it is;
Bearing much more heart-pleasing fruit than sugar or honey it is.

**(W-C 35)**

[1] "...grief on the horizon..." Hafiz says drink wine! Far from being escapism in the conventional sense, to drink wine means resort to the spiritual bliss that removes worries and negative thoughts that themselves are the cause of the problems.

[2] "...the water of life and Khizr..." See the glossary for Khizr. The water of (eternal) life is said to be hidden in darkness.

[3] "...Allah ho Akbar..." The first words of the call to prayer – also indicating the end of the Ramadan fast at sunset.

[4] "...a sweet branch..." This is probably a reference to Shaks-i-Nabat (literally meaning a branch of sugar) a beautiful woman who inspired some of Hafiz's ghazals.

Baaghe maraa che haajate sarvo senovbar ast
Shemshaade khaane parvare man az ke kamtar ast
باغ مرا چه حاجت سرو و صنوبرست
شمشاد خانه پرورمن از که کمتر است

Ey naazanin sanam to che mazhab gereftei
Ket khoone maa haalaaltar az shire maadar ast
ای نازنین صنم تو چه مذهب گرفته‌ای
کت خون ما حلالتر از شیر مادر است

Chon naghshe gham ze door bebini sharaab khaah
Tash-khis kardeimo modavaa mogharrar ast
چون نقش غم ز دور بینی شراب خواه
تشخیص کرده‌ایم و مداوا مقرّر است

Az aastaane pire moghaan sar cheraa kasham
Dovlat dar in saraavo goshaayesh darin dar ast
از آستان پیر مغان سر چرا کشم
دولت درین سرا و گشایش درین در است

Di va-de daad vaslamo dar sar sharaab daasht
Emrooz taa che gooyado baazash che dar sar ast
دی وعده داد وصلم و در سر شراب داشت
امروز تا چه گوید و بازش چه در سر است

Dar raahe maa shekaste deli mikharando bas
Baazaare khodforooshi az aan sooye digar ast
در راه ما شکسته دلی میخرند و بس
بازار خود فروشی ازان سوی دیگر است

Yek ghesse bish nist ghame eshgh vin ajab
Kaz har kasi ke mishenavam naa mokarrar ast
یک قصّه بیش نیست غم عشق واین عجب
کز هرکسی که می‌شنوم نامکرّر است

Shirazo aabe rokniyo in baade khosh nasim
Eybash makon ke khaale rokhe haft keshvar ast
شیراز و آب رکنی و این باد خوش نسیم
عیش مکن که خال رخ هفت کشور است

Fargh ast azaabe khezr ke zolmaat jaaye oust
Taa aabe maa ke manba-ash allaho akbar ast
فرق است از آب خضر که ظلمات جای اوست
تا آب ما که منبعش الله اکبر است

Maa aaberooye faghro ghanaa-at nemibarim
Baa paad-shah begooy ke roozi moghaddar ast
ما آب روی فقر و قناعت نمی‌بریم
با پادشه بگوی که روزی مقدّر است

Hafez che torfe shaakhe nabaatist kelke to
Kesh mive delpazirtar az shahdo shekkar ast
حافظ چه طرفه شاخ نباتیست کلک تو
کش میوه دلپذیرتر از شهد و شکّر است

The highest paradise garden is just a retreat for the Dervishes[1]:
The source of munificence is the service of the Dervishes.

Honour bestowing talismans are the treasures concealed,
That in the merciful look of the Dervishes become revealed.

The palace of paradise, to guard the door of which, Rizwan[2] goes,
Is but a turret to view the pleasures in the Dervishes' meadows.

The ray that transforms base metals into the gold of purity,
Comes from the company of Dervishes, as an alchemy.

The sun lays down its shining crown before the glory,
That can be found keeping the Dervishes' company.

From one end of the earth to the other are the armies of tyranny,
Before time began to after time's end, the Dervishes find timely.

Inestimable, never decaying, is that wealth and sovereignty,
That, to put it simply, is the Dervishes very own treasury.

That Qarun[3] with his fabled wealth sinks still deeper below,
Maybe you read - it is jealous Dervish wrath that makes it so.

O power wielding potentate, boast not of splendour you are owning,
For gold and your very head depend on a look Dervishes are giving.

The ambitions of the world's kings in many forms appear,
But are mere mirror images of what in Dervishes appear.

Hafiz, if to drink the water of everlasting life you must;
At the door to the Dervishes' cell, its fount is that dust.

I am the slave of the Asaf[4] who in our present age is living,
Beneath whose royal finery a Dervish I am seeing.

---

**(W-C 36) The radif here is 'Dervishes'.**

[1] "...the Dervishes..." The term is popularly misused these days. A true Dervish is a Sufi of a very special kind – one who has given everything to Allah and reserved nothing for himself and therefore has the capacity to give extraordinary blessings, spiritual and material, when pleased; and inflict severe punishment on one who displeases him. In effect he gives or withholds as Allah gives or withholds, without fear of consequences.

Rovzeye kholdebarin khalvate darvishaanast

Maayeye mohtashami khedmate darvishaan ast

روضه خلدبرین خلوت درویشان است

مایه محتشمی خدمت درویشان است

Ganje ezzat ke telesmaate ajaayeb daarad

Fathe aan dar nazare rahmate darvishaanast

گنج عزّت که طلسمات عجایب دارد

فتح آن در نظر رحمت درویشان است

Ghasre ferdovs ke rezvansh be darbaani raft

Manzari az chamane noz hate darvishaanast

قصر فردوس که رضوانش به دربانی رفت

منظری از چمن نزهت درویشان است

Anche zar mishavad az partove aan ghalbe siyaah

Kimiyaaeest ke dar sohbate darvishan ast

آن چه زر می‌شود از پرتو آن قلب سیاه

کیمیائیست که در صحبت درویشان است

Anke pishash benahad taaje takabbor khorshid

Kebriaeest ke dar heshmate darvishaanast

آنکه پیشش بنهد تاج تکبّر خورشید

کبریائیست که در حشمت درویشان است

Az karaan ta be karaan lashkare zolm ast vali

Az azal ta be abad forsate darvishaan ast

از کران تا به کران لشکر ظلم است ولی

از ازل تا به ابد فرصت درویشان است

Dovlati ra ke nabashad gham az aasibe zavaal

Bi takallof besheno dovlate darvishaanast

دولتی راکه نباشد غم از آسیب زوال

بی تکلّف بشنو دولت درویشان است

Ganje Gharoon ke foroo miravad az ghahr hanooz

Sadmei az asare gheirate darvishaan ast

گنج قارون که فرو می رود از قهر هنوز

صدمه ای از اثر غیرت درویشان است

Ey tavaangar maforoosh in hame nekhvat ke to raa

Saro zar dar kanafe hemmate darvishanast

ای توانگر مفروش این همه نخوت که ترا

سر و زر در کنف همّت درویشان است

Rooye maghsood ke shaahaan be doaa mitalaband

Moz-herash aayeneye tal-ate darvishaanast

روی مقصود که شاهان به دعا می‌طلبند

مظهرش آینه طلعت درویشان است

Hafez injaa be adab baash ke soltaniyo molk

Hame az bandegiye hazrate darvishaanast

حافظ اینجا به ادب باش که سلطانی و ملک

همه از بندگی حضرت درویشان است

Bandeye aasafe ahdam ke darin saltanatash

Soorate khaajegiyo sirate darvishaanast

بنده آصف عهدم که درین سلطنتش

صورت خواجگی و سیرت درویشان است

---

[2] "...Rizwan..." The gate keeper of paradise.

[3] "...Qarun..." See glossary in this volume. Here Hafiz is saying it was because Qarun offended a Dervish that h suffered his fate of being swallowed by the earth.

[4] "...Asaf..." See the glossary in this volume.

Wine cup in hand my beloved came, drunk, into the Magian's lair;
With a narcissus-like eye[1] that intoxicated the wine drinkers there.

In the hoof of that one's horse the crescent moon one can see,
In that towering presence small seemed the height of the fir tree.

How to give news of myself - when no news comes to me,[2]
How to say I don't see that one - when I see that one constantly.

When you rose up - the candle flame in the heart of friends died out,
When you sat down – there rose up from the sighted ones a great shout.

If amber has a musk scented quality then it's been in your hair somehow,
If the indigo dye[3] is an archer then it's from mixing with your eyebrow.

O return please, so that Hafiz renewed signs of life may show;
Though the arrow flies not back, once it has left the archer's bow.

**(W-C 37)**
  1 "...narcissus like eye..." See commentary 2 in (W-C 2).
  2 "...no news comes to me..." The meaning of this is that the poet has become unaware of himself because of
  his absorption in the beloved.
  3 "...indigo dye..." This is used to colour the eyebrow. The overall theme is that it is the beloved alone that
  counts and anything which has value receives that value from the beloved.

Dar deire moghaan aamad yaaram ghadahi dar dast
Mast az meyo meikhaaraan az nargese mastash mast

در دیر مغان آمد یارم قدحی در دست
مست از می و میخواران از نَرگس مستش مست

Dar na-le samande ou shekle mahe nov peidaa
Vaz ghadde bolande ou baalaaye senovbar past

در نعل سمند او شکل مه نو پیدا
وز قدّ بلند او بالای صنوبر پست

Aakher be che gooyam hast az khod khabaram chon nist
Vaz bahre che gooyam nist baa vey nazaram chon hast

آخر به چه گویم هست از خود خبرم چون نیست
وز بهر چه گویم نیست با وی نظرم چون هست

Sham-e dele damsaazaan benshast cho ou barkhaast
Vafghaan ze nazar baazaan barkhaast cho ou benshast

شمع دل دمسازان بنشست چو او برخاست
و افغان ز نظربازان برخاست چو او بنشست

Gar ghaaliye khosh boo gasht dar gisooye ou pichid
Var vasme Kamaan kash gasht dar abrooye ou peivast

گر غالیه خوش بو گشت در گیسوی اوپیچید
ور وسمه کمانکش گشت در ابروی او پیوست

Baaz aay ke baaz aayad omre shodeye Hafez
Har chand ke naayad baaz tiri ke beshod az shast

بازآی که بازآید عمر شده حافظ
هر چند که ناید باز تیری که بشد از شست

That sleepy, sullen, seductive look, in those narcissus-like eyes,
And that wayward curl midst tousled hair, have purpose I surmise.

When mother's milk your lips still made moist, I used to say this;
'Sugar at the salt-mine's[1] mouth': your sweet lip not lacking purpose is.

A long life I wish you certainly; for your eyelashes arrows are,
From your eyebrow's bow, not aimed without purpose they are.

From the sorrow of separation, in grief's grip it seems you are,
O heart, your cries, groans and moans - not without purpose they are.

Last night from your street, a scent to the rose-bed blew,
O rose, that ripped collar was not without its purpose too.

Hid from the herd by the heart, the pain love inflicts on us is,
But Hafiz, this tear-filled eye, not without a purpose it is.

**(W-C 38) The radif here is "Purpose..."**
   This Ghazal is not in book one of Khanlari, neither is it in Avery or Saberi; suggesting there is doubt about its
   authenticity. It is included by us on account of what we see as its intrinsic beauty.
   [1] "...salt-mine..." Salt is the symbol of purity. One can thus read these lines as saying that sweetness serves the
   purpose of attracting to purity.

Khaabe aan nargese fattane to bi chizi nist
خواب آن نرگس فتّان تو بی چیزی نیست

Taabe aan zolfe parishaane to bi chizi nist
تاب آن زلف پریشان تو بی چیزی نیست

Az labat shir ravaan bood ke man migoftam
از لبت شیر روان بود که من می‌گفتم

In shekar gerde namakdaane to bi chizi nist
این شکر گرد نمکدان تو بی چیزی نیست

Jaan deraziyye to baadaa ke yaghin midaanam
جان درازیّ تو بادا که یقین می‌دانم

Dar kamaan naavake mojgaane to bi chizi nist
در کمان ناوک مژگان تو بی چیزی نیست

Mobtalaaee be ghame mehnato andoohe feraagh
مبتلایی به غم و محنت ایّام فراق

Ey del in naale o afghaane to bi chizi nist
ای دل این ناله و افغان تو بی چیزی نیست

Doosh baad az sare kooyash be golestaan bogzasht
دوش باد از سر کویش به گلستان بگذشت

Ey gol in chaake garibaane to bi chizi nist
ای گل این چاک گریبان تو بی چیزی نیست

Darde eshgh ar che del az khalgh nahaan midaarad
درد عشق ار چه دل از خلق نهان می‌دارد

Hafez in dideye geryaane to bi chizi nist
حافظ این دیده گریان تو بی چیزی نیست

O sermoniser, sort yourself out, what's the commotion, pray?
Today my hand gave my heart away, what did yours do today?

Although love's intoxication to a ruined state brought me,
The foundation of my prosperity that ruin turned out to be.

O heart, at the beloved's violence don't cry, saying, 'Injustice!'
It is the beloved gave you this and the beloved is justice.

The beloved's slender waist, from nothing God brought it,
It is such a subtlety that no one created has discovered it.

Your street's beggar for eight paradises has no need,
A captive to you, so from both worlds that one is freed.

Whilst your lip leaves my desire unfulfilled, as in (kissing) the Ney,
My ear hears only vain wind from what worldly folk say.

Hafiz, no more stories, no more charm-filled words breath out,
For many such magical  tales, linger in the memory, no doubt.

**(W-C 39)**
This is ostensibly a ghazal full of conventional love imagery. Try reading it, however, as if it is describing the process of birth. In that case the slender waist is the umbilical cord, the heart given away is the child, the beloved's violence is the act of procreation, often seen retrospectively as undesirable due to labour pains, etc. Within the ghazal one must accept varying perspectives. For example is the line "My ear hears only vain wind from what worldly folk say" from the perspective of the newborn infant?
Based on this it is our contention that the idea of Hafiz's ghazals as a string of loosely connected, albeit beautiful, pearls does not do full justice to his inspired genius and spiritual profundity. There is always a main spiritual theme (not just in the radif), however well hidden.

Boro be kaare khod ey vaaez in che faryaadast      برو به کار خود ای واعظ این چه فریادست

Maraa fetaad del az rah to raa che oftaadast      مرا فتاد دل از ره تو را چه افتادست

Agar che mastiye eshgham kharaab kard vali      اگرچه مستی عشقم خراب کرد ولی

Asaase hastiye man zaan kharaab aabaad ast      اساس هستی من زان خراب آباد است

Delaa manaal ze bidaado jovre yaar ke yaar      دلا منال ز بیداد و جور یار که یار

To raa nasib hamin karde asto in daad ast      تو را نصیب همین کرده است و این داد است

Miyaane ou ke khodaa aafaride ast az hich      میان او که خدا آفریده است از هیچ

Daghigheist ke hich aafaride nagshaadast      دقیقه‌ایست که هیچ آفریده نگشادست

Gedaaye kooye to az hasht khold mostaghnist      گدای کوی تو از هشت خلد مستغنیست

Asire bande to az har do aalam aazad ast      اسیر بند تو از هر دو عالم آزاد است

Be kaam taa naresaanad maraa labash chon naay      به کام تا نرساند مرا لبش چون نای

Nasihate hame aalam be gooshe man baad ast      نصیحت همه عالم به گوش من بادست

Boro fesaane makhaano fosoon madam Hafez      برو فسانه مخوان و فسون مدم حافظ

Kazin fesaanevo afsoon maraa basi yaad ast      کزین فسانه و افسون مرا بسی یاد است

The ruby lip so full! Yet thirsty for my blood the beloved's lip is,
The surrender of my life to gain the sight of you, my labour is.

One who saw the eyelashes of that dark-eyed heart-breaker,
Would feel ashamed if, of my desire, they were an ill speaker.

Camel-driver, not that exit, carry my goods and me further,
At the end of my lane is the beloved's way, go there rather.[1]

I am slave to my fortunate stars, for when fidelity is in short supply,
The faithful love of that intoxicated beauty has purchased me.

The tray of perfume bottles and cascading hair that's like amber,
Is but one flavour from the flavours of my sweet essence maker.

From your gate like a breeze don't blow me away, O gardener,
For it's my pomegranate-red tears that give the rose bed water.

Of sweetness and rose water, the beloved's lip is the provider,
Its cure the narcissus' eye for the love-sick heart did order.

That one who taught Hafiz how the art of the ghazal to refine,
Is a sweetly spoken, subtle speaker and a good friend of mine.[2]

*(W-C 40) The radif here is "Of mine is"*
[1] *"...carry...further..." As we might say – go the extra mile; advice sometimes given to the disciple by the spiritual guide in their spiritual struggle.*
[2] *"...one who taught..." Hafiz refines his ghazals in the way inspired by Hazrat Ali who was instrumental in giving the gift of true poetry to him.*

La-le siraabe be khoon teshne labe yaare manast

Vaz peye didane ou daadane jaan kaare manast

لعل سیراب به خون تشنه لب یار من است

وز پی دیدن او دادن جان کار من است

Sharm az aan chashme siyah baadasho mojgaane deraaz

Har ke del bordane ou dido dar enkaare manast

شرم از آن چشم سیه بادش و مژگان دراز

هر که دل بردن او دید و در انکار من است

Sarebaan rakht be darvaaze mabar kaan sare kooy

Shaah raahist ke sar manzele deldaare manast

ساربان رخت به دروازه مبر کان سر کوی

شاهراهیست که سرمنزل دلدار من است

Bandeye taale-e khisham ke dar in ghahte vafaa

Eshghe aan looliye sarmast vafaadaare manast

بنده طالع خویشم که در این قحط وفا

عشق آن لولی سرمست وفادار من است

Tableye atre golo dorje abir afshaanash

Feize yek shamme ze booye khoshe attare manast

طبله عطر گل و درج عبیرافشانش

فیض یک شمّه ز بوی خوش عطّار من است

Baaghbaan hamcho nasimam ze dare baagh maraan

Kaabe golzaare to az ashke cho golnaare man ast

باغبان همچو نسیمم ز درباغ مران

کآب گلزار تو از اشک چو گلنار من است

Sharbate ghando golaab az labe yaaram farmood

Nargese ou ke tabibe dele bimaare manast

شربت قند و گلاب از لب یارم فرمود

نرگس او که طبیب دل بیمار من است

Aanke dar tarze ghazal nokte be Hafez aamookht

Yaare shirin sokhane naadere goftaare manast

آن که در طرز غزل نکته به حافظ آموخت

یار شیرین سخن نادره گفتار من است

It's the time when passion for beauties[1] is my religion,
In this work my broken-heart in joy has gone.

To see your ruby, a soul-seeing eye one must gain,
How should my world-seeing eye this high station attain.

Be my dear friend! For space's adorner and time's beautifier,
Are both your moon-like face and my star-like tears' cluster.

Since your love taught me the art of speaking words finely,
People speak words about us that are very complimentary[2].

Give me, O God, I pray the good fortune of poverty[3],
For this blessing brings with it grandeur and dignity.

O Lord, this Kaaba of my desire, whose spectacular show is it,
That desert thorns are like red and white roses on the way to it?

O critical preacher, don't be proud of attachment to a deputy,
For the place where the King lives is in my heart you see.

Hafiz! Speak no more of the prestige of Parvis[4] that ancient governor,
His lip[5] now serves to pour wine for my Khusrau[6], my own sweet ruler.

---

**(W-C 41) The radif here is "Of mine is"**
[1] "..beauties..." This may refer to the spiritually exalted Prophets or Saints as the next verse clearly implies.
[2] "..This ghazal may be directed to Hazrat Ali.
[3] "..poverty..." The holy Prophet Muhammed famously said "poverty is my pride"
[4] "..Parvis..." See the glossary in volume one. The name means "victorious".
[5] "..lip..." This probably refers to his skull.
[6] "...Khusrau..." This is also a reference to Parvis, but in his role as king.

Roozegaarist ke sovdaaye botaan dine manast

روزگاریست که سودای بتان دین من است

Ghame in kaar neshaate dele ghamgine manast

غم این کار نشاط دل غمگین من است

Didane lale to raa dideye jaan bin baayad

دیدن لعل تو را دیده جان بین باید

Vin kojaa martabeye chashme jahaan bine man ast

وین کجا مرتبه چشم جهان بین من است

Yaare man baash ke zibe falako zinate dahr

یار من باش که زیب فلک و زینت دهر

Az mahe rooye tovo ashke cho parvine manast

از مه روی تو و اشک چو پروین من است

Taa maraa eshghe to talime sokhan goftan daad

تا مرا عشق تو تعلیم سخن گفتن داد

Khalgh raa verde zabaan medhato tahsine manast

خلق را ورد زبان مدحت و تحسین من است

Dovlate faghr khodaayaa be man arzaani daar

دولت فقر خدایا به من ارزانی دار

Kin keraamat sababe heshmato tamkine man ast

کاین کرامت سبب حشمت و تمکین من است

Yaa rab aan kabeye maghsood tamaashaagahe kist

یا رب آن کعبه مقصود تماشاگه کیست

Ke moghilaane tarighash golo nasrine manast

که مغیلان طریقش گل و نسرین من است

Vaaeze shahne shenaas in azamat goo maforoosh

واعظ شحنه شناس این عظمت گو مفروش

Zaanke manzelgahe soltaan dele meskine manast

زانکه منزلگه سلطان دل مسکین من است

Hafez az heshmate parviz degar ghesse makhaan

حافظ از حشمت پرویز دگر قصّه مخوان

Ke labash jor-e keshe khosrove shirine manast

که لبش جرعه کش خسرو شیرین من است

By inclination the tavern corner is the place for my prayer,
The Magian Pir's prayer is the morning litany that I do there.[1]

If the tune of the morning harp I fail to hear, do not fear,[2]
In the dawn my sighs of excuse flowing like tears will appear.

Praise be to God, neither king nor beggar means anything to me,
The beggar of the dust of your doorstep is king enough for me,

Tavern or mosque, union with you[3] is what matters to me,
No other idea comes into my mind; may God my witness be.

From the moment that on this threshold my forehead I pressed,
The throne of the sun's glory was a cushion for my head to rest.

Maybe the blade of death will cut the cords of my life's tent;
Otherwise, to leave your blessed door is never my intent!

Hafiz, though you know that sin we could not have been avoiding;
Chivalrously strive to take the blame and say, "It is my own doing".

**(W-C 42) The radif here is "Of mine is"**
[1] An alternative rendering is "My morning litany is to pray for the Magian Pir".
[2] This verse can be understood in different ways; for example Hafiz could be saying that if he misses (or fails to make responses to) to the morning call to prayer....etc. He could also be meaning by dawn – the Day of Resurrection. He could also be saying that if he missed the dawn prayer his distress alone would make up for that. There are stories in the Masnevi about Mu'ahwia with the same theme.
[3] "...you..." This ghazal appears to be directed firmly at the Pir of the Magian's (meaning his spiritual guide) and is in line with the veneration for the guide practised in Sufism and disparaged by many of the orthodox. In reality the guide is only the path to God, but for the blind disciple the guide is all they need to know until they begin to truly see. Since Hafiz is one who sees clearly I take it the intent is to make a ghazal as guidance about the guide/disciple relationship.

Manam ke goosheye meykhaneh khanghahe manast

Doaaye pire Moghan verde sobhgahe manast

منم که گوشه میخانه خانقاه من است

دعای پیر مغان ورد صبحگاه من است

Garam taraaney change sabooh nist che baak

Navaaye man be sahar aahe ozr khaahe manast

گرم ترانه چنگ صبوح نیست چه باک

نوای من به سحر آه عذرخواه من است

Ze padeshaaho gedaa faaregham be hamdellaah

Kamin gedaaye dare doost paadeshahe manast

ز پادشاه و گدا فارغم بحمدالله

کمین گدای در دوست پادشاه من است

Gharaz ze masjedo meykhaaneam vesaale shomaast

Joz in khiyaal nadaarm khodaa govaahe manast

غرض ز مسجد و میخانه‌ام وصال شماست

جز این خیال ندارم خدا گواه من است

Az aan zamaan ke barin aastaan nahaadam rooy

Faraaze masnade khorshid tekyegaah man ast

از آن زمان که برین آستان نهادم روی

فراز مسند خورشید تکیه گاه من است

Magar be tighe ajal kheyme bar kanam var ni

Ramidan az dare dovlat na rasmo raahe manast

مگر به تیغ اجل خیمه برکنم ور نی

رمیدن از در دولت نه رسم و راه من است

Gonaah agar che nabood ekhtyaar maa Hafiz

To dar tarighe adab koosho goo gonaahe manast

گناه اگر چه نبود اختیار ما حافظ

تو در طریق ادب کوش و گو گناه من است

The red rose in bloom! Drunk is the bulbul too!
Time savvy Sufis[1], an invite to carousing for you!

Even though rock-solid that repentance was deemed,
It was shattered by a crystal goblet that fragile seemed.

Wine ho! For in the court of that One, independent of all need,
If guard or sultan; sober or drunk; distinction they don't heed.

In this Inn of two doors, one entrance and one exit, there is,
Whether high-arched, or low-beamed, our way of living is.

Without suffering and hardship the state of ease cannot be attained,
In timeless *Alast* testing was also decreed and as man's lot remained[1].

If existence 'is' or if it 'is not' - in the mind be content,
All the paths to perfection lead only to the non-existent.

Asaf-like pomp, a steed like the wind, and birds talking clearly![2]
Yet blown away! A noble soul in them found no profitability?

"Wing and feather"[3] you may have, but don't fly from the Way,
For sure, the highest flying arrow must bite the dust one day.

Hafiz, the tongue of your pen cannot give thanks sufficiently;
That what it inscribes passes from hand to hand so eagerly.

---

**(W-C 43)**

[1] See in the glossary under 'Alast'. A Sufi may sometimes be called the 'child of the moment' – as he or she is
unattached to what has or what will happen in chronological time, their response to any situation is based
on an awareness of eternity in the present moment.
Repentance is the first stage of the Sufi path – it is not the repentance for one particular act as much as
repentance for one's whole former life. The foundation of that repentance is smashed when it is realised, in
a true sense that in all things Allah is the Causer. This is known as the 'repentance of repentance'. The glass
that smashes it may be - as Avery points out - a reference to the glass surrounding the lamp mentioned in
the famous Light verse of the holy Qur'an since seen in God's light all appears different. The "repentance of
repentance" however is dependent on having first repented fully.
[2] This verse refers to the prophet Solomon.
[3] "..."Wing and feather"..." The flight of imagining one has the stage of repentance or indeed other spiritual
stages, instead of tasting them actually, will end in dust as Hafiz Saheb puts it.

Shekofte shod gole khamraavo gasht bolbol mast

شکفته شد گل خمری و گشت بلبل مست

Salaaye sarkhoshi ey soofiaane vaght parast

صلای سرخوشی ای صوفیان وقت پرست

Asaase tovbe ke dar mohkami cho sang nomood

اساس توبه که در محکمی چو سنگ نمود

Bebin ke jaame zojaaji che torfe ash beshkast

ببین که جام زجاجی چه طرفه‌اش بشکست

Biyaar baade ke dar baargaahe esteghnaa

بیار باده که در بارگاه استغنا

Che paasebaano che soltaan che hooshyaaro che mast

چه پاسبان و چه سلطان چه هوشیار و چه مست

Darin rebaate do dar chon zaroorat ast rahil

درین رباط دودر چون ضرورت است رحیل

Ravaagho taaghe maeeshat che sarbolando che past

رواق و طاق معیشت چه سربلند و چه پست

Maghaame eish moyassar nemishavad bi ranj

مقام عیش میسّر نمی‌شود بی‌رنج

Balaa be hokme balaa basteand ahde alast

بلی به حکم بلا بسته‌اند عهد الست

Be hasto nist maranjaan zamiro khosh mibaash

به هست و نیست مرنجان ضمیر و خوش می‌باش

Ke nistist sar anjaame har kamaal ke hast

که نیستیست سرانجام هر کمال که هست

Shokoohe aasafiyo asbe baado manteghe teir

شکوه آصفی و اسب باد و منطق طیر

Be baad rafto az ou khaaje hich tarf nabast

به باد رفت و از او خواجه هیچ طرف نبست

Be baalo par maro az rah ke tire partaabi

به بال و پر مرو از ره که تیر پرتابی

Havaa gereft zamaani vali be khaak neshast

هوا گرفت زمانی ولی به خاک نشست

Zabaane kelke to Hafez che shokre aan guyad

زبان کلک تو حافظ چه شکر آن گوید

Ke gofteye sokhanat mibarand dast be dast

که گفته سخنت می‌برند دست به دست

Wild-haired, drunk, wine jug in hand, sweating profusely,
Unkempt, garment torn, singing and laughing so carelessly.

Eyes seemingly seeking a fight; lip showing silent sorrow!
Last night at midnight you came and sat next to my pillow.

You bent gently down and whispered softly into my ear,
Sighing, "Lover are you awake or asleep as you appear?"

The knowing lover who is given wine at night in this way,
Is unfaithful to love if homage to wine he doesn't pay.

Pious man, stop going on about our drinking dregs this way,
This gift we were given on the day of Alast, we say.

Whatever was poured into our cup we drank our ration,
Whether the wine of paradise, or another concoction.

Laughter, frothing from the wine cup, your curling locks of hair,
How many vows of repentance, like Hafiz's, lie broken, there.

*(W-C 44)*
*The mystic is granted extraordinary experiences of a spiritual nature that can extend in to the physical realm too. How should he not accept and extol the reality of these. Those who have not such first-hand knowledge will find ways to explain the experiences to satisfy their rational mind – the mystic knows what he knows as surely as the doubter knows his own hand.*

Zolf aashoftevo khey kardevo khandaan labo mast

زلف آشفته و خوی کرده و خندان لب و مست

Pirhan chaako ghazal khaano soraahi dar dast

پیرهن چاک و غزل خوان و صراحی در دست

Nargesash arbade jooyo labash afsoos konaan

نرگسش عربده جوی و لبش افسوس کنان

Nim shab doosh be baaline man aamad benshast

نیم شب دوش به بالین من آمد بنشست

Sar faraa gooshe man aavardo be aavaaze hazin

سر فرا گوش من آورد و به آواز حزین

Goft key aasheghe dirineye man khaabat hast

گفت کای عاشق دیرینه من خوابت هست

Aarefi raa ke chonin saaghare shabgir dahand

عارفی را که چنین ساغر شبگیر دهند

Kaafare eshgh bovad gar nabovad baade parast

کافر عشق بود گر نبود باده پرست

Boro ey zaahedo bar dord keshaan khorde magir

برو ای زاهد و بر دردکشان خرده مگیر

Ke nadaadand joz in tohfe be maa rooze alast

که ندادند جز این تحفه به ما روز الست

Aanche ou rikht be peimaaneye maa nooshidim

آنچه او ریخت به پیمانه ما نوشیدیم

Agar az khamre behesht asto gar az baadeye mast

اگر از خمر بهشت است وگرازباده مست

Khandeye jaame meyo zolfe gereh gire negaar

خنده جام می و زلف گره گیر نگار

Ey basaa tovbe ke chon tovbeye Hafez beshekast

ای بسا توبه که چون توبه حافظ بشکست

Your curling lock tied up, a thousand hearts with just one fine hair,
A thousand 'remedy' providers from four directions were bound there.

So that to the scented breeze their soul the lovers are surrendering,
You opened the musk-pod, and then you closed the door to wanting.

With the crescent eyebrow you revealed, I was smitten,
You turned away, and that moon face became hidden[1].

The Saki filled the goblet with a wine of so many fine hues;
Images abounded; to bind us to the cup, beauty you choose.

Lord, what sang that long neck[2] the wine barrel's blood did fill,
That despite its sweet glug, glug, glugging that voice was still.

In the hidden sama[3] what note did the musician strike, in what way,
That the folk of ecstasy, even the words Hu or Ho could not say.

Hafiz, one who loves not, but wants to go on union's path,
Ties on the pilgrim garb without taking the compulsory bath[4].

---

**(W-C 45) The radif here is "Bound".**
[1] A theme here is the transient revelation that Allah gives to seeker to encourage him or her. These are called 'Hals' or temporary states.
[2] "...that long neck..." This refers to the long narrow neck of a traditional wine-pouring vessel.
[3] "...Sama..." See in the glossary.
[4] "... the compulsory bath..." 'Ghusl' or the compulsory full bath required in Islam for physical purity after sexual contact and before a sacred act such as the pilgrimage.

Zolfat hezaar del be yeki taare moo bebast

زلفت هزار دل به یکی تار مو بست

Raahe hezaar chaaregar az chaarsoo bebast

راه هزار چاره گر از چار سو بست

Taa har kasi be booye nasimi dahand jaan

تا هر کسی به بوی نسیمی دهند جان

Bogshood naafeiyo dare aarezoo bebast

بگشود نافه‌ای و در آرزو بست

Sheidaa az aan shodam ke negaaram cho maahe nov

شیدا از آن شدم که نگارم چو ماه نو

Abroo nemoodo jelvegari kardo roo bebast

ابرو نمود و جلوه گری کرد و رو بست

Saaghi be chand rang mey andar piyaale rikht

ساقی به چند رنگ می اندر پیاله ریخت

In naghshhaa negar ke che khosh dar kadoo bebast

این نقشها نگر که چه خوش در کدو بست

Yaa rab che naghme kard soraahi ke khoone khom

یا رب چه نغمه کرد صراحی که خون خم

Baa naghmehaaye ghol gholash andar galoo bebast

با نغمه‌های قلقلش اندر گلو بست

Motreb che parde saakht ke dar pardeye samaa

مطرب چه پرده ساخت که در پرده سماع

Bar ahle vajdo haal dare haayo hoo bebast

بر اهل وجد و حال در های و هو بست

Hafez har aanke eshgh navarzido vasl khaast

حافظ هر آن که عشق نورزید و وصل خواست

Ehraame tovfe kabeye del bi vozoo bebast

احرام طوف کعبه دل بی وضو بست

When God formed your eyebrow, to be so heart enticing,
By those glances of yours, my problems He was resolving.

The heart ease was taken from the garden's bird, and so was mine.
When a robe for you was woven from nargisin cloth rare and fine.

A hundred knots dissolved in the rosebud that with labour I grew,
When the breeze bestowed on its heart the deep desire for you.

Content to be bound by you the revolving sphere caused me to be,
But the rope's end reaches to your will, what profit then for me?

O do not tie my poor heart in knots, as in the musk pod seed.
I thought with your knot-loosening hair-tip a pact had been agreed.

O union bearing breeze, union comes when the beloved sends you,
Mistakenly I was trying to get union from showing fidelity to you.

I said; "O beloved, from your cruelty to another city I'll flee",
Laughter! "Go on then Hafiz your foot is not stopped by me".

*(W-C 46) The radif here is "Established"*
*The theme here in the first section appears to be that once the mystic is turned to God, the Beloved; all other worldly difficulties seem insignificant. The last three verses however show aspects of how absorbingly complex that relationship with the Beloved is*

Khodaa cho soorate abrooye delgoshaaye to bast
Goshaade kaare man andar kereshmehaaye to bast

Maraavo morghe chaman raa ze del bebord aaraam
Zamaane taa ghasabe nargeso ghabaaye to bast

Ze kaare maavo dele ghonche bas gereh bogshood
Nasime gol cho del andar peye havaaye to bast

Maraa be bande to dovraane charkh raazi kard
Vali che sood ke sar reshte dar rezaaye to bast

Cho naafe bar dele meskine man gereh mafekan
Cho ahd baa sare zolfe gereh goshaaye to bast

To khod vesaale degar boodi ey nasime vesaal
Khataa negar ke del ommid dar vafaaye to bast

Ze daste jovre to goftam ze shahr khaaham raft
Be khande goft ke Hafez boro ke paaye to bast

خدا چو صورت ابروی دلگشای تو بست
گشاد کار من اندر کرشمه‌های تو بست

مرا و مرغ چمن را ز دل ببرد آرام
زمانه تا قصب نرگس و قبای تو بست

ز کار ما و دل غنچه بس گره بگشود
نسیم گل چو دل اندر پی هوای تو بست

مرا به بند تو دوران چرخ راضی کرد
ولی چه سود که سررشته در رضای تو بست

چو نافه بر دل مسکین من گره مفکن
چو عهد با سر زلف گره گشای تو بست

تو خود وصال دگر بودی ای نسیم وصال
خطا نگر که دل امید در وفای تو بست

ز دست جور تو گفتم ز شهر خواهم رفت
به خنده گفت که حافظ برو که پای تو بست

In time's domain the friendship that cannot be faulted,
Is from the goblet of pure wine[1] and the book[2] that's recited.

Travel light, for the way to safety is narrow[3] and hard to attain;
Grab the wine cup! Life is precious and won't return again.

In this world it's not just me that feels bad because works I'm lacking[4];
Scholars too must suffer when they're not practicing their learning.

The highway seems fantastically frenzied to the eye of reason;
The world and its works are passing, not a permanent station.

Very great was my hope for union with you, one day,
But death, that thief[5], hunts hope on life's highway.

Cling to that moon-faced beauty's hair, but do not be telling,
For good luck is from Venus and Saturn bad luck is giving.

A sober Hafiz not in time's domain will they be finding,
He has drunk the wine that is of 'no end and no beginning'.

Darin zamaane rafighi ke khaali az khelalast
Soraahiye meye saafo safineye ghazalast

Jaride rov ke gozargaahe aafiyat tang ast
Piaale gir ke omre aziz bi badalast

Na man ze bi amali dar jahaan maloolamo bas
Malaalate olamaa ham ze elme bi amalast

Be chashme aghl dar in rahgozaare por aashoob
Jahaano kaare jahaan bi sabaato bi mahalast

Delam omide faraavaan be vasle rooye to daasht
Vali ajal be rahe omr rahzane amalast

Begir torreye mah-chehre eeyo ghesse makhaan
Ke sa-do nahs ze tasire zohreo zohalast

Be hich dovr nakhaahand yaaft hoshyaarash
Chonin ke Hafeze maa maste baadeye azalast

در این زمانه رفیقی که خالی از خلل است
صراحی می صاف و سفینه غزل است

جریده رو که گذرگاه عافیت تنگ است
پیاله گیر که عمر عزیز بی‌بدل است

نه من ز بی عملی در جهان ملولم و بس
ملالت علما هم ز علم بی عمل است

به چشم عقل در این رهگذار پرآشوب
جهان و کار جهان بی‌ثبات و بی‌محل است

دلم امید فراوان به وصل روی تو داشت
ولی اجل به ره عمر رهزن امل است

بگیر طرّه مه چهره ای و قصّه مخوان
که سعد و نحس ز تاثیر زهره و زحل است

به هیچ دور نخواهند یافت هشیارش
چنین که حافظ ما مست باده ازل است

Vivid in the imagination you are! So wine why bother to drink?
Tell the wine cask to go away, this wine cellar is destroyed I think.

Spill even the wine of paradise in the friend's absence, [1]
For every sweet drop thus taken is torment's very essence.

Oh no! The heart-breaker gone! My eyes to tears are given;
Even the image of that one's letter is of words on water written.

The rose that saw in your glistening cheek beauty glowing,
From an envious heart into rose-water it is dissolving.

The Way! Awesome and stretching out forever,
The vast sky - its mirage reflected in the sea, as in a river.

Open O eye! Be awake and be alert! No false securities feel;
If you close in sleep, torrents of troubles become more real.

Your beloved passes by, quite near and openly,
But veiled from you, who only strangers can see.

In no corner of my brain will you find counselling,
In each cell harp and rebab are wordlessly singing.

If Hafiz is a glance-catching Rend[2] and lover - so what!
In many strange things the young engage - do they not?

---

**(W-C 48) The order of verses presented here differs from Khanlari and Avery.**
  [1] *"...even the wine of paradise..." Following Bibi Rabia many mystics prefer not to seek paradise or run from hell. Their concern is only with the true Beloved or Friend.*
  [2] *"...Rend..." Profligate.*

Maa raa ze khiaale to che parvaaye sharaabast
Khom goo sare khod gir ke khom khaane kharaabast

ما را ز خیال تو چه پروای شراب است
خم گو سر خود گیر که خمخانه خراب است

Gar khamre behesht ast berizid ke bi doost
Har sharbate azbam ke dahi eine azaabast

گر خمر بهشت است بریزید که بی دوست
هر شربت عذبم که دهی عین عذاب است

Afsoos ke shod delbaro dar dideye geryaan
Tahrire khiaale khate ou naghshe bar aabast

افسوس که شد دلبر و در دیده گریان
تحریر خیال خط او نقش بر آب است

Gol bar rokhe rangine to taa lotfe aragh did
Dar aatashe rashkaz ghame del gharghe golaabast

گل بر رخ رنگین تو تا لطف عرق دید
در آتش رشک ازغم دل غرق گلاب است

Raahe to che raahist ke az ghaayate tazim
Daryaaye mohite falakash eyne saraabast

راه تو چه راهیست که از غایت تعظیم
دریای محیط فلکش عین سراب است

Bidaar sho ey dide ke imen natavaan bood
Zin seile damaadam ke dar in manzele khaabast

بیدار شو ای دیده که ایمن نتوان بود
زین سیل دمادم که در این منزل خواب است

Mashooghe ayaan migozarad bar to valikan
Aghyaar hami binad azaan baste neghaabast

معشوقه عیان می گذرد بر تو ولیکن
اغیار همی بیند از آن بسته نقاب است

Dar konje demaagham matalab jaaye nasihat
Kin hojre poraz zamzameye chango robaabast

در کنج دماغم مطلب جای نصیحت
کاین حجره پر از زمزمه چنگ و رباب است

Hafez che shod ar aashegho rend asto nazar baaz
Bas tovre ajab laazeme ayaame shabaabast

حافظ چه شد ار عاشق و رند است ونظرباز
بس طور عجب لازم ایّام شباب است

Now, on the palm, the cup of pure wine, the rose displays,
The bulbul sings its praises in a hundred thousand ways.

Seek the book of verses, go, and alone in the wilderness stay,
Let academics 'explain explanations'[1] in their academic way.

Follow the way of the Anqa[2], alone on Kaf[3] and from people stay away,
From Kaf, all around the globe goes what the corner-sitters say.

The top religious cleric got drunk and his legal decision was this,
"Wine is illicit, but not as bad as corruption in charitable endowments is".

There's no choice between dregs and purified wine. Drink, anyway!
Whatever the Saki gives is sure to be full of grace in some way.

The fantasies of pretenders and vain rivals are reminders,
Of the story of the mat-weaver and the gold-cloth weavers.[4]

Hafiz stay silent! Like red-gold hide these fine points[5] away,
Because the city's banker is also a currency forger today.

**(W-C 49)**
[1] "...'explain explanations..." This refers to commentaries on commentaries of the holy Book.
[2] "...Anqa (or Simurgh)..." See the glossary in this volume
[3] "... Kaf..." See the glossary in this volume.
[4] "...gold-cloth weavers ..." Hafiz speaks of his verses as gold-cloth as distinct from the uninspired poetry of many poets who only weave grass mats.
[5] "...these fine points..." Hafiz's poetry conceals spiritual truth under the guise of beautiful turns of phrase and delightful metaphors.

Konoon ke bar kafe gol jaame baadeye saafast
Be sad hezaar zabaan bolbolash darovsaafast

كنون كه بر كف گل جام باده صاف است
به صد هزار زبان بلبلش در اوصاف است

Bekhaah daftare ash-aaro raahe sahraa gir
Che vaghte madresevo bahse kashfe kashaafast

بخواه دفتر اشعار و راه صحرا گیر
چه وقت مدرسه و بحث کشف کشّاف است

Bebor ze khalgho ze anghaa ghiyaase kaar begir
Ke seyte gooshshineshinaan ze ghaaf taa ghaafast

ببر ز خلق و زعنقا قیاس کار بگیر
که صیت گوشه نشینان ز قاف تا قاف است

Faghihe madrese di mast boodo fatvaa daad
Ke mey haraam vali beh ze maale ovghaafast

فقیه مدرسه دی مست بود و فتوی داد
که می حرام ولی به ز مال اوقاف است

Be dordo saaf toraa hokm nist khosh darkash
Ke harche saghiye maa kard eyne altaafast

به درد و صاف تو را حکم نیست خوش درکش
که هر چه ساقی ما کرد عین الطاف است

Hadise modaiaano khiyaale hamkaaraan
Hamaan hekaayate zardoozo booriaa baafast

حدیث مدّعیان و خیال همکاران
همان حکایت زردوز و بوریاباف است

Khamoosh Hafezo in noktehaaye chon zare sorkh
Negaah daar ke ghallabe shahr sarrafast

خموش حافظ و این نکته‌های چون زر سرخ
نگاه دار که قلّاب شهر صرّاف است

For one in solitude, what need for the splendid vista remains?
If the beloved's street is here, what need for wilderness remains?

O dear one, by the need that you certainly have for the All-mighty,
Take a moment finally, and ask what exactly our need might be.

O sovereign of beauty, for the sake of God, we are consumed utterly,
Finally we plead for you to ask, what this beggar's need may be.

We are need's masters, and require no tongue for requesting,
In the presence of the Merciful, what need of petitioning?

If your intention is to take our life, no excuses are you requiring;
When one owns all the goods and chattels, what need for stealing?

The world-displaying cup is the illumined mind of the friend,
So for me to reveal what is necessary, what's the need in the end?

The time is passed when I needed favours from the ocean's master,
When the pure pearl is gained, what need for the ocean thereafter?

O poor lover, when the beloved's life-giving lip you attain;
To petition for any other dispensation, what need should remain?

O hypocrite pretender, go away! Nothing in common have we;
When friends are present what need is there for those with enmity.

Hafiz complete your song, for skill is its own announcer,
I see no need to dispute with the argumentative pretender.

**(W-C 51) The radif here is "Need".**
. The seeker has need of means to attain what is sought – when it is found what is the need for those means?

Khalvat gozide raa be tamaashaa che haajatast  
Chon kooye doost hast be sahraa che haajatast

خلوت گزیده را به تماشا چه حاجت است  
چون کوی دوست هست به صحرا چه حاجت است

Jaanaa be haajati ke to raa hast baa khodaay  
Kaakher dami bepors ke maa raa che haajatast

جانا به حاجتی که تو را هست با خدای  
کآخر دمی بپرس که ما را چه حاجت است

Ey paadshaahe hosn khodaa raa besookhtim  
Aakher soaal kon ke gedaa raa che haajatast

ای پادشاه حسن خدا را بسوختیم  
آخر سؤال کن که گدا را چه حاجت است

Arbaabe haajatimo zabaane soaal nist  
Dar hazrate karim tamannaa che haajatast

ارباب حاجتیم و زبان سوال نیست  
در حضرت کریم تمنّا چه حاجت است

Mohtaaje ghesse nist garat ghasde jaane maast  
Chon rakht az aane tost be yaghmaa che haajatast

محتاج قصّه نیست گرت قصد جان ماست  
چون رخت از آن تست به یغما چه حاجت است

Jaame jahaan namaast zamire monire doost  
Ezhaare ehtiyaaj khod aanjaa che haajatast

جام جهان نماست ضمیر منیر دوست  
اظهار احتیاج خود آن جا چه حاجت است

Aan shod ke baare mennate mallah bordami  
Govhar cho dast daad be daryaa che haajatast

آن شد که بار منّت ملّاح بردمی  
گوهر چو دست داد به دریا چه حاجت است

Ey aasheghe gedaa cho labe rooh bakhshe yaar  
Midaanadat vazife taghaazaa che haajatast

ای عاشق گدا چو لب روح بخش یار  
می‌داندت وظیفه تقاضا چه حاجت است

Ey moddaee boro ke ma raa baa to kaar nist  
Ahbaab haazerand be a-daa che haajatast

ای مدّعی برو که مرا با تو کار نیست  
احباب حاضرند به اعدا چه حاجت است

Hafez to khatm kon ke honar khod ayaan shaved  
Baa moddaaee nezaao mohaakaa che haajatast

حافظ تو ختم کن که هنر خود عیان شود  
با مدّعی نزاع و محاکا چه حاجت است

The garden is a court of joy, and the company is pleasingly fine;
May it be a pleasing time for the rose and so for drinkers of wine.

The dawn breeze brings, each moment, our pleasing soul's scent,
Oh yes, O yes, the perfume of the desiring ones is fragrant,

The rose didn't remove the veil but got ready to go from here,
O, bulbul cry out, for the heart-hurt ones are pleasing to hear.

Give good news to the night bird, who in love's way is singing,
The friend finds night-waking and weeping, very pleasing.

As, in the market of the world, happiness is in such short supply,
The Rend 'robin-hoods' are pleasing; and that is the reason why.

These noble words into my ear, the tongue of the lily was pouring,
"In this cloistered world, the unburdened do work that's pleasing."

Hafiz, to abandon the world is the way to a heart that's happy,
So don't think for a moment the world-owners live pleasingly.

**(W-C 52) The radif here is "Is pleasant"**
[1] "...Those who have delivered the burden of their life into God's Hands are the ones whose every work is
pleasing.

Sahne bostaan zovgh bakhsho sohbate yaaraan khoshast

صحن بستان ذوق بخش و صحبت یاران خوش است

Vaghte gol khosh baad kaz vey vaghte meykhaaraan khoshast

وقت گل خوش باد کز وی وقت میخواران خوش است

Az sabaa har dam mashaame jaane maa khosh mishavad

از صبا هر دم مشام جان ما خوش می شود

Ari ari tibe anfaase havaadaaraan khoshast

آری آری طیب انفاس هواداران خوش است

Naagoshoode gol neghaab aahange rehlat saaz kard

ناگشوده گل نقاب آهنگ رحلت ساز کرد

Naale kon bolbol ke golbaange del afgaaraan khoshast

ناله کن بلبل که گلبانگ دل افگاران خوش است

Morghe shab khaan raa beshaarat baad kandar raahe eshgh

مرغ شب خوان را بشارت باد کاندر راه عشق

Doost raa baa naaleye shabhaaye bidaaraan khoshast

دوست را با ناله شبهای بیداران خوش است

Nist dar baazaare aalam khoshdeli var zaan ke hast

نیست در بازار عالم خوشدلی ور زانکه هست

Shiveye rendyyio khosh baashiyye ayyaaraan khoshast

شیوه رندیّ و خوش باشیّ عیّاران خوش است

Az zabaane soosane aazaadeam aamad be goosh

از زبان سوسن آزاده ام آمد به گوش

Kandar in deire kohan kaare sabokbaaraan khoshast

کاندرین دیر کهن کار سبکباران خوش است

Hafezaa tarke jahaan goftan tarighe khosh delist

حافظا ترک جهان گفتن طریق خوش دلیست

Taa napendaari ke ahvaale jahaan daaraan khoshast

تا نپنداری که احوال جهانداران خوش است

O Lord! this light giving candle coming from whose[1] house is?
It has burnt up my soul! Ask whose very life that dear one is.

That one who is my heart and faith and religion overturning,
Is sharing whose bed; and with whom is presently dwelling?

The ruby wine of that lip, from my lip may it be not far, ever,
That wine for whose soul is it? The cup to whom does that one offer?

To whom has fortune given that candle radiating joy for companion,
Ask God for which moth it burns so bright in invitation?

Though everyone tries to charm by all kinds of incantation,
Who knows for whose tender heart the beloved has an inclination?

O Lord that Venus browed, moon-faced and sovereign one,
Whose precious pearl and incomparable jewel is that one?

I said, 'Without you, a sigh comes from the heart of Hafiz,'
Disguising a laugh, the beloved[2] asked, "For whom such madness is?"

---

**(W-C 53) The radif here is 'Of whom is'.**
  [1] W-C suggests this is an early ghazal. It is conceivable that it relates to his unrequited love for Shaks-i-
  Nabat.
  [2] "...the beloved..." Avery suggests this could refer to the patron who is hearing the ghazal sung.

Yaa rab in sham-e delafrooz ze kaashaaneye kist  
Jaane maa sookht beporsid ke jaanaaneye kist  

يا رب اين شمع دل افروز ز كاشانه كيست  
جان ما سوخت بپرسيد كه جانانه كيست  

Haaliaa khaane bar andaaze delo dine man ast  
Taa hamaaghooshe ke mibaashado hamkhaaneye kist  

حاليا خانه براندازِ دل و دين من است  
تا هم آغوش كه مى باشد و همخانه كيست  

Baadeye la-le labash kaz labe man door mabaad  
Raahe roohe kevo peimaan dehe peimaaneye kist  

باده لعل لبش كز لب من دور مباد  
راح روح كه و پيمان ده پيمانه كيست  

Dovlate sohbate aan sham-e sa-aadat partov  
Baaz porsid khodaa raa ke be parvaaneye kist  

دولت صحبت آن شمع سعادت پرتو  
بازپرسيد خدا را كه به پروانه كيست  

Midamad har kasash afsooniyo maloom nashod  
Ke dele naazoke ou maayele afsaaneye kist  

مى‌دمد هر كسش افسونى و معلوم نشد  
كه دل نازك او مايل افسانه كيست  

Yaa rab aan shaah vashe maah rokhe zohre jabin  
Dorre yektaaye kevo govhare yekdaaneye kist  

يا رب آن شاه وش ماه رخ زهره جبين  
درّ يكتاى كه و گوهر يكدانه كيست  

Goftam aah az dele divaaneye Hafez bi to  
Zire lab khande zanaan goft ke divaaneye kist  

گفتم آه از دل ديوانه حافظ بى تو  
زير لب خنده زنان گفت كه ديوانه كيست

It is unmannerly[1] if skill before the beloved we are displaying,
So the tongue is still, though the mouth Arabic eloquence[2] is showing.

The beauty's face is hid; but fetching eye-play the beast is making,
Reason was burnt - "What 'father of wonders' is this - it's amazing!"

Don't ask why this turning sphere cherishes the meaner kind,
Its desire fulfilling is a sham; in its giving no sense you will find.

In this world's garden what rose was picked without thorn attached,
Even Mustapha, the glorious lamp, with Abu Lahab's[2] fire is linked.

I don't give a bean for the Khanqah's[4] grand portico or Sufi Lodging,
My palace is the tavern; my tower the foot of the wine-jug[5] I am kissing.

The beauty of the 'daughter of the grape', in our eye's light hidden it is;
 (As wine is, by the glass and in the red grape), in the lens and the iris.

Now seek a remedy for your pain in that ruby red wine;
Poured from the crystal carafe into an Aleppo glass so fine.

Bring wine, for I am forever asking help, as does Hafiz,
When weeping at dawn and supplicating at midnight he is.

**(W-C 54) The radif here is "Is".**
[1] "...Unmannerly..."- See glossary under 'adab'.
[2] "...Arabic eloquence is showing..." It is possible that this is a reference to the holy Prophet and his inspiration when receiving the words of Allah in the holy Qur'an. The holy Prophet was known as 'Ummiy' (one not trained in the skill of language) yet produced under inspiration the most pure Arabic. To hear divine inspiration one must be silent within and without.
[3] "...Abu Lahab..." This refers to a man who was a fierce enemy of the holy Prophet Muhammed and was thus destined for the fire of hell.
[4] "... Khanqah's..." See the glossary in this volume.
[5] "...Wine-jug..." This is a possible reference to his Pir or guide.

Agarche arze honar pishe yaar bi adabist

اگر چه عرض هنر پیش یار بی‌ادبیست

Zabaan khamoosh valiken dahaan por az arabist

زبان خموش ولیکن دهان پر از عربیست

Pari nahofte rokho div dar kereshmeye hosn

پری نهفته رخ و دیو در کرشمه حسن

Besookht aghl ze heirat ke in che bolajabist

بسوخت عقل زحیرت که این چه بلعجبیست

Sabab mapors ke charkh az che sefle parvar shod

سبب مپرس که چرخ از چه سفله پرور شد

Ke kaam bakhshiye ou ra bahaane bi sababist

که کام بخشی او را بهانه بی سببیست

Dar in chaman gole bi khaar  kas nachid aari

در این چمن گل بی خار کس نچید آری

Cheraaghe mostafavi ba sharaare bulahabist

چراغ مصطفوی با شرار بولهبیست

Be nim jov nakharam taaghe khaaneghaaho rebaat

به نیم جو نخرم طاق خانقاه و رباط

Maraa ke mastabe eivaano paaye khom tanabist

مراکه مصطبه ایوان و پای خم طنبیست

Jamaale dokhtare raz noore chashme maast magar

جمال دختر رز نور چشم ماست مگر

Ke dar neghaabe zojajiyyo pardeye enabist

که در نقاب زجاجیّ و پرده عنبیست

Davaaye darde khod aknoon az aan mofarrah jooy

دوای درد خود اکنون از آن مفرّح جوی

Ke dar soraahiye chiniyyo saaghare halabist

که در صراحی چینیّ و ساغر حلبیست

Biar mey ke cho Hafez modaamam estezhaar

بیار می که چو حافظ مدامم استظهار

Be geryeye sahariyyo niyaaze nimshabist

به گریه سحریّ و نیاز نیم شبیست

What better than joy, good company, the garden and a spring day?
But where is the Saki? Tell us what is the cause of this delay?

Every moment of pleasure that arrives, loot consider it to be,
Delay is denial, who knows what the end of this business will be.

We are bound to life by a single hair, so use your head well;
Present grief is enough for now, destiny's grief who can tell?

In the water of life and Iram's garden[1] what meaning can there be,
That is not found in a riverbank and glass of wine tasting pleasantly.

The sober fellow and the inebriate are both of the same family,
Whose look will reach our heart? What's the choice to be?

What does the silent sky know of the mystery the screen may hide,
Would be sage, what anger with the Screen-holder is from your side?

If He understands not His slaves and their many foolish mistakes,
How is it that Mercy and Compassion as qualities the All-mighty takes?

The puritan sought from Kauther[2] to drink; Hafiz to the wine-cup went;
Let us see to which of these is inclined, the One Who is Omnipotent.

---

**(W-C 55) The radif here is "Is what?"**
  [1] "...Iram's garden..." The people of Ad, associated with Iram, are mentioned in the holy book (89:6). They were famous for lofty columned buildings. Avery (pp103) points out that this refers to a city built to imitate paradise.
  [2] "...Kauther..." This is a fountain in paradise.
  Though it would be easy to read this ghazal as extolling the transitory pleasures of life one need only understand the pleasures referred to as spiritual ones to gain a different perspective. Orthodox religion tends to see spiritual pleasure only as those waiting for us after death. Hafiz finds spiritual pleasures that have the taste of eternity, in this life as well.

Khoshtar ze eysho sohbato baagho bahaar chist  خوشتر ز عیش و صحبت و باغ و بهار چیست
Saaghi kojaast goo sababe entezaar chist  ساقی کجاست گو سبب انتظار چیست

Har vaghte khosh ke dast dahad moghtanam shomaar  هر وقت خوش که دست دهد مغتنم شمار
Kas raa voghoof nist ke anjaame kaar chist  کس را وقوف نیست که انجام کار چیست

Peivande omr baste be mooist hoosh daar  پیوند عمر بسته به مویست هوش دار
Ghamkhaare khish baash ghame roozegaar chist  غمخوار خویش باش غم روزگار چیست

Ma-niyye aabe zendegiyo rovzeye eram  معنیّ آب زندگی و روضه ارم
Joz tarfe jooybaaro meye khoshgavaar chist  جز طرف جویبار و می خوشگوار چیست

Mastoor o mast har do cho az yek ghabileand  مستور و مست هر دو چو از یک قبیله‌اند
Maa del be eshveye ke dahim ekhtiaar chist  ما دل به عشوه که دهیم اختیار چیست

Raaze daroone parde che daanad falak khamoosh  راز درون پرده چه داند فلک خموش
Ey moddaee nezaae to baa pardedaar chist  ای مدّعی نزاع تو با پرده دار چیست

Sahvo khataaye bande garash nist etebar  سهو و خطای بنده گرش نیست اعتبار
Ma-niyye lotfo rahmate parvardegaar chist  معنیّ لطف و رحمت پروردگار چیست

Zaahed sharaabe kovsar o Hafez piaale khaast  زاهد شراب کوثر و حافظ پیاله خواست
Taa dar miaane khaasteye kerdegaar chist  تا در میانه خواسته کردگار چیست

My moon left the city this week. In my eyes a year it seems like!
Separation - O how hard it is! You have no idea what it's like!

In that bright cheek, my eye's pupil, reflected I can see,
Like a black musk-scented mole that image seemed to me.

Milk-fresh the beloved's lip seems to be and sugar-sweet,
But every eyelash is a murderer, if that glance you meet.

In the city everyone points you out for your generosity,
Sadly, in care for strangers, such amazing neglect I see.

Certainly there is a jewel of minute indivisible particularity[1];
The proof is your lip, so very small yet there for all to see.

They gave the good news that your return will pass by here,
O change not your mind, a good omen in this does appear.

How is it that such a mountain of grief Hafiz must be dragging?
Weary and groaning, his body a constant lament is becoming.

*(W-C 56) The radif here is "Is".*
[1] *"...minute indivisible particularity..." A point of complex mystical philosophy that cannot be explained in a short commentary.*

Maaham in hafte shod az shahro be chashmam saalist

ماهم این هفته شد از شهر و به چشمم سالیست

Haale hejraan to che daani ke che moshkel haalist

حال هجران تو چه دانی که چه مشکل حالیست

Mardome dide ze lotfe rokhe ou dar rokhe ou

مردم دیده ز لطف رخ او در رخ او

Akse khod did gomaan bord ke meshkin khaalist

عکس خود دید گمان برد که مشکین خالیست

Michekad shir hanooz az labe hamchon shekarash

می‌چکد شیر هنوز از لب همچون شکرش

Garche dar shivegari har mojeash ghattalist

گر چه در شیوه گری هر مژه‌اش قتّالیست

Ey ke angosht namaee be karam dar hame shahr

ای که انگشت نمایی به کرم در همه شهر

Vah ke dar kaare gharibaan ajabat ehmaalist

وه که در کار غریبان عجبت اهمالیست

Ba-d az inam nabovad shaaebe dar jovhare fard

بعد از اینم نبود شایبه در جوهر فرد

Ke dahaane to baraan nokte khosh estedlaalist

که دهان تو بران نکته خوش استدلالیست

Mojde daadand ke bar maa gozari khaahi kard

مژده دادند که بر ما گذری خواهی کرد

Niyyate kheir magardaan ke mobaarak faalist

نیّت خیر مگردان که مبارک فالیست

Koohe andoohe feraaghat be che hilat bekeshad

کوه اندوه فراقت به چه حیلت بکشد

Hafeze khaste ke az naale tanash chon naalist

حافظ خسته که از ناله تنش چون نالیست

Though wine is arousing and the rose-scented breeze, inviting,
In music and drunkenness indulge not, the censor is watching.

If a jug of wine and beautiful consort comes to you - take care;
Drink with reason, for the times are dangerous - so be aware.

Up the wide sleeve of the patched robe, the wine jug be hiding,
For like the red-eyed wine jug, this time is for blood shedding.

With our eye's tears we will wash wine from the robe of piety;
Because it is now the season for the practice of pious austerity.

The uplifted sky, is a sieve, through which blood is falling,
Heads and crowns of kings are the small things that it is passing.

From its inverted bowl don't look for a time of pleasure,
For dregs are mixed with wine in the pure head of the wine jar.

Hafiz, Iraq and Fars you own due to your fine poetry;
Baghdad and Tabriz, your time is coming, of a surety.

*(W-C 57) The radif here is "Is".*

*There were occasions when particular rulers closed wine shops and forbade drinking. See the notes by Avery pp.75. W-C gives a more mystical explanation pp141. It is also possible to regard this ghazal as saying that there are times when the external situation meant spiritual joys must be hidden. The principle of concealing one's faith was established at the start of historical Islam as a legitimate response to persecution. Here Hafiz applies this principle to the joys of spiritual intoxication.*

Agarche baade farahbakhsho baad gol bizast
Be baange chang makhor mey ke mohtaseb tizast
اگر چه باده فرح بخش و باد گلبیز است
به بانگ چنگ مخور می که محتسب تیز است

Soraahe-iyo harifi garat be chang oftad
Be aghl noosh ke ayyam fetne angizast
صراحیی و حریفی گرت به چنگ افتد
به عقل نوش که ایّام فتنه انگیز است

Dar aastine moragha piaale penhaan kon
Ke hamcho chashme soraahi zamaane khoon rizast
در آستین مرقّع پیاله پنهان کن
که همچو چشم صراحی زمانه خون‌ریز است

Ze range baade beshooeem kherghehaa dar ashk
Ke movseme varao roozegaare parhizast
ز رنگ باده بشوئیم خرقه ها در اشک
که موسم ورع و روزگار پرهیز است

Sepehre bar shode parvizanist khoon afshaan
Ke rizeash sare kasraavo taaje parvizast
سپهر برشده پرویزنیست خون افشان
که ریزه‌اش سر کسری و تاج پرویز است

Majooy eyshe khosh az dovre vaajgoone sepehr
Ke saafe in sare khom jomle dordi aamizast
مجوی عیش خوش از دور واژگون سپهر
که صاف این سر خم جمله دردی آمیز است

Araagho paars gerefti be shere khosh Hafez
Biaa ke novbate baghdaado vaghte tabrizast
عراق و پارس گرفتی به شعر خوش حافظ
بیا که نوبت بغداد و وقت تبریز است

O bulbul, if your desire is to join me in being a lover, then weep!
We are both weeping lovers and it is our work is to weep.

In the land[1] where the scented breeze of the beloved's hair is blowing,
The musk-pods of Tartar can have no occasion for boasting.

Bring wine so we can dye the garment of our hypocrisy,
For we are drunk on the cup of pride yet we call it sobriety.

Envisaging your hair's beauty, the unseasoned cannot start to do,
To go beyond the (causal) chain is the thing subtle ones bravely do.

The source from which love arises is a deep and subtle mystery,
Neither the ruby lip, nor the down of green youth is its identity.[2]

Eye, hair, cheek or moles do not in themselves give anyone beauty,
Hearts become obsessed in the myriad fine points of its subtlety.

Those naked Kalanders[3] in the way of Haqiqat; they would not part,
With a bean, for the satin coat of one who has not the heart's art.

Your threshold is reached with much difficulty – yes,
It is difficult to mount up to the sky of joyousness.

I slept and saw that look in your eye, in a dream at dawn – great!
It is so good when the state of sleep is better than the waking state.

Hafiz do not annoy the beloved; put a lid on your weeping!
Eternal salvation relies on minimising any heart-hurting.

*(W-C 58) The radif here is "Is".*
    [1] *"...In the land..." This is possibly a reference to the unseen world.*
    [2] *"...Neither metaphors nor the beauties of this world can convey the beauty of the Unseen.*
    [3] *"...Kalanders..." Some mystics in the Sufi tradition took to a wandering lifestyle and the abandonment even of clothes. See Sarmad and His Rubaiyat in the Bibliography.*

Benaal bolbol agar baa manat saare yaarist
Ke maa do aasheghe zaarimo kaare maa zaarist
بنال بلبل اگر با منت سر یاریست
که ما دو عاشق زاریم و کار ما زاریست

Dar aan zamin ke nasimi vazad ze torreye doost
Che jaaye dam zadane naafehaaye taataarist
دران زمین که نسیمی وزد ز طرّه دوست
چه جای دم زدن نافه‌های تاتاریست

Biyaar baade ke rangin konim jaameye zargh
Ke maste jaame ghoroorimo naam hoshyaarist
بیار باده که رنگین کنیم جامه زرق
که مست جام غروریم و نام هشیاریست

Khiaale zolfe to pokhtan na kaare khaamaanast
Ke zire selsele raftan tarighe ayyarist
خیال زلف تو پختن نه کارخامان است
که زیر سلسله رفتن طریق عیّاریست

Latife ist nahaani ke eshgh az aan khizad
Ke naame aan na labe la-lo khatte zangaarist
لطیفه‌ایست نهانی که عشق ازآن خیزد
که نام آن نه لب لعل و خطّ زنگاریست

Jamaale shakhs na chashm asto rooyo aarezo khat
Hezaar nokte dar in kaaro bare deldaarist
جمال شخص نه چشم است وروی و عارض وخط
هزار نکته در این کار و بار دلداریست

Mojarradaane tarighat be nim jov nakharand
Ghabaaye atlase aan kas ke az honar aarist
مجرّدان طریقت به نیم جو نخرند
قبای اطلس آن کس که از هنر عاریست

Bar aastaane to moshkel tavaan resid aari
Orooj bar falake sarvari be doshvaarist
بر آستان تو مشکل توان رسید آری
عروج بر فلک سروری به دشواریست

Sahar kereshmeye chashmat be khaab mididam
Zehi maraatebe khaabi ke beh ze bidaarist
سحر کرشمه چشمت به خواب می‌دیدم
زهی مراتب خوابی که به ز بیداریست

Delash be naale mayaazaar o khatm kon Hafez
Ke rastegaariye jaavid dar kam aazaarist
دلش به ناله میازار و ختم کن حافظ
که رستگاری جاوید در کم آزاریست

O pious man, so pure, condemn not us love-crazy drunkards,
After all you will not be charged with another's crime afterwards.

Whether I am good or bad, look to yourself;
We will each reap what we have sown our self.

In sobriety or intoxication the beloved is sought by all,
Mosque or church or synagogue, every place is love's hall.

On the brick at the foot of the tavern door, my head I submitted.
Critic, if this seems strange, best take a brick to your own head.

Of grace, given before time began[1], make me not despair,
Who is right or wrong, behind the screen, are you aware?

I am not alone in this, letting fall the veil of piety,
Father's[2] hand also let slip paradise's timeless purity.

If you are well disposed to this then what a goodly disposition,
And if your nature is so inclined then excellent your inclination.

O Hafiz, if on the day of death you reach for a wine cup,
From the tavern's street, to paradise, they will snatch you up.

**(W-C 59)**
[1] "...before time began..." This refers to The Day of Alast. See the glossary in this volume.
[2] "...Father's hand..." Adam.

Eybe rendaan makon ey zaahede paakize seresht
عیب رندان مکن ای زاهد پاکیزه سرشت

Ke gonaahe degari bar to nakhaahand nevesht
که گناه دگری بر تو نخواهند نوشت

Man agar nikamo gar bad to boro khod raa koosh
من اگر نیکم و گر بد تو برو خود را کوش

Har kasi aan deravad aaghebate kaar ke kesht
هر کسی آن درود عاقبت کار که کشت

Hame kas taalebe yaarand che hoshyaaro che mast
همه کس طالب یارند چه هشیار و چه مست

Hame jaa khaaneye eshgh ast che masjed che kenesht
همه جا خانه عشق است چه مسجد چه کنشت

Sare taslime mano kheshte dare meikadehaa
سر تسلیم من و خشت در میکده‌ها

Moddaee gar nakonad fahme sokhan goo saro khesht
مدّعی گر نکند فهم سخن گو سر و خشت

Naaomidam makon az saabegheye lotfe azal
ناامیدم مکن از سابقه لطف ازل

To pase parde che daani ke ke khoob asto ke zesht
تو پس پرده چه دانی که که خوب است و که زشت

Na man az khalvate taghvaa be dar oftaadamo bas
نه من از خلوت تقوا به درافتادم و بس

Pedaram niz beheshte abad az dast behesht
پدرم نیز بهشت ابد از دست بهشت

Gar nahaadat hame in ast zehi nik nahaad
گرنهادت همه این است زهی نیک نهاد

Var sereshtat hame in ast zehi khoob seresht
ور سرشتت همه این است زهی خوب سرشت

Hafezaa rooze azal gar be kaf aari jaami
حافظا روز اجل گر به کف آری جامی

Yeksar az kooye kharaabaat boro taa be behesht
یک سر از کوی خرابات برو تا به بهشت

Now from the rose-garden the scent of paradise is wafted by the breeze,
Uniting joy-giving wine, me, and my beloved who is pure as the Houris[1].

To boast of his kingdom, today, the beggar may surely be allowed,
His banquet hall, the big field, his pavilion the shade-giving cloud.

The lawned garden reveals spring's pleasant, present, story,
To prefer a promise, to cash in hand, is the ignorant man's folly.

Don't expect, from the enmity of this world, fidelity or a dim light,
A synagogue's lamp the candle of true worship will not ignite.

Let wine expand the house of the heart, for in this narrow backyard,
The ruined world intends to make a brick from our dust in the graveyard.

Do not scold a drunk like me for the black marks recorded,
Who can say what destiny has written on one's own forehead.

From the bier of Hafiz do not withdraw your foot,
He goes to paradise even though in sin, head to foot.[2]

*(W-C 60)*
[1] *"...Houris..." See glossary in this volume under Huri.*
[2] *"...This line was the one drawn out by a child when Hafiz died and there was questions as to whether he should be buried as a Muslim. (See introduction).*

Konoon ke midamad az boostaan nasime behesht
Mano sharaabe farah bakhsho yaare hoor seresht

كنون كه مى‌دمد از بوستان نسيم بهشت
من و شراب فرح بخش و يار حورسرشت

Gedaa cheraa nazanad laafe saltanat emrooz
Ke kheime saayeye abr asto bazmgah labe kesht

گدا چرا نزند لاف سلطنت امروز
كه خيمه سايه ابر است و بزمگه لب كشت

Chaman hekaayate ordibehesht migooyad
Na aaref ast ke nesye kharido naghd behesht

چمن حكايت ارديبهشت مى‌گويد
نه عارف است كه نسيه خريد و نقد بهشت

Vafaa majooy ze doshman ke partovi nadahad
Cho sham-e sovme-e afroozi az cheraaghe kenesht

وفا مجوى ز دشمن كه پرتوى ندهد
كه شمع صومعه افروزى از چراغ كنشت

Be mey emaarate jaan kon ke in jahaane kharaab
Bar aan sarast ke az khaake maa besaazad khesht

به مى عمارت جان كن كه اين جهان خراب
بر آن سر است كه از خاك ما بسازد خشت

Makon be naame siyaahi malaamate mane mast
Ke aagah ast ke taghdir bar sarash che nevesht

مكن به نامه سياهى ملامت من مست
كه آگه است كه تقدير بر سرش چه نوشت

Ghadam darigh madaar az jenaazeye Hafez
Ke garche gharghe gonaah ast miravad be behesht

قدم دريغ مدار از جنازه حافظ
كه گر چه غرق گناه است مى‌رود به بهشت

Fragrant early morning breeze, tell me, the beloved rests where?
The abode of that moon - that lover-slaying rogue - is where?

The night is dark, the desert track of the valley of Aiman[1]is where,
Where is the fire of Tur? The appointed place of visions is where?

Whoever came into this ruined world was marked for ruination,
In the tavern don't ask where the sober man is or about his situation.

Of the folk of good news is one who knows the unspoken sign well;
Many fine points. Where is he who knows mysteries and doesn't tell?

Each and every hair tip of mine has business connecting to you;
Where then are we? Where the critic who has no dealings with you?

Reason got lost in seeking to know where it is - that musk laden hair.
The heart retreated from us; the eyebrow of its beloved is where?[2]

The Saki, the musician and the wine cup, are all here, ready,
But there is no joy without the beloved: so where can that one be?

Hafiz, care not if the autumn gale blasts the world's green field,
Consider well, the rose without a thorn, where is it concealed?

---

*(W-C 62) The radif here is 'Is where'*
[1] *"...Aiman..." This is the valley in which Prophet Moses saw the burning bush – near Mount Tur.*
[2] *..."The eyebrow..." This is the arch – about which Khwaja Muinuddin Hasan Chishti says: 'The heart of those following the haqiqat, when it is tuned and turned towards the real purpose it is called an arch by the enlightened ones.' (See; "The Meditations of. Khwaja Muinuddin Hasan Chishti" in the bibliography.)*

Ey nasime sahar aaraam gahe yaar kojaast

Manzele aan mahe aashegh koshe ayyar kojaast

ای نسیم سحر آرامگه یار کجاست

منزل آن مه عاشق کش عیّار کجاست

Shabe taar asto rahe vaadiye ayman dar pish

Aatashe toor kojaa movede didaar kojaast

شب تار است و ره وادی ایمن در پیش

آتش طور کجا موعد دیدار کجاست

Har ke aamad be jahaan naghshe kharaabi darad

Dar kharaabaat maporsid ke hoshyaar kojaast

هر که آمد به جهان نقش خرابی دارد

در خرابات مپرسید که هشیار کجاست

Aankas ast ahle beshaarat ke eshaarat daanad

Noktehaa hast basi mahrame asraar kojaast

آن کس است اهل بشارت که اشارت داند

نکته‌ها هست بسی محرم اسرار کجاست

Har sare mooye maraa baa to hezaran kaarast

Maa kojaaeemo malaamatgare bikaar kojaast

هر سر موی مرا با تو هزاران کار است

ما کجائیم و ملامت گر بیکار کجاست

Aghl divaane shod aan selseleye moshkin koo

Del ze maa gooshe gereft abrooye deldaar kojaast

عقل دیوانه شد آن سلسله مشکین کو

دل ز ما گوشه گرفت ابروی دلدار کجاست

Baadevo motrebo gol jomle mohayyast vali

Eish bi yaar mohayyaa nashavad yaar kojaast

باده و مطرب و گل جمله مهیّاست ولی

عیش بی یار مهیّا نشود یار کجاست

Hafez az baade khazaan dar chamane dahr maranj

Fekre maghool befarmaa gole bi khaar kojaast

حافظ از باد خزان در چمن دهر مرنج

فکر معقول بفرما گل بی خار کجاست

The great arc into which your arched eyebrow was drawn,
With intent of taking the blood of helpless me it was drawn.

Wine-drunk, dripping sweat, when in the garden-walk[1] was it you came,
That the red arghavan by drops of your sweat is set aflame?

One boastful bragging glance the narcissus did cast,
Your eye released a hundred calamities into the world fast.

Shamed by the temerity of whoever likened it to your face,
From the wind's hand, into its mouth, dust the lily did embrace.

The violet was plaiting the lovely hair, with which she impresses,
Suddenly the dawn breeze told the story of your lovely tresses.

From a sense of pious caution I'd not seen wine or musicians,
Desire for both came from the attraction to the young Magians.

Now we wash the robe of religion with the ruby red wine,
What timeless eternity has decreed, one cannot decline.

When love was *the* colour, the two worlds had no colouring,
Mutual love is not a pattern that recent time is innovating.

Perhaps this ruined state was, for Hafiz, an opening really,
Cast into the Magian wine in the time before eternity.

Now the world shapes itself according to whatever I am desiring.
Me, into the service of the great Soul of the world time is casting[2].

*(W-C 63) The radif here is 'Cast'*
  [1] *"..garden..." For the various garden symbols see the glossary.*
  [2] *This verse suggests that having united with God the entire universe therefore operates according to his desire since God's Wish and Hafiz's desire are one.*

Khami ke abrooye shookhe to dar kamaan andaakht
Be ghasde khoone mane zaare naatavaan andaakht
خمی که ابروی شوخ تو در کمان انداخت
به قصد خون من زار ناتوان انداخت

Sharaab khordevo khey karde key shodi be chaman
Ke aabe rooye to aatash dar arghavaan andaakht
شراب خورده و خوی کرده کی شوی به چمن
که آب روی تو آتش در ارغوان انداخت

Be yek kereshme ke narges be khod forooshi kard
Faribe chashme to sad fetne dar jahaan andaakht
به یک کرشمه که نرگس به خودفروشی کرد
فریب چشم تو صد فتنه در جهان انداخت

Ze sharme aanke be rooye to nesbatash kardand
Saman be daste sabaa khaak dar dahaan andaakht
ز شرم آن که به روی تو نسبتش کردند
سمن به دست صبا خاک در دهان انداخت

Banafshe torreye maftoole khod gereh mizad
Sabaa hekaayate zolfe to dar miyaan andaakht
بنفشه طرّه مفتول خود گره می‌زد
صبا حکایت زلف تو در میان انداخت

Man az va-ra meyo motreb nadidami zin pish
Havaaye moghbachegaanam dar ino aan andaakht
من از ورع می و مطرب ندیدمی زین پیش
هوای مغبچگانم در این و آن انداخت

Konoon be aabe meye la-l kherghe mishooyam
Nasibeye azal az khod nemitavaan andaakht
کنون به آب می لعل خرقه می‌شویم
نصیبه ازل از خود نمی‌توان انداخت

Nabood range do aalam ke naghshe olfat bood
Zamaane tarhe mahabbat na in zamaan andaakht
نبود رنگ دو عالم که نقش الفت بود
زمانه طرح محبّت نه این زمان انداخت

Magar goshaayeshe Hafez dar in kharaabi bood
Ke bakhsheshe azalash dar meye moghaan andaakht
مگر گشایش حافظ در این خرابی بود
که بخشش ازلش در می مغان انداخت

Jahaan be kaame man aknoon shavad ke dovre zamaan
Maraa be bandegiye khaajeye jahaan andaakht
جهان به کام من اکنون شود که دور زمان
مرا به بندگی خواجه جهان انداخت

In the street of the tavern every traveller on the Way knows,
That if he thinks to knock on another door, towards ruin he goes[1].

Whosoever found a way to reach the threshold of the tavern,
The mysteries of that place, from wine's bounty he did learn.

Only to that one will time award the cap of drunken revelries,
Who, realises this cap is the glory of the universal mysteries.

Expect no rituals from us, save observances of those madly in love,
For our order's Sheykh knows wisdom is a sin in the way of love.

Whoever read the Saki's inscription, mysteries of the two worlds knows,
 To him, the pictures seen in Jamshid's cup[2] the road dust also shows.

From the eye of the Saki my heart did not, for a safe life, sue,
For the tyranny of the fearless black-hearted Turk my heart knew.

From the violence my birth star shows, my eye wept at dawn,
So much, that the moon must have known and to us Venus was drawn.

Happy the sight that knows that the cup's lip and the Saki's face,
Are like the crescent moon of one night; and the full moon's face.

The story of Hafiz, and the cup he secretly drinks from too,
What of the policeman and the censor? The King also knew.

A high Monarch is one who knows the nine heavenly vaults the model are,
That concealed in the curving forms of the archways of his court also are.[3]

**(W-C 64) The radif here is 'Knew'.**
[1] "...to knock on another door..." It is axiomatic on the Sufi Way to remain loyal to one guide and to follow one path. Flirtation with other mystical paths leads to disaster for the disciple.
[2] "...Jamshid's cup..." See glossary in this volume. For the advanced mystic the hidden world that can be seen in Jamshid's cup can be seen in any brick or object.
[3] "...nine heavenly vaults the model..." The apparently invisible nine heavens can be seen as manifest in physical creation by the spiritual monarch.

Be kooye meikade har saaleki ke rah daanest
Dari degar zadan andisheye tabah daanest

به کوی میکده هر سالکی که ره دانست
دری دگر زدن اندیشه تبه دانست

Bar aastaaneye meikhaane har ke yaaft rahi
Ze feize jaame mey asraare khaanghah daanest

بر آستانه میخانه هر که یافت رهی
ز فیض جام می اسرار خانقه دانست

Zamaane afsare rendi nadaad joz be kasi
Ke sarfaraaziye aalam dar in kolah daanest

زمانه افسر رندی نداد جز به کسی
که سرفرازی عالم در این کله دانست

Varaaye taa-ate divaanegaan ze maa matalab
Ke sheikhe mazhabe maa aagheli gonah daanest

ورای طاعت دیوانگان ز ما مطلب
که شیخ مذهب ما عاقلی گنه دانست

Har aanke raaze do aalam ze khatte saaghar khaand
Romooze jaame jam az naghshe khaake rah daanest

هر آنکه راز دو عالم ز خطّ ساغر خواند
رموز جام جم از نقش خاک ره دانست

Delam ze nargese saaghi amaan nakhaast be jaan
Cheraa ke shiveye aan torke del siyah daanest

دلم ز نرگس ساقی امان نخواست به جان
چراکه شیوه آن ترک دل سیه دانست

Ze jovre kovkabe taale sahargahaan chashmam
Chenaan gerist ke naahid dido mah daanest

ز جور کوکب طالع سحرگهان چشمم
چنان گریست که ناهید دید و مه دانست

Khosh aan nazar ke labe jaamo rooye saaghi raa
Helaale yekshabevo maahe chaardah daanest

خوش آن نظر که لب جام و روی ساقی را
هلال یک شبه و ماه چارده دانست

Hadise Hafezo saaghar ke mizanad penhaan
Che jaaye mohtasebo shahne paadshah daanest

حدیث حافظ و ساغر که می‌زند پنهان
چه جای محتسب و شحنه پادشه دانست

Boland martabe shaahi ke noh ravaaghe sepehr
Nemoonei ze khame taaghe baargah daanest

بلندمرتبه شاهی که نه رواق سپهر
نمونه‌ای ز خم طاق بارگه دانست

My heart's fire burnt in my chest; for the beloved it is longing,
It was such a fire in the heart, that the whole house it was consuming.

In separation from that heart-ravisher my very body melted utterly,
In love for the beloved's face my very life was burned completely.

Whoever's sight the hair tip of that Pari-faced beauty enchained,
For love-mad me they will by the heart's distress be consumed.

The heart's burning, how in tears of fire it burns, see,
So that last night from love the candle burnt like a moth for me.

That compassionate one is my friend and certainly no stranger to me,
Since I went out of myself, even strangers behave compassionately.

The water of the wine house carried away the cloak of austerity,
The fire of the wine house then burned up my reason rapidly.

The cup of my heart was broken, when repentance became mine;
My liver's[1] like an empty fiery tulip, with neither tavern nor wine.

Critic - enough palaver! Draw back and see how the pupil of my eye,
Pulled religion's cloak off and burnt it with a grateful sigh[2].

Hafiz, leave convoluted converse and for a while just drink the wine,
It stole sleep last night, and burnt up the candle of this life of mine.

---

*(W-C 65) The radif here is 'Consumed'.*
[1] *"...the liver's like..." The liver is the root of the faculty of the body. (See Shah Wali Ullah's description in "The Sacred Knowledge", in the bibliography).*
[2] *These lines are controversial and open to many interpretations – here we have taken the view that he is drawing back from theological debate and saying, 'See as if from the perspective of the candle flame burning away the wax, (modesty-covering religion, suitable for most situations)', The sigh being the smoke rising from the flame. Equally he could be referring to winning an argument with a more orthodox Sufi and talking about burning up that person's argument; and more likely both at once. The custom, it is said, was for Sufis in disagreement was to meet in a circle of peers to thrash out the disagreement. The final verse would of course follow naturally from this interpretation. There are however other interpretations possible.*

Sineam zaatashe del dar ghame jaanaane besookht
Aatashi bood dar in khaane ke kaashaane besookht

سینه ام زآتش دل در غم جانانه بسوخت
آتشی بود درین خانه که کاشانه بسوخت

Tanam az vaaseteye dooriye delbar begodaakht
Jaanam az aatashe mehre rokhe jaanaane besookht

تنم از واسطه دوری دلبر بگداخت
جانم از آتش مهر رخ جانانه بسوخت

Har ke zanjire sare zolfe pari rooye to did
Dele sovdaa zadeash bar mane divaane besookht

هر که زنجیر سر زلف پری روی تو دید
دل سودازده اش بر من دیوانه بسوخت

Sooze del bin ke ze bas aatashe ashkam dele sha-m
Doosh bar man ze sare mehr cho parvaane besookht

سوز دل بین که ز بس آتش اشکم دل شمع
دوش بر من ز سر مهر چو پروانه بسوخت

Aashnaaee na gharib ast ke delsooze man ast
Chon man az khish beraftam dele bigaane besookht

آشنائی نه غریب است که دلسوز من است
چون من از خویش برفتم دل بیگانه بسوخت

Khergheye zohde maraa aabe kharaabaat bebord
Khaaneye aghle maraa aatashe khomkhaane besookht

خرقه زهد مرا آب خرابات ببرد
خانه عقل مرا آتش خمخانه بسوخت

Chon piaale delam az tovbe ke kardam beshekast
Hamcho laale jegaram bi meyo peymaane besookht

چون پیاله دلم از توبه که کردم بشکست
همچو لاله جگرم بی می وپیمانه بسوخت

Maajaraa kam kon o baaz aa ke maraa mardome chashm
Kherghe az sar be dar aavard o be shokraane besookht

ماجرا کم کن و بازآ که مرا مردم چشم
خرقه از سر به درآورد و به شکرانه بسوخت

Tarke afsaane begoo Hafez o mey noosh dami
Ke nakhoftim shab o sha-m be afsaane besookht

ترک افسانه بگو حافظ و می نوش دمی
که نخفتیم شب و شمع به افسانه بسوخت

The sparkling of wine[1], to the knowledge seeker, a mystery retailed,
The essence of each soul's nature, to that one, this ruby unveiled.

Only the early dawn bird, the rose petal's true value got to know,
For not to everyone that reads it does a page its full import show.

O to you, who try to learn love's sign from reason's book;
Sadly, I say, by this means, into its subtle nature you cannot look.

Bring wine! Of the flower of the world's garden, no boast will make,
One who knows the devastating attack the autumn wind can make.

I offered both the worlds, to my long-serving heart,
Except love for you, all else it turned away from, for its part.

Stone and clay become ruby and cornelian, with the holy gaze,
Of one who knows the value of what the breeze from Yemen[2] says.

The time of paying regard to what the people say has passed,
Since the guardian of public morals my secret joy guessed.

That one's kindness sees our ease as being outside of time's domain,
If it weren't so then how would our heart's desperations remain?

This precious jewel of verse is mined from his mind by Hafiz,
On it the stamp of being nurtured by a second Asaf[3] there is.

---

**(W-C 66) The radif here is 'Knew'.**
[1] "...the sparkling is possibly a reference to the Divine Tajalli or First Emanation; or the reflection on the wine of a ray of light given a more universal significance.
[2] "..Yemen..." See the glossary in this volume.
[3] "...Asaf..." See the glossary in this volume.

Soofi az partove mey raaze nahaani daanest
صوفی از پرتو می راز نهانی دانست

Govhare har kas az in lal tavaani daanest
گوهر هر کس از این لعل توانی دانست

Ghadre majmooeye gol morghe sahar daanado bas
قدر مجموعه گل مرغ سحر داند و بس

Ke na har koo varaghi khaand ma-aani daanest
که نه هر کاو ورقی خواند معانی دانست

Ey ke az daftare aghl aayate eshgh aamoozi
ای که از دفتر عقل آیت عشق آموزی

Tarsam in nokte be tahghigh nadaani daanest
ترسم این نکته به تحقیق ندانی دانست

Mey biyaavar ke nanaazad be gole baaghe jahaan
می بیاور که ننازد به گل باغ جهان

Har ke ghaarat gariye baade khazaani daanest
هر که غارتگری باد خزانی دانست

Arze kardam do jahaan bar dele kaar oftaade
عرضه کردم دو جهان بر دل کارافتاده

Bejoz az eshghe to baaghi hame faani daanest
بجز از عشق تو باقی همه فانی دانست

Sango gel raa konad az yomne nazar la-lo aghigh
سنگ و گل را کند از یمن نظر لعل و عقیق

Har ke ghadre nafase baade yamaani daanest
هر که قدر نفس باد یمانی دانست

Aan shod aknoon ke ze afsoose avaam andisham
آن شد اکنون که زافسوس عوام اندیشم

Mohtaseb niz dar in eyshe nahaani daanest
محتسب نیز درین عیش نهانی دانست

Lotfash aasaayeshe maa maslahate vaght nadid
لطفش آسایش ما مصلحت وقت ندید

Varna az jaanebe maa delnegaraani daanest
ورنه از جانب ما دل نگرانی دانست

Hafez in govhare manzoom ke az tab angikht
حافظ این گوهر منظوم که از طبع انگیخت

Asare tarbiyate aasafe saani daanest
اثر تربیت آصف ثانی دانست

By your beauty, allied to fine manners, captive the world was taken,
Yes, by means of forming alliances, the world captive can be taken.

The secret of the secluded ones[1] the candle thought of revealing.
Thank God! The heart's secret its tongue of flame was burning.

Compared to the fire hidden in my chest that burns fiercely,
The sun in the sky seems to be but a spark that burns gently.

The rose wanted to boast of the friend's scent and beauty,
The mouth held its breath, for fear of the breeze's envy.

On the rim of the circle of the compass, at ease I was staying,
At last to the centre point I was taken by time's revolving.

That day, in desire of a wine-cup, my life's harvest was burnt up,
Fired up by seeing the Saki's cheek reflected in the cup I took up.

To the Magian's street I would go, joyfully sleeve-waving; shaking out,
From this skirt, disasters accumulated for the Final Days of sorting out[2].

Drink wine! At work's end, one who at the world gave a true look,
Made light of so much grief, and a heavy jug of wine they took.

On the rose leaf it is written, with the blood of the tulip as ink,
"Wine, deep-red, like the arghavan, the mature ones drink".

Seize the moment! For when the world went into its commotion,
The Sufi stuck to the cup and departed from that sad condition.

Hafiz, grace trickles like water out from your poetry,
How is it finicky distinctions some take up from envy?

**(W-C 67) The radif here is 'Took' or "Take".**
[1] "...secluded ones..." This refers to the Khilvatis (see the glossary in this volume).
[2] "...To the Magian's street...sorting out..." We have taken a particular meaning from this verse – as follows. The difficulties encountered in this life may stand us in good stead on the days between the rise of Prophet Muhammed and the Day of Judgement. The poet says – I will distribute the benefit of these freely (so full of joy am I). Difficulties encountered and endured are positive in the context of Judgement.

Hosnat be ettefaaghe malaahat jahaan gereft
Aari be ettefaagh jahaan mitavaan gereft

حسنت به اتّفاق ملاحت جهان گرفت
آری به اتّفاق جهان می‌توان گرفت

Efshaaye raaze khalvate maa khaast kard sha-m
Shokre khodaa ke serre delash dar zabaan gereft

افشای راز خلوت ما خواست کرد شمع
شکر خدا که سرّ دلش در زبان گرفت

Zin aatashe nahofte ke dar sineye man ast
Khorshid sho-leist ke dar aasemaan gereft

زین آتش نهفته که در سینه من است
خورشید شعله‌ایست که در آسمان گرفت

Mikhaast gol ke dam zanad az rango booye doost
Az gheirate sabaa nafasash dar dahaan gereft

می‌خواست گل که دم زند از رنگ و بوی دوست
از غیرت صبا نفسش در دهان گرفت

Aasoode bar kenaar cho pargaar mishodam
Dovraan cho noghte aaghebatam dar miyaan gereft

آسوده بر کنار چو پرگار می‌شدم
دوران چو نقطه عاقبتم در میان گرفت

Aan rooz eshghe saaghare mey kharmanam besookht
Kaatash ze akse aareze saaghi dar aan gereft

آن روز عشق ساغر می خرمنم بسوخت
کاتش ز عکس عارض ساقی در آن گرفت

Khaaham shodan be kooye meikade aastin feshaan
Zin fetnehaa ke daamane aakher zamaan gereft

خواهم شدن به کوی مغان آستین فشان
زین فتنه‌ها که دامن آخرزمان گرفت

Mey khor ke har ke aakhere kaare jahaan bedid
Az gham sabok bar aamado ratle geraan gereft

می خور که هر که آخر کار جهان بدید
از غم سبک برآمد و رطل گران گرفت

Bar barge gol be khoone shaghaayegh neveshteand
Kaankas ke pokhte shod meye chon arghavaan gereft

بر برگ گل به خون شقایق نوشته‌اند
کان کس که پخته شد می چون ارغوان گرفت

Forsat negar ke fetne cho dar aalam ooftaad
Soofi be jaame mey zado az gham karaan gereft

فرصت نگر که فتنه چو در عالم اوفتاد
صوفی به جام می زد و از غم کران گرفت

Hafez cho aabe lotf ze nazme to michekad
Haased chegoone nokte tavaanad baraan gereft

حافظ چو آب لطف ز نظم تو می‌چکد
حاسد چگونه نکته تواند بران گرفت

Come Saki! The veil has been taken off by the beloved,
The work of the Khilvati's[1] lamp has once again restarted.

That candle has once more lifted up its head; face shining;
And youth came and took away from the Pir his ageing.

Love cast a saucy glance so that piety was diverted,
From the friend came kindness, so the enemy retreated.

What a deceitful and sweet heart-catching word you utter,
It seems your pistachio mouth[2] has coated speech with sugar.

For the burden of grief that has weighed on our heart,
God sent one with the breath of Jesus to lift and depart.

Every beauty whose cypress stature belittled the sun and moon,
When you came, recalled they had to be elsewhere - and soon.

The vaults of the seven heavens with this tale resounded,
See that short-sighted one, too short he thought it sounded.

From whom did you learn this prayer, Hafiz, that a kind destiny,
Made an amulet of your verse, so that taken as gold it would be.[3]

---

**(W-C 68) The radif here is 'Kindled' and 'Took'.**
 [1] "...Khilvati's..."These are reclusive mystics.
 [2] "...pistachio mouth..." This is a common metaphor for the mouth taken from its lip-like shape and small size.
 [3] "...Made an amulet of your verse..." A clear indication that far from being merely beautiful poetry there is a depth to Hafiz's ghazals that goes beyond any overt meanings that may be read into it. The recitation alone, as with the holy book itself,  has spiritual power. This is the justification for our inclusion of the original Farsi in transliteration. To enable those who cannot read the original script to be benefitted by it.

Saaghi biyaa ke yaar ze rokh parde bar gereft
Kaare cheraaghe khalvatiaan baaz dar gereft

ساقی بیا که یار ز رخ پرده برگرفت
کار چراغ خلوتیان باز درگرفت

Aan sha-me sar gerefte degar chehre bar forookht
Vin pire saal khorde javaani ze sar gereft

آن شمع سرگرفته دگر چهره برفروخت
وین پیر سالخورده جوانی ز سر گرفت

Aan eshve daad eshgh ke taghvaa ze rah beraft
Vaan lotf kard doost ke doshman hazar gereft

آن عشوه داد عشق که تقوی ز ره برفت
وان لطف کرد دوست که دشمن حذر گرفت

Zenhaar az aan ebaarate shirine delfarib
Gooee ke peste-ye to sokhan dar shekar gereft

زنهار از آن عبارت شیرین دلفریب
گوئی که پسته تو سخن در شکر گرفت

Baare ghami ke khaatere maa khaste karde bood
Isaa dami khodaa beferestaado bar gereft

بار غمی که خاطر ما خسته کرده بود
عیسی دمی خدا بفرستاد و برگرفت

Har hoorvash ke bar maho khor hosn miforookht
Chon to dar aamadi peye kaari degar gereft

هرحورروش که بر مه و خور حسن می‌فروخت
چون تو درآمدی پی کاری دگر گرفت

Zin ghesse haft gombade aflaak por sedaast
Kootah nazar bebin ke sokhan mokhtasar gereft

زین قصّه هفت گنبد افلاک پرصداست
کوته نظر ببین که سخن مختصر گرفت

Hafez to in doaa ze ke aamookhti ke bakht
Taviz kard shere toraavo be zar gereft

حافظ تو این دعا ز که آموختی که بخت
تعویذ کرد شعر ترا و به زر گرفت

A bulbul had in his beak a rose petal of pleasant colouring,
Yet was wailing and weeping profusely anyway, from longing.

I said, "You are united with your desire so why such bitter crying?"
He replied, "The beloved's show of beauty holds me here grieving".

If the beloved sat not with us poor beggars, what to say?
Royalty is prosperous and holds us poor beggars at bay.

The beautiful beloved is immune to our wailing supplication,
Happy is one who holds wealth with that one's sanction.[1]

Arise! So we can offer up our very life for that artist's pen,
From whose turning compass all these wonderful images have arisen.

If you're a follower of the path of love don't consider ill-fame,
Pawned for wine was the robe of Sheikh Sanaan's pious name[2].

Happy the time of that Kalander[3] who retained in wandering,
Held under his girdle, the beads which named the Great King.

Beneath the palace roof of that Houri-natured[4] heavenly beauty,
Hafiz's eye beholds streams that beneath paradise flow freely[5].

*(W-C 69) The radif here is 'held' or 'hold'.*
[1] *"...who holds wealth..." This reminds one of Imam Ghazali's description of four classes of people; the wise poor man, the foolish poor man, the wise wealthy man and the foolish wealthy man. Perhaps the most blessed one is he who has wealth and the wisdom to use it well. Next comes the wise poor man, third comes the foolish rich man, and least comes the foolish poor man.*
[2] *"...Sheikh Sanaan..." (D.1159 AD). He is said to have deserted Islam for the love of a beautiful Christian woman, but continued the use of the rosary of the 99 beautiful names of Allah (see next verse). See also 'Conference of the Birds by Fariduddin Attar – there are variations on this story.*
[3] *"...Kalandar..." See glossary in this volume.*
[4] *"...Houri-natured..." See glossary in this volume under Huri or Houri.*
[5] *"...beneath paradise..." Streams are spoken of in the holy Qur'an as flowing beneath paradise.*

Bolboli barge goli khosh rang dar menghaar daasht

Vandar aan bargo navaa khosh naalehaaye zaar daasht

بلبلی برگ گلی خوش رنگ در منقار داشت

و اندران برگ و نوا خوش ناله‌های زار داشت

Goftamash dar eine vasl in naalevo faryaad chist

Goft maa raa jelveye mashoogh dar in kaar daasht

گفتمش در عین وصل این ناله و فریاد چیست

گفت ما را جلوه معشوق در این کار داشت

Yaar agar nanshast baa maa nist jaaye eteraaz

Paad shaahi kaamraan bood az gedaayaan aar dasht

یار اگر ننشست با ما نیست جای اعتراض

پادشاهی کامران بود از گدایان عار داشت

Dar nemigirad niyaazo naaze maa baa hosne doost

Khorram aan kaz naazaninaan bakhte barkhordaar daasht

در نمی‌گیرد نیاز و ناز ما با حسن دوست

خرّم آن کز نازنینان بخت برخوردار داشت

Khiz ta bar kelke aan naghaash jaan afshaan konim

Kin hame naghshe ajab dar gardeshe pargaar daasht

خیز تا بر کلک آن نقّاش جان افشان کنیم

کاین همه نقش عجب در گردش پرگار داشت

Gar moride raahe eshghi fekre badnaami makon

Sheikhe san-aan kherghe rahne khaaneye khammar daasht

گر مرید راه عشقی فکر بدنامی مکن

شیخ صنعان خرقه رهن خانه خمّار داشت

Vaghte aan shirin ghalandar khosh ke dar atvaare seir

Zekre tasbihe malek dar halgheye zonnaar daasht

وقت آن شیرین قلندر خوش که در اطوار سیر

ذکر تسبیح ملک در حلقه زنّار داشت

Chashme Hafez zire ghasre baame aan hoori seresht

Shiveye jannaate tajri tahtehal anhaar daasht

چشم حافظ زیر بام قصر آن حوری سرشت

شیوه جنّات تجری تحتها الانهار داشت

You saw that only tyranny and violence the beloved would show;
Pacts were made and broken, but pity for our anguish? Oh no!

O Lord, don't charge that one, not even for catching and killing -
The bird, my heart; nor because the sanctuary's[1] life that one is ignoring.

It was because of my bad luck that this violence came to me,
Otherwise my beloved shows nothing but a kind liberality.

Those who have not felt the contempt that beloved showed me,
Everywhere such a one goes, for them no respect will there be.

O Saki, bring wine, please! To the earnest preacher, say,
"Deny not! Even Jamshid had not the cup[2] we have today."

Every pilgrim who did not go towards your sacred door,
Sadly travelled in the valley, but your holy enclave[3] never saw.

Hafiz, the trophy of felicity for the fine art of poetry is yours alone,
The pretender had not the skill, though by him this was not known.

---

**(W-C 70) The radif here is 'Have not'.**
   [1] *"...the sanctuary..." Hunting is forbidden in the sacred enclosure of Mecca. Here of course Hafiz is likening the heart to a sacred place.*
   [2] *"...Jamshid...cup..." See the glossary in this volume.*
   [3] *"...holy enclave..." This refers to the surrounds of the Kaaba.*

Didi ke yaar joz sare jovro setam nadaasht
Beshkast ahdo az ghame maa hich gham nadaasht

دیدی که یار جز سر جور و ستم نداشت
بشکست عهد و ازغم ما هیچ غم نداشت

Yaa rab magirash ar che dele chon kabootaram
Afkando koshto ezzate seide haram nadaasht

یا رب مگیرش ار چه دل چون کبوترم
افکند و کشت و عزّت صید حرم نداشت

Bar man jafaa ze bakhte man aamad vagarna yaar
Haashaa ke rasme lotfo tarighe karam nadaasht

بر من جفا ز بخت من آمد وگرنه یار
حاشا که رسم لطف و طریق کرم نداشت

Baa in hame har aanke na khaari keshid azoo
Harjaa ke raft hich kasash mohtaram nadaasht

با این همه هر آنکه نه خواری کشید از او
هر جا که رفت هیچکسش محترم نداشت

Saaghi biaar baadevo baa mohtaseb begooy
Enkaare maa makon ke chonin jaam jam nadaasht

ساقی بیار باده و با محتسب بگوی
انکار ما مکن که چنین جام جم نداشت

Har raahro ke rah be harime darash nabord
Meskin borid vaadio rah dar haram nadaasht

هر راهرو که ره به حریم درش نبرد
مسکین برید وادی و ره در حرم نداشت

Hafez bebar to gooye sa-aadat ke moddaee
Hichash honar naboodo khabar niz ham nadaasht

حافظ ببر تو گوی سعادت که مدّعی
هیچش هنر نبود و خبر نیز هم نداشت

No sunshine from your cheek, no daylight in my life,
Nothing but the deep black night remains in my life.

For separation patience is the only remedy that I can apply,
How to apply patience, when the power to do it runs dry.

When it came to saying goodbye to you, I could only cry,
Your face seemed far, no light from you reached my eye.

From this eye's corner your image departed, and said,
"It's a great pity, that this corner is no longer inhabited".

Union with you kept the idea of death from my mind,
Now with separation from you, this I no longer find.

Soon that insidious watcher (may he remain far away),
Will start to whisper, "That shattering one did not stay."

What does it matter now if the beloved chooses to visit me,
No spark of life is in my body now, for the beloved to see.

If, from separation, no water for tears remains in my eye,
Say, "Spill the liver's blood then, or how else shall I cry",

Through grief and weeping Hafiz has abandoned laughter,
The one torn by grief loses desire for the feast thereafter.

*(W-C 71) The radif here is; "Has not remained".*

Bi mehre rokhat rooze maraa noor namaandast

Vaz omr maraa joz shabe deyjoor namaandast

بی مهر رخت روز مرا نور نماندست

وز عمر مرا جز شب دیجور نماندست

Sabr ast maraa chaareye hejre to valikan

Chon sabr tavaan kard ke maghdoor namaandast

صبر است مرا چاره هجر تو ولیکن

چون صبر توان کرد که مقدور نماندست

Hengaame vedaae to ze bas gerye ke kardam

Door az rokhe to chashme maraa noor namaandast

هنگام وداع تو زبس گریه که کردم

دور از رخ تو چشم مرا نور نماندست

Miraft khiyaale to ze chashme mano migoft

Heyhaat azin gooshe ke mamoor namaandast

می رفت خیال تو ز چشم من و می گفت

هیهات ازین گوشه که معمور نماندست

Vasle to ajal raa ze saram door hami daasht

Az dovlate hejre to konoon door namaandast

وصل تو اجل را ز سرم دور همی داشت

از دولت هجر تو کنون دور نماندست

Nazdik shodaan dam ke raghibe to begooyad

Door az darat aan khasteye ranjoor namaandast

نزدیک شد آن دم که رقیب تو بگوید

دور از درت آن خسته مهجور نماندست

Men ba-d che sood ar ghadami ranje konad doost

Kaz jaan ramaghi dar tane ranjoor namaandast

من بعد چه سود ار قدمی رنجه کند دوست

کز جان رمقی در تن رنجور نماندست

Dar hejre to gar chashme maraa aab namaanad

Goo khoone jegar riz ke ma-zoor namaandast

در هجر تو گر چشم مرا آب نماند

گو خون جگر ریز که معذور نماندست

Hafez ze gham az gerye napardaakht be khande

Maatam zade raa daaee yeye soor namaandast

حافظ ز غم از گریه نپرداخت به خنده

ماتم زده را داعیه سور نماندست

From weeping, the pupil of my eye has become bloody,
How it is for people who seek you, now do you see?

Drinking to your wine-soaked eye and lip of ruby,
In the cup of grief the ruby wine I drink is bloody.

The sun of your face, if from your place in the east,
It should rise, then an auspicious sign for me it is at least.

Farhad, only stories about Shirin's lip[2], he gives,
Majnun in the curling locks of Laila's hair lives.

Seek out my heart, for your cypress stature is heart pleasing;
Talk to me, for your gracious measured speech too is pleasing.

O Saki, some mercy for my soul from the wine's circulation,
My sorrow is from the tyranny of the sphere's revolution.

When from my hand that dearly loved one had departed,
Like the river Jihune[3] became my robe's hem, from tears shed.

How can my sad heart ever become joyful again?
Only by a power beyond any power I can attain.

Though Hafiz is beside himself, still the beloved he seeks,
Like the impoverished one who for Karun's[4] gold seeks.

---

*(W-C 72) The radif here is; "Is".*
   [1] *"...Farhad ...Shirin..." See the glossary in this volume under Farhad.*
   [2] *"...Layla and Majnun..." See the glossary in this volume*
   3 *"...Jihune..." The river Oxus.*
   4 *"...Karun..." See the glossary in this volume.*

Ze gerye mardome chashmam neshaste dar khoonast
Bebin ke dar talabat haale mardomaan choonast

ز گریه مردم چشمم نشسته در خون است
ببین که در طلبت حال مردمان چون است

Be yaade la-le to bi chashme maste meigoonat
Ze jaame gham meye la-li ke mikhoram khoonast

به یاد لعل تویی چشم مست میگونت
ز جام غم می لعلی که می‌خورم خون است

Ze mashreghe sare kooy aaftaabe tal-ate to
Agar toloo konad taaleam homayoon ast

ز مشرق سر کوی آفتاب طلعت تو
اگر طلوع کند طالعم همایون است

Hekaayate labe shirin kalaame farhaadast
Shekanje torreye leili maghaame majnoonast

حکایت لب شیرین کلام فرهاد است
شکنج طرّه لیلی مقام مجنون است

Delam bejoo ke ghadat hamcho sarv deljooyast
Sokhan bego ke kalaamat latifo movzoonast

دلم بجو که قدت همچو سرو دلجوی است
سخن بگو که کلامت لطیف و موزون است

Ze dovre baade be jaan raahati resaan saghi
Ke ranje khaateram az jovre dovre gadroon ast

ز دور باده به جان راحتی رسان ساقی
که رنج خاطرم از جور دور گردون است

Az aan zamaan ke ze changam beraft roode aziz
Kenaare daamane man hamcho roode jeihoon ast

از آن زمان که ز چنگم برفت رود عزیز
کنار دامن من همچو رود جیحون است

Chegoone shaad shavad andaroone ghamginam
Be ekhtiyaar ke az ekhtiyaar biroonast

چگونه شاد شود اندرون غمگینم
به اختیار که از اختیار بیرون است

Ze bikhodi talabe yaar mikonad Hafez
Cho moflesi ke talabkaare ganje ghaaroonast

ز بیخودی طلب یار می‌کند حافظ
چو مفلسی که طلبکار گنج قارون است

Except for your face, our eye's pupil[1] wishes not any other view,
Except remembering you, nothing else can this broken heart do.

My tear enfolds me, like the *ihram*[2] worn for circling your sanctuary[3],
Though not for a moment unsullied by my wounded heart's blood really.

Trapped and caged, as the wild bird is most frequently,
May the paradise-bird be, if in search of you not flying swiftly.

If a poor sad lover has scattered counterfeit currency,
Do not criticise him please, he has no legitimate money.

At last his hand will reach up to the lofty cypress tree,
If his spirit's searching lacks neither ardour, nor purity.

The reason I do not boast before you about Jesus' life-giving[4],
Is because he is less expert than your lip at soul refreshing.

Though I am on fire for you, no sigh escapes from me,
How can one say that by me heart stains are not born patiently.

I spoke of the tip of your lovely curl, before time's creation,
Saying, "There is no conclusion to this chain of confusion."

The desire of union with you is not in Hafiz's heart alone,
Who is there whose heart does not that desire secretly own?

---

**(W-C 73)**
   [1] *"...pupil of the eye..." See the glossary in this volume under symbols - the body.*
   [2] *"...Ihram..." See the glossary in this volume.*
   [3] *"...Sanctuary..." Haram Sharif (the Kaaba) in Mecca.*
   [4] *"... Jesus' live-giving breath..." This refers to the miraculous healing power of Lord Jesus, which is also associated with the breathing into him of the Holy Spirit by Archangel Gabriel.*

Mardome dideye maa joz be rokhat naazer nist
Dele sar gashteye maa gheire to raa zaaker nist

مردم دیده ما جز به رخت ناظر نیست
دل سرگشته ما غیر ترا ذاکر نیست

Ashkam ehraame tavaafe haramat mibandad
Garche az khoone dele rish dami taaher nist

اشکم احرام طواف حرمت می‌بندد
گر چه از خون دل ریش دمی طاهر نیست

Basteye daame ghafas baad cho morghe vahshi
Taayere sedre agar dar talabat taayer nist

بسته دام قفس باد چو مرغ وحشی
طایر سدره اگر در طلبت طایر نیست

Aasheghe mofles agar ghalbe delat kard nesaar
Makonash eib ke bar naghde ravaan ghaader nist

عاشق مفلس اگر قلب دلت کرد نثار
مکنش عیب که بر نقد روان قادر نیست

Aaghebat dast bedaan sarve bolandash beresad
Har ke raa dar talabat hemmate ou ghaaser nist

عاقبت دست بدان سرو بلندش برسد
هر که را در طلبت همّت او قاصر نیست

Az ravaan bakhshiye isaa nazanam pishe to dam
Zaanke dar rooh fazaaee cho labat maaher nist

از روان بخشی عیسی نزنم پیش تو دم
زان که در روح فزایی چو لبت ماهر نیست

Man ke dar aatashe sovdaaye to aahi nazanam
Key tavaan goft ke bar daagh delam saaber nist

من که در آتش سودای تو آهی نزنم
کی توان گفت که بر داغ دلم صابر نیست

Rooze avval ke sare zolfe to didam goftam
Ke parishaaniye in selsele raa aakher nist

روز اوّل که سر زلف تو دیدم گفتم
که پریشانی این سلسله را آخر نیست

Sare peivande to tanhaa na dele Hafez raast
Kist aan kesh sare peivande to dar khaater nist

سر پیوند تو تنها نه دل حافظ راست
کیست آن کش سر پیوند تو در خاطر نیست

Love's path is the path that is without any limit,
The soul's surrender is the only remedy given by it.

Every moment the heart dedicates to love fortunate will be,
For this goodly kind of work seeking an omen is unnecessary.

Take as plundered pleasure the hidden path of the profligate,
Like the way to the hidden treasure[1], it is strictly for the initiate.

Don't try to impose reason's prohibition; and bring wine too!
In this land that guardian of morals has no work; nothing to do.

The pure sighted one sees the new moon's slender crescent,
But sight of such a fine treasure is hid; to few eyes is it sent.

Only ask this of your eye, "Who is it that so fatally attracts you?"
Dear, there's no sin in the stars or fate; this comes from you.

It seems that all Hafiz's weeping leaves you unaffected,
Amazing! Harder than rock is the one that is stony hearted[2].

---

*(W-C 74) The radif here is; "Is not".*
   [1] *"...hidden treasure..." According to a Hadith Allah says: "I was a hidden treasure and desired to be known".*
   [2] *"...stony-hearted..." Love softens the heart so that is liked by God. Concerns and worries in the present life make the heart hard.*

Raahist raahe eshgh ke hichash kenaare nist

Aanjaa joz aanke jaan besepaarand chaare nist

راهیست راه عشق که هیچش کناره نیست
آن جا جز آن که جان بسپارند چاره نیست

Har gah ke del be eshgh dahi khosh dami bovad

Dar kaare kheir haajate hich estekhaare nist

هر گه که دل به عشق دهی خوش دمی بود
در کار خیر حاجت هیچ استخاره نیست

Forsat shemor tarigheye rendi ke in neshaan

Chon raahe ganj bar hame kas aashkaare nist

فرصت شمر طریقه رندی که این نشان
چون راه گنج بر همه کس آشکاره نیست

Maa raa be man-e aghl matarsaano mey biyaar

Kaan shahne dar velaayate maa hich kaare nist

ما را به منع عقل مترسان و می بیار
کان شحنه در ولایت ما هیچ کاره نیست

Ou raa be chashme paak tavaan did chon helaal

Har dide jaaye jelveye aan maahpaare nist

او را به چشم پاک توان دید چون هلال
هر دیده جای جلوه آن ماهپاره نیست

Az chashme khod bepors ke maa raa ke mikoshad

Jaanaa gonaahe taale o jorme setaare nist

از چشم خود بپرس که ما را که می کشد
جانا گناه طالع و جرم ستاره نیست

Nagreft dar to geryeye Hafez be hich rooy

Heiraane aan delam ke kam az sange khaare nist

نگرفت در تو گریه حافظ به هیچ روی
حیران آن دلم که کم از سنگ خاره نیست

O Saki, Eid greetings![1] May this day be a fortunate for you,
And may the promises you have made, be in your mind too.

During the time of separation, it is amazing, but true,
From friends you parted and your heart agreed to it too.

Serve the dear daughter of the vine and say, "Come on out!"
For the breath of our resolve has freed you, there's no doubt.

Your footsteps brought great gladness into the assembly,
On any heart that is not rejoicing for you, grief let there be.

This autumnal wind did not damage your garden, thankfully,
It hurt neither jasmine, cypress, nor rose, nor the box tree.

From separation you came, (far be the evil eye from you!)
With a famous fortune and the mother of good luck too.

O Hafiz, do not from the company of Noah's Ark[2] loosen your grip,
Or under a deluge of misfortune your foundation will slip.

*(W-C 75)*

[1] *"...Eid greetings..." Eid is a festival day or holiday. Probably referring here to the Eid following the fasting month since the next line speaks of a period of separation. Hafiz says the fasting did you no harm and in fact from it you gained a (spiritual) fortune.*
[2] *"...the company of Noah's Ark..." This probably refers to the religion, so Hafiz may be saying don't leave of from the religious practice of fasting.*

Saaghiyaa aamadane eid mobaarak baadat

Vaan mavaaeed ke kardi maravad az yaadat

ساقیا آمدن عید مبارک بادت

وان مواعید که کردی مرود از یادت

Dar shegeftam ke dar in moddate ayyaame feraagh

Bar gerefti ze harifaan delo del midaadat

در شگفتم که در این مدت ایّام فراق

برگرفتی ز حریفان دل و دل می‌دادت

Beresaan bandegiye dokhtar raz goo be dar aay

Ke damo hemmaate maa kard ze band aazaadat

برسان بندگی دختر رز گو به درآی

که دم و همّت ما کرد ز بند آزادت

Shaadiye majlesiaan dar ghadamo maghdame tost

Jaaye gham baad haraan del ke nakhaahad shaadat

شادی مجلسیان در قدم و مقدم تست

جای غم باد هران دل که نخواهد شادت

Shokre izad ke azin baade khazaan rakhne nayaaft

Boostaane samano sarvo golo shemshaadat

شکر ایزد که ازین باد خزان رخنه نیافت

بوستان سمن و سرو و گل و شمشادت

Chashme bad door kazaan tafraghe khosh baazaavard

Taale-e naamvaro dovlate maadar zaadat

چشم بد دور کزان تفرقه خوش باز آورد

طالع نامور و دولت مادرزادت

Hafez az dast made sohbate in kashtiye nooh

Varna toofaane havaades bebarad bonyaadat

حافظ از دست مده صحبت این کشتی نوح

ورنه طوفان حوادث ببرد بنیادت

From the sage of Caanan[1] I heard these excellent words,
"Grief at separation from the beloved finds no words".

Terrifying words the city preacher spoke, about The Last Day,
They barely hint at the words that one on departing had to say.

Of whom to seek news of the departed? In such diverse ways
Blows the wind, the messenger who only confusion conveys.

That unkind moon is the enemy's friend; very sadly,
When it came to deserting, that friend's words came so slickly.

In future the stage of contentment is mine; thanks to the rivalry[2],
My heart got used to pain from you, and left off seeking remedy.

Even if the wind says what you want to hear don't tie a knot in it,
This proverb the wind spoke, and to Solomon[3] it spoke it.

Be true, whatever fancy excuse the sky may offer you,
Who told you this ugly old hag had stopped lying to you.

"With wine matured over many years, that age-old grief repel,
Thus sow the seed of a happy heart"; the village elder said well.

Don't waste breath on 'how' or 'why'. Slaves must hear and obey,
With heart and soul, any words the sovereign beloved may say.

Who is it saying that from thought of you Hafiz retreated?
Whoever it is, he speaks lies: by me this was never said.

---

**(W-C 76) The radif here is; "Uttered".**

[1] "...the sage of Canaan..." This refers to Prophet Yaqub (Jacob) who suffered long from the separation from his beautiful son, Prophet Yusuf (Joseph). The grief he underwent are a symbol for the grief of the lover for God.

[2] "...thanks to.....rivalry', (or it could be 'the rival')..." Here we take it to refer to the rivalry of the brothers of Prophet Yusuf (Joseph) that led to separation – which in turn taught to Prophet Yaqub the lesson of accepting the Divine Will. This would seem to be the theme of the ghazal.
Indeed the entire Ghazal could be read as a meditation on Prophet Yaqub. The words that 'came so slickly' being the excuses the brothers made for Prophet Yusuf having been 'killed' by a wolf. The last verse could be Hafiz saying he has not withdrawn from his meditation on the separation of Prophet Yaqub. Even hearing news from voices of the unseen (on the wind) as Prophet Yaqub must have done, is not something to rely on or 'tie a knot in'.
The radif here which is 'uttered' or 'said' echoes the references to the various forms of spiritual messages about Prophet Joseph that Prophet Yaqub was hearing.

Shanideam sokhani khosh ke pire kan-aan goft
Feraaghe yaar na aan mikonad ke betvaan goft

شنیده‌ام سخنی خوش که پیر کنعان گفت
فراق یار نه آن می‌کند که بتوان گفت

Hadise hovle ghiyaamat ke goft vaaeze shahr
Kenaayatist ke az roozegaare hejraan goft

حدیث هول قیامت که گفت واعظ شهر
کنایتیست که از روزگار هجران گفت

Neshaane yaare safar karde az ke porsam raast
Ke harche goft baride sabaa parishaan goft

نشان یار سفرکرده از که پرسم راست
که هر چه گفت برید صبا پریشان گفت

Faghaan ke aan mahe naamehrabaane doshmandoost
Be tarke sohbate yaaraane khod che aasaan goft

فغان که آن مه نامهربان دشمن دوست
به ترک صحبت یاران خود چه آسان گفت

Mano maghaame rezaa ba-d az ino shokre raghib
Ke del be darde to khoo kardo tarke darmaan goft

من و مقام رضا بعد از این و شکر رقیب
که دل به درد تو خو کرد و ترک درمان گفت

Gereh be baad mazan gar che bar moraad vazad
Ke in sokhan be masal baad baa soleimaan goft

گره به باد مزن گر چه بر مراد وزد
که این سخن به مثل باد با سلیمان گفت

Be mohlati ke sepehrat dahad ze dast maro
To raa ke goft ke in zaal tarke dastaan goft

به مهلتی که سپهرت دهد ز دست مرو
ترا که گفت که این زال ترک دستان گفت

Ghame kohan be meye saalkhorde daf konid
Ke tokhme khoshdeli inasto pire dehghaan goft

غم کهن به می سالخورده دفع کنید
که تخم خوشدلی این است و پیر دهقان گفت

Mazan ze choono cheraa dam ke bandeye moghbel
Ghabool kard be jaan har sokhan ke jaanaan goft

مزن ز چون و چرا دم که بنده مقبل
قبول کرد به جان هر سخن که جانان گفت

Gereh be baad mazan gar che bar moraad ravad
Ke goft Hafez az andisheye to baaz aamad

که گفت حافظ از اندیشه تو باز آمد
من از این نگفته ام آن کس که گفت بهتان گفت

Man in nagofteam aan kas ke goft bohtaan goft

The bird of the garden said to the blossoming rose, at the break of day,
'Be less proud, for many a rose like you has bloomed this way.'

Laughing, the rose replied, "Truth does not make us sad,
But no true lover harsh words to the beloved ever said."

If ruby wine you desire from the cup jewelled so richly,
With the point of your eyelash pierce many a pearl and ruby[1].

The scent of love will evade the senses of anyone, eternally,
If they have not, with the face, swept clean the tavern's entry.

Last night in the garden of Iram[2], came the soft dawn breeze,
And the hyacinth's curling hair locks it happily began to tease.

 I asked Jamshid's throne "where is your cup for world-viewing?"
It replied - "It is a great pity that alert fortune has been sleeping".

The language of the tongue cannot reach up to love,
O Saki, give wine, and cut short this talk about love.

In to the ocean were cast wisdom and patience, by the tear of Hafiz.
What else can he do? The fire of love's grief - unbearably sad it is.

---

**(W-C 77)**
[1] Here Hafiz may be saying; discover the essence of many a hidden secret. But to do so you must make yourself pure if you want the scent of love.
[2] "...Iram..." See the glossary in this volume.

Sobh dam morghe chaman baa gole nov khaaste goft

صبحدم مرغ چمن با گل نوخاسته گفت

Naaz kam kon ke dar in baagh basi chon to shekoft

ناز کم کن که در این باغ بسی چون تو شکفت

Gol bekhandid ke az raast naranjim vali

گل بخندید که از راست نرنجیم ولی

Hich aashegh sokhane sakht be mashoogh nagoft

هیچ عاشق سخن سخت به معشوق نگفت

Gar tama daari az aan jaame morassa meye la-l

گر طمع داری از آن جام مرصّع می لعل

Dorro yaaghoot be noke mojeat baayad soft

درّ و یاقوت به نوک مژه‌ات باید سفت

Taa abad booye mahabbat be mashaamash naresad

تا ابد بوی محبّت به مشامش نرسد

Har ke khaake dare meikhaane be rokhsaare naroft

هر که خاک در میخانه به رخساره نرفت

Dar golestaane eram doosh cho az lotfe havaa

در گلستان ارم دوش چو از لطف هوا

Zolfe sombol be nasime sahari miaashoft

زلف سنبل به نسیم سحری می‌آشفت

Goftam ey masnade jam jaame jahaan binat koo

گفتم ای مسند جم جام جهان بینت کو

Goft afsoos ke aan dovlate bidaar bekhoft

گفت افسوس که آن دولت بیدار بخفت

Sokhane eshgh na aan ast ke aayad be zabaan

سخن عشق نه آن است که آید به زبان

Saaghiaa mey deho kootaah kon in gofto shenoft

ساقیا می ده و کوتاه کن این گفت و شنفت

Ashke Hafez kherado sabr be daryaa andaakht

اشک حافظ خرد و صبر به دریا انداخت

Che konad sooze ghame eshgh nayaarast nahoft

چه کند سوز غم عشق نیارست نهفت

My heart and faith have departed and the heart-taker has risen up,
In reproach saying, "Sit not with us, for safety you have given up."

Have you ever heard of one sitting and happily feasting,
Who has not finally risen up and in remorse is departing?

The tongue of the candle bragged brazenly about that laughing face,
By rising up nightly to burn for lovers, this fault it seeks to erase.

At the lawn's edge the rose and cypress, inspired the passing breeze,
To rise up in longing for your cheek and your lofty elegant ease.

Drunkenly, you passed by, and in the Khilvati's[1] place of isolation,
There arose, from the sight of you, the roar of the Day of Destination.

Rooted in shame, seeing the walk that you exhibit, so gracefully,
Is the cypress that in height and form had been so proud formerly.

Hafiz, throw off this religious robe and maybe you will find safety,
For fire rises up from the robe's wonder working and hypocrisy.

*(W-C 78) The radif here is; "Has risen".*
   [1] *"...Khilvati's..." See glossary in this volume.*

Delo dinam shodo delbar be malaamat bar khaast
Goft baa maa maneshin kaz to salaamat bar khaast

Ke shanidi ke dar in bazm dami khosh beneshast
Ke na dar akhere sohbat be nedaamat bar khaast

Sha-m agar zaan rokhe  khandaan be zabaan laafi zad
Pishe oshaaghe to shabhaa be gheraamat bar khaast

Dar chaman baade bahaari ze kenaare golo sarv
Be havaa daariye aan aarezo ghaamat bar khaast

Mast bogzashtiyo az khalvatiaane malakoot
Be tamaashaaye to aashoobe ghiaamat bar khaast

Pishe raftaare to paa bar nagereft az khejlat
Sarve sarkash ke be naaz az ghado ghaamat bar khaast

Hafez in kherghe biyandaaz magar jaan bebari
Kaatash az kharmane saaloose keraamat bar khaast

دل و دینم شد و دلبر به ملامت برخاست
گفت با ما منشین کز تو سلامت برخاست

که شنیدی که در این بزم دمی خوش بنشست
که نه در آخر صحبت به ندامت برخاست

شمع اگر زان رخ خندان به زبان لافی زد
پیش عشّاق تو شبها به غرامت برخاست

در چمن باد بهاری ز کنار گل و سرو
به هواداری آن عارض و قامت برخاست

مست بگذشتی و از خلوتیان ملکوت
به تماشای تو آشوب قیامت برخاست

پیش رفتار تو پا برنگرفت از خجلت
سرو سرکش که به ناز قد و قامت برخاست

حافظ این خرقه بینداز مگر جان بری
کاتش از خرمن سالوس کرامت برخاست

Your face no one ever saw, yet a thousand look-outs you have,
Concealed as a rosebud, yet a hundred bulbuls you have.

Though I seem far from you, far from you may no one be,
The hope I have, of union with you, is very near to me.

It is not so strange that I should happen to be in your street,
For in this country thousands of strangers like me one can meet.

Who became a lover that the beloved did not observe it?
Khwaja[1] there is no pain and if there were there is a doctor to cure it.

Sufi hospice or tavern - in love's way these are not different,
Whichever it is, the beloved's face a ray to it has sent.

Where the work of the cloister shining with splendour is,
The monk's chantry with the name of the cross there is.

In short, the sorrowful lament of Hafiz has not been in vain,
A very strange and wonderful story it is, and will remain.

*(W-C 79)*
   [1] *"...Khwaja..." Respected elder or great soul.*

Rooye to kas nadido hazaarat raghib hast

Dar ghonchei hanoozo sadat andalib hast

روی تو کس ندید و هزارت رقیب هست

در غنچه‌ای هنوز و صدت عندلیب هست

Har chand dooram az to ke door az to kas mabaad

Liken omide vasle toam an gharib hast

هر چند دورم از تو که دور از تو کس مباد

لیکن امید وصل تو ام عن قریب هست

Gar aamadam be kooye to chandaan gharib nist

Chon man dar in diyaar hezaaraan gharib hast

گر آمدم به کوی تو چندان غریب نیست

چون من در در این دیار هزاران غریب هست

Aashegh ke shod ke yaar be haalash nazar nakard

Ey khaaje dard nist vagar na tabib hast

عاشق که شد که یار به حالش نظر نکرد

ای خواجه درد نیست وگرنه طبیب هست

Dar eshgh khaaneghaaho kharaabaat fargh nist

Har jaa ke hast partove rooye habib hast

در عشق خانقاه و خرابات فرق نیست

هر جا که هست پرتو روی حبیب هست

Aanjaa ke kaare sovme-e raa jelve midahand

Naamoose deire raahebo naame salib hast

آنجا که کار صومعه را جلوه می‌دهند

ناموس دیر راهب و نام صلیب هست

Faryaade Hafez in hame aakher be harze nist

Ham ghessei gharibo hadisi ajib hast

فریاد حافظ این همه آخر به هرزه نیست

هم قصّه‌ای غریب و حدیثی عجیب هست

My heart got tangled in your curling locks, all by itself,
With one love-look kill it! This we have brought on our self.

If from your open-hand our heart's desire gain its satisfaction,
Be at hand: for that would be kindness in its own proper situation.

For scent, the musk of China or Chigal the rose depends not on,
But gets its muskiness from the fastenings that hold its own coat on.[1]

On your soul my sweet idol, to be like a candle I aspire,
In the depths of dark night, to extinguish my own fire.

Bulbul, when you began to speak of love, I said "Desist!"
For that rose is self-serving and acts only in self-interest.

Do not go to the houses of the worldly lords of mean intent,
Find ease in your own house, from that corner of contentment.

Hafiz burned, but in terms of the conventions of loving,
He is the height of fidelity and of promise keeping.

*(W-C 80) The radif here is; 'of itself' or 'of one's own self'.*
   [1] *"...its own coat..." Meaning the rose depends on no nothing else but itself.*

Be daame zolfe to del mobtalaaye khish tanast
Bekosh be ghamze ke inash sazaaye khish tanast

به دام زلف تو دل مبتلای خویشتن است
بکش به غمزه که اینش سزای خویشتن است

Garat ze dast bar aayad moraade khaatere maa
Be dast baash ke kheiri be jaaye khish tanast

گرت ز دست برآید مراد خاطر ما
به دست باش که خیری به جای خویشتن است

Be moshke chino chegel nist booye gol mohtaaj
Ke naafehaash ze bande ghabaaye khish tanast

به مشک چین و چگل نیست بوی گل محتاج
که نافه هاش ز بند قبای خویشتن است

Be jaanat ey bote shirine man ke hamchon sha-m
Shabaane tire moraadam fanaaye khish tanast

به جانت ای بت شیرین من که همچون شمع
شبان تیره مرادم فنای خویشتن است

Cho raaye eshgh zadi baa to goftam ey bolbol
Makon ke aan gole khodroo be raaye khish tanast

چو رای عشق زدی با تو گفتم ای بلبل
مکن که آن گل خودرو به رای خویشتن است

Maro be khaaneye arbaabe bi morovvate dahr
Ke ganje aafiyatat dar saraaye khish tanast

مرو به خانه ارباب بی مروّت دهر
که گنج عافیتت در سرای خویشتن است

Besookht Hafezo dar sharte eshghbaaziye ou
Hanooz bar sare ahdo vafaaye khishtanast

بسوخت حافظ و در شرط عشقبازی او
هنوز بر سر عهد و وفای خویشتن است

O I long to tell you the state of my heart,
O I long to hear the news of the heart.

Look you, at this crude wish of mine, to hide,
The old, old, story, from the spies who pried.

On this Night of Power[1], so blessed and holy,
I yearn to sleep with you till the day we see.

Oh dear, the desire that I have in the dark night,
Is to pierce that unique pearl[2] so tender and bright.

O gracious breeze for your holy help I plead,
For to bloom in the morning[3] is my real need.

For holy honour's sake my dearest desire is only this,
To sweep your path's dust[4] with the tip of my eyelashes.

Like Hafiz, my desire is to recite a Rend kind of poetry[5],
Irrespective of whatever that one says who has enmity.

---

**(W-C 81) The radif here is; 'Is my desire'.**

[1] The Night of Power is referred to in the holy Qur'an as a special night when a continuous flow of blessings descend on the fortunate recipient and there is peace in the soul till the dawn. It also refers to the night the Holy Qur'an was revealed. Traditionally it is thought to be one of the nights at the end of Ramadan but many mystics would say it can be any night. Hafiz himself experienced the Night of Power when receiving his gift of poetry.

[2] "...unique pearl..." This ghazal can be read as desiring the spiritual bliss that comes with the Night of Power and perhaps the unique pearl is the holy Qur'an or union with The Beloved. To pierce the pearl can also refer to finding Truth in a given situation.

[3] "...the 'morning..." This could refer to the Day of Judgement.

[4] "...sweeping the dust..." This could be referring to acquiring spiritual purity – the aspiration to clean the heart.

[5] "...a Rend kind of poetry..." For Rend see the glossary in this volume. At the end Hafiz seems to acknowledge the alternative ways of reading the poem – he is shocking the pious reader in the manner of Rends since it is possible to read this ghazal as being about human passion whilst his real intent is purely spiritual.

Haale del baa to goftanam havasast

Khabare del shenoftanam havasast

Tama-e khaam bin ke ghesseye faash

Az raghibaan nahoftanam havasast

Shabe ghadri chenin azizo sharif

Ba to taa rooz khoftanam havasast

Vah ke dordaanei chenin naazok

Dar shabe taar softanam havasast

Ey sabaa emshabam madad farmaay

Ke sahargah shekoftanam havasast

Az baraayr sharaf be noke moje

Khaake raahe to roftanam havasast

Hamcho Hafez be raghme moddaiaan

Shere rendaane goftanam havas ast

حال دل با تو گفتنم هوس است

خبر دل شنفتنم هوس است

طمع خام بین که قصّه فاش

از رقیبان نهفتنم هوس است

شب قدری چنین عزیز و شریف

با تو تا روز خفتنم هوس است

وه که دردانه‌ای چنین نازک

در شب تار سفتنم هوس است

ای صبا امشبم مدد فرمای

که سحرگه شکفتنم هوس است

از برای شرف به نوک مژه

خاک راه تو رفتنم هوس است

همچو حافظ به رغم مدّعیان

شعر رندانه گفتنم هوس است

O hoopoe[1] of the east wind, to Saba[2] I am sending you,
See from where I send, and to where I am sending you.

So sad, that in this dust-pit, a bird of your quality is grieving,
So I am sending you to the heaven where fidelity is nesting.

In love's path there is no such thing as 'far' or 'near'.
I send a prayer, as to me you are so visible and clear.

A caravan of benedictions for your welfare, I send morn and eve,
In the company of the north wind and the east wind they leave.

So that land of your heart, is not ruined by grief's armies,
I am sending to you the soul of my life to pay off these.

O Saki, come! The unseen messenger this news did explain,
"I send the cure of union to you, so have patience in pain!"

O silent sharer in my heart, hidden so well from view,
Prayers I will say for you, and also greetings I send too.

The Creator's handiwork in your own face can be seen,
For I send to you the mirror where God's display is seen.

So the musicians may relay the feelings I have for you,
Well worded ghazals I send you with fine melodies too.

Hafiz, our gathering is singing songs for your welfare,
Hurry up, I sent a horse to bring you, and a coat to wear.

*(W-C 82) The radif is "I send to you".*
[1] *"...hoopoe..." See the glossary in this volume.*
[2] *"...Saba..." See the glossary in this volume.*
*The story of Solomon sending a messenger bird (Hoopoe) to Bilqis the Queen of Sheba and ultimately bringing her to know the Unity of Allah is found in (Qur'an 27). Here however Hafiz also seems to be using the story as a model for speaking of love at a distance and/or connection to the Unseen.*

Ey hod hode sabaa be sabaa miferestamat

Bengar ke az kojaa be kojaa miferestamat

ای هدهد صبا به سبا می‌فرستمت

بنگر که از کجا به کجا می‌فرستمت

Heif ast taayeri choto dar khaakdaane gham

Zinjaa be aasmaane vafaa miferestamat

حیف است طایری چو تو در خاکدان غم

زینجا به آسمان وفا می‌فرستمت

Dar raahe eshgh marhaleye ghorbo bo-d nist

Mibinamat ayaano doaa miferestamat

در راه عشق مرحله قرب و بعد نیست

می‌بینمت عیان و دعا می‌فرستمت

Har sobho shaam ghaafelei az doaaye kheir

Dar sohbate shomaalo sabaa miferestamat

هر صبح و شام قافله‌ای از دعای خیر

در صحبت شمال و صبا می‌فرستمت

Taa lashkare ghamat nakonad molke del kharaab

Jaane azize khod be navaa miferestamat

تا لشکر غمت نکند ملک دل خراب

جان عزیز خود به نوا می‌فرستمت

Saaghi biyaa ke haatefe gheibam be mojde goft

Baa dard sabr kon ke davaa miferestamat

ساقی بیا که هاتف غیبم به مژده گفت

با درد صبر کن که دوا می‌فرستمت

Ey ghaayeb az nazar ke shodi hamneshine del

Miguyamat doaa o sanaa miferestamat

ای غایب از نظر که شدی همنشین دل

می‌گویمت دعا و ثنا می‌فرستمت

Dar rooye khod tafarroje son-e khodaay kon

Kaeeneye khodaay nomaa miferestamat

در روی خود تفرّج صنع خدای کن

کآیینهٔ خدای نما می‌فرستمت

Ta motrebaan ze shovghe manat aagahi dahand

Ghovlo ghazal be saazo navaa miferestamat

تا مطربان ز شوق منت آگهی دهند

قول و غزل به ساز و نوا می‌فرستمت

Hafez soroode majlese maa zekre kheire tost

Beshtaab kon ke asbo ghabaa miferestamat

حافظ سرود مجلس ما ذکر خیر توست

تعجیل کن که اسب و قبا می‌فرستمت

You are hidden from view, so to God I am entrusting you,
You inflamed my soul, but as friend of my heart, I hold you.

Until my shirt becomes a shroud that's trodden under the dust,
To imagine I would stop from holding to your robe is unjust.

Reveal the Mihrab[1] of your eyebrow so in the dawn prayer,
Round your neck my raised hands can go in prayer.

If necessary I will even go to Harut[2], the magician of Babylon,
A hundred kinds of sorcery will perform, so you I can summon.

Fickle healer I wish and wait to die in front of you,
Just ask who is sick - I am a patient waiting for you.

From my eyes, in a hundred rivulets, water over my chest, is flowing,
I hold on to the hope that seeds of love in your heart will be growing,

O Hafiz, wine, a mistress, and profligacy are not really quite *you*,
Still you continue do all of these and I continue to pardon you.

*(W-C 83) The radif is "You".*
[1] *"..Mihrab..." The prayer arch of Muslims that is oriented towards Mecca.*
[2] *"..Harut..." See the glossary in this volume.*

Ey ghaayeb az nazar be khodaa misepaaramat
Jaanam besookhtiyyo ze jaan doost daaramat

ای غایب از نظر به خدا می‌سپارمت
جانم بسوختیّ وزجان دوستدارمت

Taa daamane kafan nakesham zire paaye khaak
Baavar makon ke dast ze daaman bedaaramat

تا دامن کفن نکشم زیر پای خاک
باور مکن که دست ز دامن بدارمت

Mehraabe abrooyat benamaa ta sahar gahi
Daste doaa bar aaramo dar gardan aaramat

محراب ابرویت بنما تا سحرگهی
دست دعا برآرم و در گردن آرمت

Gar baayadam shodan sooye haroote baabeli
Sad goone jaadovi bekonam taa biyaaramat

گر بایدم شدن سوی هاروت بابلی
صد گونه جادوئی بکنم تا بیارمت

Khaaham ke pish miramat ey bivafaa tabib
Bimaar baaz pors ke dar entezaaramat

خواهم که پیش میرمت ای بیوفا طبیب
بیمار بازپرس که در انتظارمت

Sad jooye aab basteam az dide dar kenaar
Bar booye tokhme mehr ke dar del bekaaramat

صد جوی آب بسته‌ام از دیده در کنار
بر بوی تخم مهر که در دل بکارمت

Hafez sharaabo shaahedo rendi na vaz-e tost
Fel jomle mikoniyyo foroo migozaaramat

حافظ شراب و شاهد و رندی نه وضع تست
فی الجمله می‌کنیّ و فرو می‌گذارمت

O Lord, I pray find some means so that in safety and security,
My beloved may return to release me from the grip of infamy.

Bring the dust from the path of the dear one, who is away travelling,
So my world-seeing eye will be where that one is safely staying.

 Be just!  On six sides[1] of this path they bar the way to me,
That mole, down, hair, face, cheek, and statuesque form that I see.

Have some mercy I pray, as I am in your hands today,
Tears of repentance are useless tomorrow, when I return to clay.

To one who wastes breath trying to be love's rationaliser,
The only thing we have to say is; 'Go in safety and prosper.'

Dervish, towards sword-wielding beauties feel no ill-will,
For this tribe receive the full blood price[2] for those they kill.

Burn the cloak of religious piety; for the arch of the Saki's eyebrow,
Shatters the prayer arch where the pious preachers make their bow.

God forbid that I should moan of your violence and tyranny,
The unfairness of the delicate ones is all kindness and generosity.

With regard to the tip of your hair locks, that which Hafiz has to say,
He does not curtail, it extends all the way, to the Judgement Day.

**(W-C 84)**
[1] "...On six sides ..." Six directions – in other words in every direction (up, down, left, right, before and behind) –
implying spatiality.
[2] "...blood price..." Money paid by the murderers to kin and relatives when someone is murdered.

Yaa rab sababi saaz ke yaaram be salaamat

Baaz aayado berhaanadam az bande malaamat

یا رب سببی ساز که یارم به سلامت

بازآید و برهاندم از بند ملامت

Khaake rahe aan yaare safar karde biyaarid

Ta chashme jahaan bin konamash jaaye eghaamat

خاک ره آن یار سفرکرده بیارید

تا چشم جهان بین کنمش جای اقامت

Faryaad ke az shesh jahatam raah bebastand

Aan khaalo khato zolfo rokho aarezo ghaamat

فریاد که از شش جهتم راه ببستند

آن خال و خط و زلف و رخ و عارض و قامت

Emrooz ke dar daste toam marhamati kon

Fardaa ke shodam khaak che sood ashke nedaamat

امروز که در دست توام مرحمتی کن

فردا که شدم خاک چه سود اشک ندامت

Ey aanke be taghriro bayaan dam zani az eshgh

Maa baa to nadaarim sokhan kheiro salaamat

ای آن که به تقریر و بیان دم زنی از عشق

ما با تو نداریم سخن خیر و سلامت

Darvish makon naale ze shamshire ahebba

Kin taayefe az koshte setaanand gharaamat

درویش مکن ناله ز شمشیر احبّا

کاین طایفه از کشته ستانند غرامت

Dar kherghe zan aatash ke khame abrooye saaghi

Bar mishekanad goosheye mehraabe emaamat

در خرقه زن آتش که خم ابروی ساقی

بر می‌شکند گوشه محراب امامت

Haashaa ke man az jovro jafaaye to benaalam

Bidaade latifaan hame lotf asto keraamat

حاشا که من از جور و جفای تو بنالم

بیداد لطیفان همه لطف است و کرامت

Kootah nakonad bahse sare zolfe to Hafez

Peivaste shod in sel sele taa rooze ghiaamat

کوته نکند بحث سر زلف تو حافظ

پیوسته شد این سلسله تا روز قیامت

For my heart's beloved, complaint and gratitude both blend,
If love's finer points you know, then to my tale attend.

Without thanks, service I gave, and gave for free,
O Lord! Ungrateful may the one I serve never be.

To the dry-lipped Rend ones even water no one will give,
Those versed in the ways of holy men, here no longer live.

My friend you took honour from me, but at your door I will be,
Better anger from the friend, than kindness from the enemy.

Entangled in those curling locks of hair, try not to be,
O heart, there the severed heads of innocent lovers see.

Your eye-glance drained our blood; approved by you!
Dear, seek not to protect illicit blood taking as you do.

Extremely dark is the night and my way I cannot see,
From your corner O star come; give light to guide me.

Whichever way I turned I encountered only more horror,
Beware this desert! An endless trek filled with terror.

To this long lonely road no end can ever be envisaged,
A hundred thousand stages[1] and you have hardly started!

Love may hear your cry and rescue you, if, in the manner of Hafiz,
You recite the holy Qur'an in the fourteen different styles there is.

**(W-C 85)**
[1] "...stages..." See under Maqam in the glossary in this volume.

Zaan yaare del navaazam shokrist baa shekaayat
Gar nokte daane eshghi khosh beshno in hekaayat

زان یار دلنوازم شکریست با شکایت
گر نکته دان عشقی خوش بشنواین حکایت

Bi mozd boodo mennat har khedmati ke kardam
Yaa rab mabaad kas raa makhdoome bi enaayat

بی مزد بود و منّت هر خدمتی که کردم
یا رب مباد کس را مخدوم بی عنایت

Rendaane teshne lab raa jaami nemidahad kas
Gooee vali shenaasaan raftand azin velaayat

رندان تشنه لب را جامی نمی‌دهد کس
گوئی ولی شناسان رفتند از این ولایت

Harchand bordi aabam rooy az darat nataabam
Jovr az habib khoshtar kaz moddaee ra-aayat

هر چند بردی آبم روی از درت نتابم
جور از حبیب خوشتر کز مدّعی رعایت

Dar zolfe chon kamandash ey del mapich kaanjaa
Sarhaa boride bini bi jormo bi jenaayat

در زلف چون کمندش ای دل مپیچ کانجا
سرها بریده بینی بی جرم و بی جنایت

Chashmat be ghamze maa raa khoon khordo mipasandi
Jaanaa ravaa nabaashad khoonriz ra hemaayat

چشمت به غمزه ما را خون خورد و میسندی
جانا روا نباشد خونریز را حمایت

Dar in shabe siyaaham gom gasht raahe maghsood
Az gooshei boroon aay ey kovkabe hedaayat

در این شب سیاهم گم گشت راه مقصود
از گوشه‌ای برون آی ای کوکب هدایت

Az har taraf ke raftam joz vahshatam nayafzood
Zenhaar azin biyaabab vin raahe bi nahaayat

از هر طرف که رفتم جز وحشتم نیفزود
زنهار از این بیابان وین راه بی‌نهایت

In raah raa nahaayat soorat kojaa tavaan bast
Kesh sad hezaar manzel bishast dar bedaayat

این راه را نهایت صورت کجا توان بست
کش صد هزار منزل بیش است در بدایت

Eshghat rasad be faryaad var khod besaane Hafez
Ghoraan ze bar bekhaani dar chaardah ravaayat

عشقت رسد به فریاد ور خود بسان حافظ
قرآن ز بر بخوانی در چارده روایت

Always drunk on the scent the breeze brings from your curl, I am;
Each moment ruined by the deceit of the magic in your eye, I am.

O Lord, will so much patience lead us, one of these nights,
To your eyebrow, the prayer arch where our eye a candle lights?

The black tablet[1] of the eye's vision is very dear and the reason is,
For the soul it's the book in which the picture of your black mole is.

If, once and forever, the world you would beautify entirely,
Tell the breeze to lift the veil from your face, for a second only.

If you want the custom of 'dying out' from the world to disappear,
Toss your head; thousands of lives will drop out of each hair.

Two wretched ones are hopelessly drunk - the dawn breeze and I,
The breeze from your hair's scent; and I, from the spell in your eye.

Great! The himmat[2] of Hafiz is high, with both the worlds at his feet,
For nothing comes into his eye, other than the dust of your street.

**(W-C 86)**
[1] *"..black tablet..." This refers to the pupil of the eye.*
[2] *"..Himmat..." See the glossary in this volume. Here the meaning may be that the eye which beholds the beloved's dust (the unseen) sees beyond either this world or the next when it is forcefully directed – hence the power it perceived to have. Clearly the theme is the eye (perception).*

Modaamam mast midaarad nasime ja-de gisooyat

مدامم مست می‌دارد نسیم جعد گیسویت

Kharaabam mikonad har dam faribe chashme jadooyat

خرابم می‌کند هر دم فریب چشم جادویت

Pas az chandin shakibaaee shabi yaa rab tavaan didan

پس از چندین شکیبائی شبی یا رب توان دیدن

Ke sham-e dide afroozim dar mehraabe abrooyat

که شمع دیده افروزیم در محراب ابرویت

Savaade lovhe binesh ra aziz az bahre aan daaram

سواد لوح بینش را عزیز از بهر آن دارم

Ke jaan raa noskhei bashad ze naghshe khaale hendooyat

که جان را نسخه‌ای باشد ز نقش خال هندویت

To gar khaahi ke jaavidaan jahaan yek sar biyaaraaee

تو گر خواهی که جاویدان جهان یکسر بیارائی

Sabaa raa goo ke bardaarad zamaani borgha az rooyat

صبا را گو که بردارد زمانی برقع از رویت

Vagar rasme fanaa khaahi ke az aalam bar andaazi

و گر رسم فنا خواهی که از عالم براندازی

Bar afshaan taa foroo rizad hezaaraan jaan ze har mooyat

برافشان تا فروریزد هزاران جان ز هر مویت

Mano baade saaba meskin do sargardaane bi haasel

من و باد صبا مسکین دو سرگردان بی‌حاصل

Man az afsoone chashmat masto ou az booye gisooyat

من از افسون چشمت مست و او از بوی گیسویت

Zehi hemmat ke Hafez raast kaz donyaavo az oghbaa

زهی همّت که حافظ راست کز دنیی و از عقبی

Nayaamad hich dar chashmash bejoz khaake sare kooyat

نیامد هیچ در چشمش بجز خاک سر کویت

Thanks God! In such a way is the tavern door open,
That turned toward it can be my face of supplication.

The jugs enjoy the shouts of ecstatic intoxication!
They are full of real wine[1], not mere hallucination.

From the beloved; turbulence, pride and intoxication,
From us; helplessness, weakness and supplication.

This mystery we concealed from common detection,
But with my knowing friend have free communication.

The helix-like spiral of the beloved's hair needs long explanation,
For there is no way to simplify it or to make an abbreviation.

Majnun's heavy heart, finding in Layla's[2] lock's such fascination,
Or Mahmud's cheek[3], and Ayaz's foot; these give an indication.

My eyes are stitched up like a falcon's hood to prevent distraction,
Because only in seeing your cheek do I find the real satisfaction.

Whoever towards the Kaaba of your street their face is turning,
Through the qibla[4] of your eyebrow's arch, is actually praying.

Hafiz's burnt heart! O people of the assembly, its explanation,
Seek from the candle that melts and burns to give illumination.

---

**(W-C 87) The radif is "Is".**
[1] "...real wine..." Being 'full of real wine' can be read literally as referring to physical fermented wine or of course the reverse since 'real' can mean spiritually real, not illusory worldly physical wine which merely causes hallucinations..
[2] "...Layla (Laila)..." For Laila and Majnun see glossary in this volume.
[3] "...Mahmud..." Mahmud (d.1030AD) was a warrior king of great repute who had a slave called Ayaz – their loving relationship often used as symbols for true love.
[4] "...Qibla..." This refers to the direction of the Kaaba in Mecca from any given point.

Al mennato lellah ke dare meikade baazast

Zaan roo ke mara bar dare ou rooye niyaazast

المنّة لله که در میکده باز است

زان رو که مرا بر در او روی نیاز است

Khomhaa hame dar joosho khorushand ze masti

Vaan mey ke dar aanjaast haghighat na majaaz ast

خم‌ها همه در جوش و خروشند ز مستی

وان می که در آن جاست حقیقت نه مجاز است

Az vey hame mastiyyo ghorur asto takabbor

Vaz maa hame bichaaregiyo ajzo niyazast

از وی همه مستیّ و غرور است و تکبّر

وز ما همه بیچارگی و عجز و نیاز است

Raazi ke bare gheir nagoftimo nagooeem

Baa doost begueem ke ou mahrame raazast

رازی که بر غیر نگفتیم و نگوئیم

با دوست بگوئیم که او محرم راز است

Sharhe shekane zolfe kham andar khame jaanaan

Kootah natavaan kard ke in ghesse deraazast

شرح شکن زلف خم اندر خم جانان

کوته نتوان کرد که این قصّه دراز است

Baare dele Majnoono khame torreye leili

Rokhsaareye mahmoodo kafe paaye ayaazast

بار دل مجنون و خم طرّه لیلی

رخساره محمود و کف پای ایاز است

Bar dookhteam dide cho baaz az hame aalam

Ta dideye man bar rokhe zibaaye to baazast

بردوخته‌ام دیده چو باز از همه عالم

تا دیده من بر رخ زیبای تو باز است

Dar kabeye kooye to har aankas ke daraayad

Az ghebleye abrooye to dar eine namaazast

در کعبه کوی تو هر آن کس که درآید

از قبله ابروی تو در عین نماز است

Ey majlesiyaan sooze dele Hafeze meskin

Az sha-m beporsid ke dar soozo godaazast

ای مجلسیان سوز دل حافظ مسکین

از شمع بپرسید که در سوز و گداز است

The products of the workshop, of being and place, are nothing,
Bring wine, for causes in the world do not produce any thing[1].

The intent of life, and the heart, is the Beloved's goodly company,
This is how it is; and if not - in heart and life no value can there be.

Depend not for favours, even on the shade of Sidhra[2] or Tuba tree,
In them too is no value, if you see well, O swaying cypress tree.

Fortune is that which draws near without the heart's blood spilling,
Otherwise the garden of heaven gained by toil amounts to nothing.

Only five short days' favour you have here, more or less,
So rest peacefully awhile; time will make it valueless.

O Saki, on the lips of the ocean of death, our waiting is,
Regard it well! From lip to mouth no distance there is.

About being eaten up by sorrows, weeping and wailing,
There is no value at all in any explanations I am giving.

O pious zealot, there is no value in the sport of pride,
Mosque and Magian temple no distance does divide.

The name of Hafiz is accepted, written in the role of honour too,
But for the profligates writing of profit and loss has no value.

---

**(W-C 88) The radif is "All else is nothing".**
  [1] "...for causes in the world do not produce anything..." Mevlana Rumi says in the Masnevi that the whole of
  the Qur'an is dedicated to removing the idea that 'causes' cause anything. There is only one Causer.
  [2] "...Sidhra/Tuba tree..." See the glossary in this volume.

Haasele kaargahe kovno makaan in hame nist
Baade pish aar ke asbaabe jahaan in hame nist

حاصل کارگه کون و مکان این همه نیست
باده پیش آر که اسباب جهان این همه نیست

Az delo jaan sharafe sohbate jaanaan gharaz ast
Hame aanast vagar ni delo jaan in hame nist

از دل و جان شرف صحبت جانان غرض است
همه آن است و گرنی دل و جان این همه نیست

Mennate sedrevo toobaa ze peye saaye makesh
Ke cho khosh bengari ey sarve ravaan in hame nist

منّت سدره و طوبی ز پی سایه مکش
که چو خوش بنگری ای سرو روان این همه نیست

Dovlat aan ast ke bi khoone deloftad be kenaar
Varna baa sa-yo amal baaghe jenaan in hame nist

دولت آن است که بی خون دل افتد به کنار
ور نه با سعی عمل باغ جنان این همه نیست

Panj roozi ke dar in marhale mohlat daari
Khosh biaasaay zamaani ke zamaan in hame nist

پنج روزی که در این مرحله مهلت داری
خوش بیاسای زمانی که زمان این همه نیست

Bar labe bahre fanaa montazerim ey saaghi
Forsati daan ke ze lab taa be dahaan in hame nist

بر لب بحر فنا منتظریم ای ساقی
فرصتی دان که ز لب تا به دهان این همه نیست

Dard-mandiyye mane sookhteye zaaro nezaar
Zaaheran haajate taghriro bayaan in hame nist

دردمندیّ من سوخته زار و نزار
ظاهرا حاجت تقریر و بیان این همه نیست

Zaahed imen masho az baaziye gheirat zenhaar
Ke rahe sovme-e taa deire moghaan in hame nist

زاهد ایمن مشو از بازی غیرت زنهار
که ره صومعه تا دیر مغان این همه نیست

Naame Hafez raghame nik paziroft vali
Pishe rendaan raghame soodo ziaan in hame nist

نام حافظ رقم نیک پذیرفت ولی
پیش رندان رقم سود و زیان این همه نیست

What kindness, when a drop from your pen showed, unexpectedly,
What was due to us for our service, according to your generosity.

With the pen nib you inscribed, many times, salaams to me,
May the abode of time, bereft of your writings not ever be.

I do not call your recalling of heart-sad me, a mistake,
 For in wise accounting your pen no error can make.

Don't hold me in contempt, you should be grateful,
That the eternal Fortune made you so honourable.

Come, and on the tip of the curl of your hair, I promise it,
My head at your feet stays, though from the body they tear it.

Our state you may get to know, only when, on the morrow[1],
The tulip blooms from debris of the victims of love's sorrow.

Of your hair the Saba[2] wind to every rose is carrying the story.
How did the watcher allow a tell-tale into your place of glory?

What sorrow can you feel for ones whose hearts are grieving,
When, from Jamshid's cup, Khizr's[3] clear water fortune is giving?

Living at your door is my heart, please guard it well,
After all God has kept you free from grieving as well.

O breeze, be happy always, your breath from Jesus is,
And life it breathed into a poor broken-hearted Hafiz.

**(W-C 89) The radif is "You".**
[1] "..Morrow..." This implies; on the Day of Judgement. In this case Hafiz seems to be saying the inner state of the lover of God will only become apparent then.
[2] "..Saba..." This refers to the breeze that carries the divine secrets that can be heard by the ear of the heart.
[3] "..Khizr's .water..." See the glossary in this volume.

Che lotf bood ke naagaah rash-heye ghalamat
Hoghooghe khedmate maa arze kard bar karamat

چه لطف بود که ناگاه رشحه قلمت
حقوق خدمت ما عرضه کرد بر کرمت

Be noke khaame ragham kardei salaame maraa
Ke kaarkhaaneye dovraan mabaad bi raghamat

به نوک خامه رقم کرده‌ای سلام مرا
که کارخانه دوران مباد بی رقمت

Nagooyam az mane bidel be sahv kardi yaad
Ke dar hesaabe kherad nist sahv bar ghalamat

نگویم از من بیدل به سهو کردی یاد
که در حساب خرد نیست سهو بر قلمت

Maraa zalil magardaan be shokre in tovfigh
Ke daasht dovlate sarmad aziz o mohtaramat

مرا ذلیل مگردان به شکر این توفیق
که داشت دولت سرمد عزیز و محترمت

Biyaa ke baa sare zolfat gharaar khaaham kard
Ke gar saram beravad bar nadaaram az ghadamat

بیا که با سر زلفت قرار خواهم کرد
که گر سرم برود برندارم از قدمت

Ze haale maa delat aagah shavad vali vaghti
Ke laale bardamad az khaake koshtegaane ghamat

ز حال ما دلت آگه شود ولی وقتی
که لاله بردمد از خاک کشتگان غمت

Sabaa ze zolfe to baa har goli hadisi raand
Raghib key rahe ghammaaz daad dar haramat

صبا ز زلف تو با هر گلی حدیثی راند
رقیب کی ره غمّاز داد در حرمت

To raa ze haale dele khastegaan che gham ke modaam
Hami dahand sharaabe khezer ze jaame jamat

ترا ز حال دل خستگان چه غم که مدام
همی دهند زلال خضر ز جام جمت

Delam moghime dare tost hormatash midaar
Be shokre aanke khodaa daashtast mohtaramat

دلم مقیم در توست حرمتش می دار
به شکر آنکه خدا داشتست محترمت

Hamishe vaghte to ey isiye sabaa khosh baad
Ke jaane Hafeze del khaste zende shod be damat

همیشه وقت تو ای عیسی صبا خوش باد
که جان حافظ دلخسته زنده شد به دمت

O chaste beloved![1] Who now unfastens your veil, for you?
O paradise bird! Who gives grain and water to you?

I cannot sleep for it eats at my liver, this wondering -
On whose chest you rest, and where you are sleeping!

You don't come asking after this Dervish? I fear one thing:
That you are indifferent[2], neither forgiving nor punishing.

The way of lovers, was changed by that eye that is inebriated,
It is obvious from all this that from you wine is inebriated.

That arrow, your glance, glanced off my heart, missing me,
Reveal to me the true design you again have in mind for me.

Loudly I raised complaint! You never heard my intense wailing,
O my idol, it must be a high place indeed, where you're residing.

Be sensible, in the vast desert, very far is the water pool,
So do not be fooled by the mirage of the tricky ghoul.

O heart, in what way will you tread the path of later years,
In such a rapid rush of follies you spent your young years.

O you heart-igniting palace in which our love lives,
O Lord, let not time ruin what, to you, love gives.

Hafiz is not the slave who flees from his master's approach.
Be kind; come back; or else I am ruined by your reproach.

**(W-C 90) The radif is "You".**
   [1] According to W-C this ghazal refers to a time when Hafiz's wife left to return to her father's house. As ever
   Hafiz finds a universal timeless meaning in a local temporal event.
   [2] "...you are indifferent..." Hatred is often thought of as the opposite of affection, but actually both are strong
   emotions – the opposite of affection is indifference.

Ey shaahede ghodsi ke keshad bande neghaabat     ای شاهد قدسی که کشد بند نقابت

Vey morghe beheshti ke dahad daanevo aabat     وی مرغ بهشتی که دهد دانه و آبت

Khaabam beshod az dide dar in fekre jegar sooz     خوابم بشد از دیده درین فکر جگرسوز

Kaaghooshe ke shod manzelo ma-vaagahe khaabat     کاغوش که شد منزل و ماواگه خوابت

Darvish nemiporsiyo tarsam ke nabaashad     درویش نمی‌پرسی و ترسم که نباشد

Andisheye aamorzesho parvaaye savaabat     اندیشه آمرزش و پروای ثوابت

Raahe dele osh shaagh zad aan chashme khomaarin     راه دل عشّاق زد آن چشم خمارین

Peidaast azin shive ke mast ast sharaabat     پیداست ازین شیوه که مست است شرابت

Tiri ke zadi bar delam az ghamze khataa raft     تیری که زدی بر دلم از غمزه خطا رفت

Taa baaz che andishe konad raaye savaabat     تا باز چه اندیشه کند رای صوابت

Har naalevo faryaad ke kardam nashanidi     هر ناله و فریاد که کردم نشنیدی

Peidaast negaaraa ke boland ast jenaabat     پیداست نگارا که بلند است جنابت

Door ast sare aab darin baadiye hosh daar     دور است سر آب درین بادیه هش دار

Taa ghoole biyaabaan nafaribad be saraabat     تا غول بیابان نفریبد به سرابت

Taa dar rahe piri be che aaeen ravi ey del     تا در ره پیری به چه آئین روی ای دل

Baari be ghalat sarf shod ayyaame shabaabat     باری به غلط صرف شد ایّام شبابت

Ey ghasre delafrooz ke manzel gahe onsi     ای قصر دل افروز که منزلگه انسی

Yaa rab makonaad aafate ayyaam kharaabat     یا رب مکناد آفت ایّام خرابت

Hafez na gholaamist ke az khaaje gorizad     حافظ نه غلامیست که از خواجه گریزد

Lotfi kono baaz aa ke kharaabam ze etaabat     لطفی کن و بازآکه خرابم ز عتابت

That Turk[1], with the heavenly face, who passed us by last night,
What fault in us, that mistakenly to China that one took flight?

As soon as that possessor of the world-seeing eye had departed,
None can imagine what I passed through, or how many tears shed.

Not even the candle felt the heat my heart last night was feeling,
Nor candle smoke like the sigh that from my liver to head was rising.

Parted from your face, from the eye's corner a fountain was gushing,
In the flood of tears from my eye, a deluge of disasters was passing.

When separation's sorrow came and stayed, we lost our footing,
In pain we remained, when from our hand, the cure was passing.

The heart declared that by prayer one could again gain union,
But a lifetime had passed in giving prayer my constant attention.

Why would I put on pilgrim dress where I find not even the Qibla?[2]
If Safa[3] has not purity why to strive so urgently to reach to Marwah?

Yesterday, when the kind doctor, from feelings of pity, saw me,
He said I had passed beyond the reach of any medical directory.

O friend turn your foot towards Hafiz's abode and visit him there,
Before, from this house of passing away, he passes on elsewhere.

---

**(W-C 91) The radif is "Passed".**
   [1] "-Turk..." This can refer to the Beloved, though often an 'imperious' manifestation of the Beloved. ·
   [2] "...Qibla..." This refers to the direction of the Kaaba in Mecca from any given point.
   [3] Part of the pilgrimage rites in Islam is the walking urgently between two small hills – Safa (purity) and
   Marwah, seven times – these are located close to the Kaaba. There is a play on words here – since this
   process is called Sa-y – which also means striving. The pilgrim has to walk quickly, almost running, for part
   of the distance.

Aan torke pari chehre ke doosh az bare maa raft
Ayaa che khataa did ke az raahe khataa raft

آن ترک پری چهره که دوش از بر ما رفت
آیا چه خطا دید که از راه خطا رفت

Taa raft ma raa az nazar aan noore jahaan bin
Kas vaaghefe maa nist ke az dide chehaa raft

تا رفت مرا از نظر آن نور جهان بین
کس واقف ما نیست که از دیده چها رفت

Bar sha-m naraft az gozare aatashe del doosh
Aan dood ke az sooze jegar bar sare maa raft

بر شمع نرفت ازگذر آتش دل دوش
آن دود که از سوز جگر بر سر ما رفت

Door az rokhe ou dambedam az cheshmeye chashmam
Seilaabe sereshk aamado toofaane balaa raft

دور از رخ او و دم بدم از چشمه چشمم
سیلاب سرشک آمد و طوفان بلا رفت

Az paay fetaadim cho aamad ghame hejraan
Dar dard bemaandim cho az dast davaa raft

از پای فتادم چو آمد غم هجران
در درد بماندیم چو از دست دوا رفت

Del goft vesaalash be doaa baaz tavaan yaaft
Omrist ke omram hame dar kaare doaa raft

دل گفت وصالش به دعا باز توان یافت
عمری ست که عمرم همه در کار دعا رفت

Ehraam che bandim cho aan gheble na injaast
Dar sa-y che kooshim cho az marve safaa raft

احرام چه بندیم چو آن قبله نه اینجاست
در سعی چه کوشیم چو از مروه صفا رفت

Di goft tabib az sare hasrat cho maraa did
Heihaat ke ranje to ze ghaanoone shafaa raft

دی گفت طبیب از سر حسرت چو مرا دید
هیهات که رنج تو ز قانون شفا رفت

Ey doost be porsidane Hafez ghadami neh
Zaan pish ke gooyand ke az daare fanaa raft

ای دوست به پرسیدن حافظ قدمی نه
زان پیش که گویند که از دار فنا رفت

I find no other shelter in the world, but this doorstep of yours,
No bastion of protection for my head, but this door of yours.

When the enemy draws the sword, the shield we let slip,
Except for grief-stricken wailing, we have no sword at our hip,

From the street of wine-houses why would I turn my face away?
There is nothing better in this world for me than this way.

If time's vagaries set ablaze the harvest of my whole life,
Let it burn; for less than a blade of grass is all this strife.

I'm the slave of the drunken narcissus eye of that cypress-tall one,
Who is drunk on the wine of pride, so gives glances at no one.

Do whatever you wish, but not so as to injure anyone,
For in our Shariat[1] law there is no other real sin but this one.

O king of the country of beauty draw in your rein do,
For there is no way that has not a justice seeker too.

Everywhere I look the pitfalls of the Way I can see,
And only in your curling hair locks is shelter for me.

The treasure of Hafiz's heart to every black curl and mole, give not,
 For the power to receive this, not every kind of blackness has got.

---

**(W-C 92) The radif is "Is none".**
 [1] "...Shariat..." This is the code of behaviour derived from the holy Qur'an and the Hadiths of the holy Prophet
 and is incumbent on Muslims. Here Hafiz sums it up perfectly as a system for avoiding doing harm.

Joz aastaane toam dar jahaan panaahi nist        جز آستان توام در جهان پناهی نیست

Sare maraa bejoz in dar havaale gaahi nist        سر مرا بجز این در حواله گاهی نیست

Adoo cho tigh keshad man separ biyandaazam        عدو چو تیغ کشد من سپر بیندازم

Ke teere maa bejoz az naaleiyyo aahi nist        که تیر ما بجز از ناله‌ای و آهی نیست

Cheraa ze kooye kharaabaat rooy bar taabam        چرا ز کوی خرابات روی برتابم

Kazin beham be jahaan hich rasmo raahi nist        کز این به ام به جهان هیچ رسم وراهی نیست

Zamaane gar bezanad aatasham be kharmane omr        زمانه گر بزند آتشم به خرمن عمر

Begoo besooz ke bar man be barge kaahi nist        بگو بسوز که بر من به برگ کاهی نیست

Gholaame nargese jammaashe aan sahi ghaddam        غلام نرگس جمّاش آن سهی قدّم

Ke az sharaabe ghoroorash be kas negaahi nist        که از شراب غرورش به کس نگاهی نیست

Mabaash dar peye aazaaro harche khaahi kon        مباش در پی آزار و هر چه خواهی کن

Ke dar shariate maa gheir az in gonaahi nist        که در شریعت ما غیر از این گناهی نیست

Enaan keshide ro ey paadeshaahe keshvare hosn        عنان کشیده رو ای پادشاه کشور حسن

Ke nist bar sare raahi ke daad khaahi nist        که نیست بر سر راهی که دادخواهی نیست

Chonin ke az hame soo daame raah mibinam        چنین که از همه سو دام راه می‌بینم

Beh az hemaayate zolfat maraa panaahi nist        به از حمایت زلفت مرا پناهی نیست

Khazineye dele Hafez be zolfo khaal made        خزینه دل حافظ به زلف و خال مده

Ke kaarhaaye chenin hadde har siyaahi nist        که کارهای چنین حدّ هر سیاهی نیست

O Saki, bring wine, for the month of fasting has now passed by,
Give wine in the cup, to the season of good repute, say goodbye.

The 'fortuitous time' we missed, let us compensate for it;[1]
For a life passed without wine cup and long necked goglet.

How long, like aloes wood[2], in the fire of repentance to burn,
Give wine, for life has been passed in rawness I discern.

Make me drunk so that, from self being parted, I am not knowing,
Who, on the plain of imagination, has been, or is, coming or going.

In the desperate hope of a drink from your precious wine cup,
In the tavern every morning and evening I offered prayer up.

A great surge of life has reached to this dead heart,
The scent of wine the breeze brought gave life to my heart.

The pious one from pride did not find the way to travel safely,
But the Rend, by way of need reached the home of security.

The currency of my heart's earning; I spent all of it on wine,
It was counterfeit coinage, so it was spent on the illegal wine.

Don't try to advise our Hafiz of the merits of the path of austerity;
A love-lost one, whose palate has tasted much sweeter wine, happily!

**(W-C 93) The radif is "Has passed".**
[1]'Fortuitous time' refers to the prescribed time for prayers – if this is missed compensatory prayers may be
offered to make this up. Used here to indicate life spent without spiritual wine.
[2]Aloes wood is Incense, burned in a dish to ward of misfortunes.

Saaghi biaar baade ke maahe siyaam raft

Dar deh ghadah ke movseme naamooso naam raft

ساقی بیار باده که ماه صیام رفت

درده قدح که موسم ناموس و نام رفت

Vaghte aziz raft biyaa taa ghazaa konim

Omri ke bi hozoore soraahiyyo jaam raft

وقت عزیز رفت بیا تا قضا کنیم

عمری که بی حضور صراحیّ و جام رفت

Dar taabe tovbe chand tavaan sookht hamcho ood

Mey deh ke omr dar sare sovdaaye khaam raft

در تاب توبه چند توان سوخت همچو عود

می ده که عمر در سر سودای خام رفت

Mastam kon anchonaan ke nadaanam ze bikhodi

Dar arseye khiyaal ke aamad kodaam raft

مستم کن آن چنان که ندانم ز بیخودی

در عرصه خیال که آمد کدام رفت

Bar booye aanke jor-eye jaamat be maa resad

Dar mastabe doaaye to har sobh o shaam raft

بر بوی آن که جرعه جامت به ما رسد

در مصطبه دعای تو هر صبح و شام رفت

Del raa ke morde bood hayaati be jaan rasid

Taa booee az nasime meyash dar mashaam raft

دل را که مرده بود حیاتی به جان رسید

تا بوئی از نسیم میاش در مشام رفت

Zaahed ghoroor daasht salaamat nabord raah

Rend az rahe niyaaz be darossalam raft

زاهد غرور داشت سلامت نبرد راه

رند از ره نیاز به دارالسّلام رفت

Naghde deli ke bood maraa sarfe baade shod

Ghalbe siyaah bood az aan dar haraam raft

نقد دلی که بود مرا صرف باده شد

قلب سیاه بود از آن در حرام رفت

Digar magoo nasihate Hafez ke rah nayaaft

Gom gashtei ke baadeye naabash be kaam raft

دیگر مگو نصیحت حافظ که ره نیافت

گمگشته ای که باده نابش به کام رفت

In the Way, vision of your face our travelling companion is,
Perfume from your hair always, intimations to our soul gives.

To critics whose claim is that love is forbidden really,
Our perfect argument is your face's beauty[1].

See what words the apple (dimple) of your chin has to say,
"Many a Yusuf of Egypt[2] fell into our well this way."

If your long hair does not reach all the way to our hand,
The cause is our misfortune and the short reach of our hand.

To the guard of your private door may it please you to say;
"One of those corner sitters our dust's colour does display.

"If that beggar Hafiz knocks at that door where you stand sentry,
Open! Year upon year, to our moon-like face he seeks entry."

Although it seems the Beloved is veiled from our sight,
That one is always and ever in our tranquil heart's sight.

*(W-C 97)*
  [1] *"...is your face's beauty..." The Hadith says, 'God is beautiful and He loves beauty'.*
  [2] *"...Many a Yusuf of Egypt..." Prophet Yusuf (Joseph) was renowned for his physical beauty – he was cast into a well by jealous brothers.*

Khiyaale rooye to dar har tarigh hamrahe maast
Nasime mooye to peivande jaane aagahe maast

خیال روی تو در هر طریق همره ماست
نسیم موی تو پیوند جان آگه ماست

Be raghme moddaiyaani ke man-e eshgh konand
Jamaale chehreye to hojjate movajjahe maast

به رغم مدّعیانی که منع عشق کنند
جمال چهره تو حجّت موجّه ماست

Bebin ke sibe zanakhdaane to che migooyad
Hezaar yoosofe mesri fetaade dar chahe mast

ببین که سیب زنخدان تو چه می‌گوید
هزار یوسف مصری فتاده در چه ماست

Agar be zolfe deraaze to daste maa naresad
Gonaahe bakhte parishaano daste kootahe maast

اگر به زلف دراز تو دست ما نرسد
گناه بخت پریشان و دست کوته ماست

Be haajebe dare khalvat saraaye khaas begoo
Felaan ze gooshe neshinaane khaake dargahe maast

به حاجب در خلوت سرای خاص بگو
فلان ز گوشه نشینان خاک درگه ماست

Agar be saali Hafez dari zanad begoshaay
Ke saalhaast ke moshtaaghe rooye chon mahe maast

اگر به سالی حافظ دری زند بگشای
که سال‌هاست که مشتاق روی چون مه ماست

Be soorat az nazare maa agar che mahjoob ast
Hamishe dar nazare khaatere morrafahe maast

به صورت از نظر ما اگر چه محجوب است
همیشه در نظر خاطر مرفّه ماست

Beloved if a fault from your musk-scented hair passed, so be it,
And if from your Hindu dark mole a harsh act passed, so be it.

If a wool-wearer's harvest was burnt by love's lightning, so be it;
If violence to a poor beggar the prosperous king showed, so be it.

If the look of the beloved bore away a heart, so be it,
If between soul and beloved something happened, so be it.

The critics and carpers may complain much - so be it;
If in our circle anything doubtful passed, well, so be it.

In Tariqat's[1] way the heart suffers no grief, bring wine, so be it;
Every impurity of heart you see, into purity passes, so be it.

O heart for love-playing firm of foot you must be, so be it;
If a worry, or if harshness came to pass, it came; so be it.

Admonish those who censure Hafiz for leaving; say, "So be it,"
Who can bind the foot of a free man? If he moved on, so be it!"

*(W-C 98) The radif here is; "Passed, it passed"*
    [1] *"..Tariqat..." See the glossary in this volume.*

Gar ze daste zolfe moshkinat khataaee raft raft

گرزدست زلف مشکینت خطائی رفت رفت

Var ze hendooye shomaa bar maa jafaaee raft raft

ور ز هندوی شما بر ما جفائی رفت رفت

Barghe eshgh ar kharmane pashmine pooshi sookht sookht

برق عشق ار خرمن پشمینه پوشی سوخت سوخت

Jovre shaahi kaamraan gar bar gedaaeee raft raft

جور شاهی کامران گر بر گدائی رفت رفت

Gar deli az ghamze ee deldaar baari bord bord

گر دلی از غمزه دلدار باری برد برد

Var miaane jaano jaanaan maajaraaee raft raft

ور میان جان و جانان ماجرائی رفت رفت

Az sokhan chinaan malaalathaa padid aamad vali

از سخن چینان ملالتها پدید آمد ولی

Chon miaane hamneshinaan naasezaaee raft raft

چون میان همنشینان ناسزائی رفت رفت

Dar tarighat ranjeshe khaater nabaashad mey biyaar

در طریقت رنجش خاطر نباشد می بیار

Har kodoorat raa ke bini chon safaaee raft raft

هر کدورت را که بینی چون صفائی رفت رفت

Eshgh baazi raa tahammol baayad ey del paay daar

عشقبازی را تحمّل باید ای دل پای دار

Gar malaali bood boodo gar khataaee raft raft

گر ملالی بود بود و گر خطائی رفت رفت

Eibe Hafez goo makon vaaez ke raft az khaaneghaah

عیب حافظ گو مکن واعظ که رفت از خانقاه

Paaye aazaadaan nabandand ar be jaaee raft raft

پای آزادان نبندند ار به جایی رفت رفت

We sipped not from that ruby lip, before the beloved departed,
Before that one's moon-face we fully saw, from it we were parted.

One might say that one's interest in our company just went away,
Packing belongings before we even arrived, that one went away.

The Fatiha and holy Prophet's Yemen prayer we were so much reciting,
We blew the Qur'an's 'closing part'[1] toward the beloved departing.

With a glance that said, "It is not your reproaches that make me go away",
The beloved went. So we bought that look, but that one did not stay.

Proudly, that one sauntered into the meadow of beauty and of grace,
Into that garden of union we dare not go, and the beloved left our place.

Just like Hafiz, all night long, in distress, we cried bitterly,
We could not even say farewell, the beloved had left so quickly.

**(W-C 100) The radif is "and He departed".**
　This is a Ghazal about the death of an infant son.
　[1]Closing verses of the holy Qur'an: the Sura of unity. 'Blowing' is the custom of passing the benefit of the
　verse on to another - by blowing on that person after reciting.

Sharbati az labe la-lash nacheshidimo beraft

Rooye mah peikare ou sir nadidimo beraft

شربتی از لب لعلش نچشیدیم و برفت

روی مه پیکر او سیر ندیدیم و برفت

Gooee az sohbate maa nik be tang aamade bood

Baar bar basto be gardash naresidim o beraft

گویی از صحبت ما نیک به تنگ آمده بود

بار بربست و به گردش نرسیدیم و برفت

Bas ke maa faatehevo herze yamaani khaandim

Vaz peyash sooreye ekhlaas damidimo beraft

بس که ما فاتحه و حرز یمانی خواندیم

وز پی اش سوره اخلاص دمیدیم و برفت

Eshve midaad kea z kooye malaamat naravim

Didi akher ke chenin eshve kharidimo beraft

عشوه می داد که از کوی ملامت نرویم

دیدی آخر که چنین عشوه خریدیم و برفت

Shod chamaan dar chamane hosno letaafat liken

Dar golestaane vesaalash nachamidimo beraft

شد چمان در چمن حسن و لطافت لیکن

در گلستان وصالش نچمیدیم و برفت

Hamcho Hafez hame shab naalevo zaari kardim

Key darighaa be vedaa-ash naresidimo beraft

همچو حافظ همه شب ناله و زاری کردیم

کای دریغا به وداعش نرسیدیم و برفت

Those spiralling locks of hair; none but fell into their snare;
Did anyone find a path and yet not find that calamity there?

Perhaps your face is a divine mirror, brightly shining!
O God, yes; and in it there is not hypocrisy, or lying.

The piety-punching preacher forbids your excellent face,
He has neither respect for God nor any shame before your face.

For God's sake do not make your locks of hair even more fair;
No night but ends in tangles, when the dawn breeze comes there.

O heart igniting candle, return, for when your face is absent,
At the banquet of the kindred souls no light or purity is present.

Beloved, handsome treatment of visitors brings reputation,
In your city, for such fine manners, is there no inclination?

Yesterday before that one left I asked to keep to promises given,
The reply; 'O, Sir, you don't get it, these days fidelity is forsaken'.

Since your eye captures the corner sitter's heart,
To follow after you cannot be a sin on our part.

If the Pir of the Magians[1] were to be my spiritual guide - so what!
There is no head in which the mystery of God's presence is not.

If one challenges the sun, saying 'I am the fountain of light!'
The great know that to say so, an obscure star has no right.

In the cell of the pious priest or in the retreat of Hafiz,
Except your eyebrow's curve no other prayer arch there is.

*(W-C 102) The radif here is; "is none".*

Kas nist ke oftaadeye aan zolfe do taa nist

کس نیست که افتاده آن زلف دوتا نیست

Dar rah gozare kist ke in daame balaa nist

در رهگذر کیست که این دام بلا نیست

Rooye to magar aayeneye lotfe elaahist

روی تو مگر آینه لطف الهیست

Haghaa ke chonin asto dar in rooyo riyaa nist

حقّا که چنین است و درین روی وریا نیست

Zaahed dahadam pand ze rooye to zehi rooy

زاهد دهدم پند ز روی تو زهی روی

Hichash ze khodaa sharmo ze rooye to hayaa nist

هیچش ز خدا شرم و ز روی تو حیا نیست

Az bahre khodaa zolf mapiraay ke maa raa

از بهر خدا زلف مپیرای که ما را

Shab nist ke sad arbade baa baade sabaa nist

شب نیست که صد عربده با باد صبا نیست

Baaz aay ke bi rooye to ey sha-me del afrooz

بازآی که بی روی تو ای شمع دل افروز

Dar bazme harifaan asare nooro safaa nist

در بزم حریفان اثر نور و صفا نیست

Timaare gharibaan sababe zekre jamil ast

تیمار غریبان سبب ذکر جمیل است

Jaanaa magar in ghaaede dar shahre shomaa nist

جانا مگر این قاعده در شهر شما نیست

Di mishodo goftam sanamaa ahd be jaay aar

دی می‌شد و گفتم صنما عهد به جای آر

Goftaa ghalati khaaje dar in ahd vafaa nist

گفتا غلطی خواجه در این عهد وفا نیست

Chon chashme to del mibarad az gooshe neshinaan

چون چشم تو دل می‌برد از گوشه نشینان

Dombaale e to boodan gonah az jaanebe maa nist

دنبال تو بودن گنه از جانب ما نیست

Gar pire moghaan morshede man shod che tafaavot

گر پیر مغان مرشد من شد چه تفاوت

Dar hich sari nist ke serri ze khodaa nist

در هیچ سری نیست که سرّی ز خدا نیست

Goftan bare khorshid ke man cheshmeye nooram

گفتن بر خورشید که من چشمه نورم

Daanand bozorgaan ke sezaavaare sohaa nist

دانند بزرگان که سزاوار سها نیست

Dar sovmeeye zaahedo dar khalvate soofi

در صومعه زاهد و در خلوت حافظ

Joz goosheye abrooye to mehraabe doaa nist

جز گوشه ابروی تو محراب دعا نیست

From your beaming face arises the light in each and every eye,
Depending on the salve of your doorstep's dust is every eye.

Those with true insight, they see your face, do they not?
There is no head in which the secret of your hair is not.

Any wonder that red my secret-revealing tears are running?
There is no veil-remover that is not ashamed to be unveiling.

To ensure no speck of dust should settle on your robe of purity,
No path is seen that a torrent of tears has not made dust free.

So that evening gossip is not about the scent of your black hair,
There is no dawn I don't talk to the breeze about this affair.

About luck being both good and bad I sorrow, but if it were not
Everyone who is on your way some benefit would not have got.

O sweet fountain, from shame before your lip so sweet,
There is no sugar that is not drowned in water and sweat.

Water from these eyes has blessing from the dust of your door;
There is no door dust that is not indebted to the dust of your door.

I have a kind of existence, in the reputation that I have,
Except for that weakness, no existence do I really have.

Even the lion becomes foxy in the desert of love for you,
O there is no danger not found on the way towards you.

It is not wise counsel to reveal openly the nature of the mystery,
Or in the Rend's gathering all kinds of rumour there would be.

In spite of Hafiz not being happy with you about this,
The truth is every skill that exists in your possession is.

*(W-C 103) The radif here is; "is not, that is not".*

Rovshan az partove rooyat nazari nist ke nist
Mennate khaake darat bar basari nist ke nist

روشن از پرتو رویت نظری نیست که نیست
منّت خاک درت بر بصری نیست که نیست

Naazere rooye to saaheb nazaraanand aari
Serre gisooye to dar hich sari nist ke nist

ناظر روی تو صاحب نظرانند آری
سرّ گیسوی تو در هیچ سری نیست که نیست

Ashke man gar ze ghamat sorkh bar aamad che ajab
Khejel az kardeye khod parde dari nist ke nist

اشک من گر ز غمت سرخ برآمد چه عجب
خجل از کرده خود پرده دری نیست که نیست

Taa be daaman naneshinad ze nasimash gardi
Seil khiz az nazaram rah gozari nist ke nist

تا به دامن ننشیند ز نسیمش گردی
سیل خیز از نظرم رهگذری نیست که نیست

Taa dam az shaame sare zolfe to har jaa nazanad
Baa sabaa gofto shanidam sahari nist ke nist

تا دم از شام سر زلف تو هر جا نزند
با صبا گفت و شنیدم سحری نیست که نیست

Man az in taale-e shooride be ranjam var na
Bahremand az sare kooyat degari nist ke nist

من از این طالع شوریده برنجم ور نه
بهره مند از سر کویت دگری نیست که نیست

Az hayaaye labe shirine to ey cheshmeye noosh
Gharghe aabo aragh aknoon shekari nist ke nist

از حیای لب شیرین تو ای چشمه نوش
غرق آب و عرق اکنون شکری نیست که نیست

Abe chashmam ke bar ou mennate khaake dare tost
Zire sad mennate ou khaake dari nist ke nist

آب چشمم که بر او منّت خاک در توست
زیر صد منّت او خاک دری نیست که نیست

Az vojoodam ghadari naamo neshaan hast ke hast
Var na az za-f dar aanjaa asari nist ke nist

از وجودم قدری نام و نشان هست که هست
ور نه از ضعف در آن جا اثری نیست که نیست

Shir dar baadiyeye eshghe to roobaah shavad
Aah az in raah ke dar vey khatari nist ke nist

شیر در بادیه عشق تو روباه شود
آه از این راه که در وی خطری نیست که نیست

Maslahat nist ke az parde boroon oftad raaz
Varna dar majlese rendaan khabari nist ke nist

مصلحت نیست که از پرده برون افتد راز
ور نه در مجلس رندان خبری نیست که نیست

Ghey razin nokte ke Hafez ze to naa khosh nood ast
Dar saraa paaye vojoodat honari nist ke nist

غیر از این نکته که حافظ ز تو ناخشنود است
در سراپای وجودت هنری نیست که نیست

Your spiralling locks of hair ensnare both faith and infidelity,
This is a little thing coming from the workshop of Divinity.

Though your beauty is a beautiful miracle,
The story of your glance is more magical.

How can one remove oneself from your eye's stare,
That in ambush with a bow is always waiting there?

Your black eye, a hundred "congratulations" is deserving,
For it is the master of the subtle magic of lover-slaying.

The science of love's form is a science that is amazing;
For under the lowest earth the highest heaven is existing.

You may think the evil-speaker has died intact,
But the two recording angels[1] were there in fact.

Hafiz, from the snare of that hair don't feel secure,
It caught your heart and is eyeing your religion for sure.

**(W-C 105)**
[1] "...two recording angels..." As with other traditions Muslims believe there are angels recording our every
action, thought or impulses. At death a person is questioned by two angels (Munkar and Nakir) and either
the door to hell or to paradise is opened.

Khame zolfe to daame kofro dinast
خم زلف تو دام کفر و دین است

Ze kaarestaane ou yek shamme inast
ز کارستان او یک شمّه این است

Jamaalat mojeze hosn ast liken
جمالت معجز حسن است لیکن

Hadise ghamzeat sehre mobinast
حدیث غمزه‌ات سحر مبین است

Ze chashme shookhe to jaan key tavaan bord
ز چشم شوخ تو جان کی توان برد

Ke daaem baa kamaan andar kamin ast
که دایم با کمان اندر کمین است

Bedaan chashme siyah sad aafarin baad
بدان چشم سیه صد آفرین باد

Ke dar aashegh koshi sehr aafarinast
که در عاشق کشی سحرآفرین است

Ajab elmist elme heiate eshgh
عجب علمیست علم هیئت عشق

Ke charkhe hashtomash haftom zaminast
که چرخ هشتمش هفتم زمین است

Napendaari ke badgoo rafto jaan bord
نپنداری که بدگو رفت و جان برد

Hesaabash ba keramol kaatebinast
حسابش با کرام الکاتبین است

Masho Hafez ze keide zolfash imen
مشو حافظ ز کید زلفش ایمن

Ke del bordo konoon dar bande dinast
که دل برد و کنون در بند دین است

The fast, done! The time of Eid, begun; hearts rejoicing!
In the tavern the wine bubbles up, so let's be asking.

The time has passed of the heavy austerity boasters,
Risen up, the time of celebration for love's carousers.

One who drinks wine the way we do, to criticism is impervious,
To the delirious drunken lover no fault or defect is obvious.

The wine drinker who is open-faced and doesn't hide it,
Is better than a hardship boasting two-faced hypocrite.

We are not hypocrites, nor are we friends thereof,
'Who knows the secrets of all hearts,'[1] is witness thereof.

We obey God and do not do any harm to anyone at all,
A thing called unlawful, we do not say it is lawful.

How does it harm if we drink a glass or two of wine together,
Wine is the blood of grapes, not the blood of you my brother.

It is not a fault that will cause you any injury;
And if a fault? Say, "Who from all fault is free?"

*(W-C 106)*
  [1] *"...Who knows the secrets of all hearts..." This refers of course to Allah.*

Rooze yek soo shodo eid aamado delhaa barkhaast

Mey ze khom khaane be joosh aamado mi baayad khaast

روزه یک سو شد و عید آمد و دلها برخاست

می ز خمخانه به جوش آمد و می باید خواست

Novbeye zohd forooshaane geraan jaan begozasht

Vaghte rendiyyo tarab kardane rendaan barjaast

نوبه زهدفروشان گرانجان بگذشت

وقت رندیّ و طرب کردن رندان برجاست

Che malaamat bovad aan raa ke chonin baade khorad

In che eyb ast bedin bikheradi vin che khataast

چه ملامت بود آن را که چنین باده خورد

این چه عیب است بدین بیخردی وین چه خطاست

Baade nooshi ke dar ou rooyo riyaaee nabovad

Behtar az zohd forooshi ke dar ou rooyo riyaast

باده نوشی که در او روی و ریائی نبود

بهتر از زهدفروشی که درو روی و ریاست

Ma na mardaane riyaaeemo harifaane nefaagh

Aanke ou aaleme ser ast bedin haal gavaast

ما نه مردان ریائیم و حریفان نفاق

آنکه او عالم سرّست برین حال گواست

Farze izad begozaarimo be kas bad nakonim

Vaanche gooyand ravaa nist nagooeem ravaast

فرض ایزد بگزاریم و به کس بد نکنیم

وانچه گویند روا نیست نگوئیم رواست

Che shaved gar mano to chand ghadah baade khorim

Baade az khoone razaan ast na az khoone shomaast

چه شودگر من و تو چند قدح باده خوریم

باده از خون رزانست نه از خون شماست

In che eyb ast kaz aan eyb khelal khaahad bood

Var bovad niz che shod mardome bi eyb kojaast

این چه عیبست کزان عیب خلل خواهد بود

ور بود نیز چه شد مردم بیعیب کجاست

My dear, if the words of the pure-hearted you're not getting,
The fault is that this kind of talk you are not used to receiving.

Neither to this world nor to the next obeisence am I making,
God be praised for this contention  my poor head is making.

I know not who within this shattered heart is,
I am silent, but my heart shouting excitedly is.

My heart leapt from this veil: 'Hey musician where are you?'
Hey - sing, because of that note my work is a sweet tune too.

To the work of the world I gave no attention, but your face,
To these sweet eyes, made it seem a nicely decorated place.

I imagined I had moved on; sleepless with thoughts my head is;
A hundred-night hangover! O say then where the tavern is!

Stained with the blood of my heart my place of retreat is,
If you give Ghusl[1] with red wine, from your hand truth it is.

In the Magians[2] sanctuary high their regard for me is,
On acount of the fire that in my heart permanently is.

The tune the musician played under cover of night, tell what it is!
Life passed on but still in my head that melody playing is.

Last night in my heart your voice of love they declared in me,
And that voice filling my breast with desire still seems to be.


**(W-C 109) The radif here is; "Is".**
  [1] "...Ghusl..." This refers to the full bath taken by Muslims after sexual contact.
  [2] "...Magian's..." Magians are associated with fire-worship.

Cho beshnavi sokhane ahle del magoo ke khataast

چو بشنوی سخن اهل دل مگو که خطاست

Sokhan shenaas ne ee delbaraa khataa injaast

سخن شناس نئی دلبرا خطا اینجاست

Saram be donyee yo oghbi foroo nemiaayad

سرم به دنیی و عقبی فرو نمی‌آید

Tabaa rakallah azin fetnehaa ke dar sare maast

تبارک الله ازین فتنه‌ها که در سر ماست

Dar andaroone mane khaste del nadaanam kist

در اندرون من خسته دل ندانم کیست

Ke man khamooshamo ou dar faghaano dar ghovghaast

که من خموشم و او در فغان و در غوغاست

Delam ze parde boroon shod kojaaee ey motreb

دلم ز پرده برون شد کجائی ای مطرب

Benaal haan ke azin parde kaare maa be navaast

بنال هان که ازین پرده کار ما به نواست

Maraa be kaare jahaan hargez eltefaat nabood

مرا به کار جهان هرگز التفات نبود

Rokhe to dar nazare man chonin khoshash aaraast

رخ تو در نظر من چنین خوشش آراست

Nakhofteam ze khiyali ke mipazam shabhaast

نخفته‌ام ز خیالی که می‌پزم شبهاست

Khomaare sad shabe daaram sharaab khaane kojaast

خمار صدشبه دارم شرابخانه کجاست

Chenin ke sovme-e aaloode shod ze khoone delam

چنین که صومعه آلوده شد ز خون دلم

Garam be baade beshooeed hagh be daste shomaast

گرم به باده بشوئید حق به دست شماست

Az aan be deire moghaanam aziz midaarand

از آن به دیر مغانم عزیز می‌دارند

Ke aatashi ke namirad hamishe dar dele maast

که آتشی که نمیرد همیشه در دل ماست

Che saaz bood ke benvaakht doosh aan motreb

چه ساز بود که بنواخت دوش آن مطرب

Ke raft omro demaagham hanooz por ze havaast

که رفت عمر ودماغم هنوز پر ز هواست

Nedaaye eshghe to doosham dar andaroon daadand

ندای عشق تو دوشم در اندرون دادند

Fazaaye sine ze shovgham hanooz por ze sedaast

فضای سینه ز شوقم هنوز پر ز صداست

For our pain there is no cure at all, O please justice!
To our separation no end in sight, O please justice!

Both religion and heart they ravished; even on our life they prey,
Justice! On those tyrannical beauties, mete out justice I say.

For the price of just a kiss our life they demand,
Those heart ravishing beauties! Its justice I demand.

Those heathen-hearted ones drank our life blood they do,
O true believers what's the solution? Only justice will do.

Each night and day, free from self, as Hafiz is,
In all-consuming grief I have sought just justice.

*(W-C 110) The radif here is; "Justice".*
 *This ghazal is not included by Avery or Khanlari.*

Darde maa raa nist darmaan al ghiyaas
Hejre maa raa nist paayaan al ghiyaas

Dino del bordando ghasde jaan konand
Al ghiyaas az jovre khoobaan al ghiyaas

Dar bahaaye boosei jaani talab
Mikonand in delsetaanaan al ghiyaas

Khoone ma khordand in kaafar delaan
Ey mosalmaanaan che darmaan al ghiyaas

Hamcho Hafez roozo shab bi khishtan
Gashteam soozaano geryaan al ghiyaas

درد ما را نیست درمان الغیاث
هجر ما را نیست پایان الغیاث

دین و دل بردند و قصد جان کنند
الغیاث از جور خوبان الغیاث

در بهای بوسه‌ای جانی طلب
می‌کنند این دلستانان الغیاث

خون ما خوردند این کافردلان
ای مسلمانان چه درمان الغیاث

همچو حافظ روز و شب بی خویشتن
گشته‌ام سوزان و گریان الغیاث

My heart, desiring so ardently the face of Farrukh,[1]
Is tumbling in confusion, like the hair of Farrukh.

Except for one Hindu slave - that black hair,
Sight of Farrukh's face no one else can share.

Good fortune follows blackness, for that black servant constantly,
Travels on the shoulder of Farrukh on every single journey.

The cypress of the garden would tremble, like the willow tree,
If the heart enticing stature of Farrukh it should happen to see.

Bring the wine, deep crimson like the arghavan, O Saki,
To drink to the enchantment in Farrukh's eye we see.

My body is bent like a drawn bow from long misery,
 Of the shape of the eyebrows of Farrukh it reminds me.

The musk of Tartary on the breeze becomes ashamed,
 At the ambergris scent for which Farrukh's hair is famed.

If to various places the heart of others may incline,
Inclined only to Farrukh is this poor heart of mine.

I am slave to anyone whose firm intention is,
To serve the black hair of Farrukh, like Hafiz.


**(W-C 114)**
   [1] "...Farrukh..." Farrukh can be the name of a man or woman. It also literally means 'glorious, auspicious, or fortunate (Avery).' It may refer to a woman who inspired Hafiz.

Dele man dar havaaye rooye farrokh
Bovad aashofte hamchon mooye farrokh

Be joz hendooye zolfash hich kas nist
Ke bar khordaar shod az rooye farrokh

Siyaahi nik bakht ast aanke daaem
Bovad hamraaho ham zanooye farrokh

Shavad chon bid larzaan sarve bostaan
Agar binad ghade deljooye farrokh

Bede saaghi sharaabe arghavaani
Be yaade nargese jaadooye farrokh

Do ta shod ghaamatam hamchon kamaani
Ze gham peivaste chon abrooye farrokh

Nasime moshke taataari khejel kard
Shamime zolfe ambar booye farrokh

Agar meile dele har kas be jaaeest
Bovad meile dele man sooye farrokh

Gholaame hemmate aanam ke baashad
Cho Hafez chaakero hendooye farrokh

دل من در هوای روی فرّخ
بود آشفته همچون موی فرّخ

بجز هندوی زلفش هیچ کس نیست
که برخوردار شد از روی فرّخ

سیاهی نیکبخت است آن که دایم
بود همراه و همزانوی فرّخ

شود چون بید لرزان سروبستان
اگر بیند قد دلجوی فرّخ

بده ساقی شراب ارغوانی
به یاد نرگس جادوی فرّخ

دوتا شد قامتم همچون کمانی
ز غم پیوسته چون ابروی فرّخ

نسیم مشک تاتاری خجل کرد
شمیم زلف عنبربوی فرّخ

اگر میل دل هر کس به جائیست
بود میل دل من سوی فرّخ

غلام همّت آنم که باشد
چو حافظ چاکر و هندوی فرّخ

O heart! You saw yet again what love's grief did,
How the beloved was and what to the faithful lover did.

O what a game that enchanter, the narcissus, started;
O dear! See how by the drunken one the sober are led.

Beloved! sunset-red my tears are from unkindness in you,
No compassion falls to my lot in this work of loving you.

Dawn came and from Layla's[1] abode up the lightening leaped,
But see what harvest the heart-broken Majnun then reaped.

O Saki give a cup of wine! O that Writer Who is well hid,
In the veil of mysteries, who knows what He did?

He designed the azure blue of the heavens, that Artist did,
In the turning of the compass hidden is what He did.

The thought of love struck the heart; Hafiz burned in grief – he did,
Just see how to a lover that one behaved – what that old friend did.

*(W-C 115) The radif here is; "What it did".*
    [1] *"...Layla (Laila)..." Layla means night but is also the name of a woman, beloved of Quais; (who is known as Majnun) from the extreme 'mad' intensity of his love.*

Didi ey del ke ghame eshgh dagar baar che kard
Chon beshod delbaro baa yaare vafaa daar che kard

دیدی ای دل که غم عشق دگربار چه کرد
چون بشد دلبر و با یار وفادار چه کرد

vah azaan nargese jadoo ke che baazi angikht
Aah azaan mast ke baa mardome hoshyaar che kard

وه از آن نرگس جادو که چه بازی انگیخت
آه ازان مست که با مردم هشیار چه کرد

Ashke man range shafagh yaaft ze bi mehriye yaar
Taale-e bi shafaghat bin ke dar in kaar che kard

اشک من رنگ شفق یافت ز بی‌مهری یار
طالع بی‌شفقت بین که در این کار چه کرد

Barghi az manzele leili bederakhshid sahar
Vah ke baa kharmane Majnoone del afgaar che kard

برقی از منزل لیلی بدرخشید سحر
وه که با خرمن مجنون دل افگار چه کرد

Saaghiyaa jaame meyam deh ke negaarandeye gheib
Nist maloom ke dar pardeye asraar che kard

ساقیا جام می‌ام ده که نگارنده غیب
نیست معلوم که در پرده اسرار چه کرد

Aanke por naghsh zad in daayereye minaaee
Kas nadaanest ke dar gardeshe pargaar che kard

آن که پرنقش زد این دایره مینائی
کس ندانست که در گردش پرگار چه کرد

Fekre eshgh aatashe gham dar dele Hafez misookht
Yaare dirine bebinid ke baa yaar che kard

فکر عشق آتش غم در دل حافظ می سوخت
یار دیرینه ببینید که با یار چه کرد

At dawn the bulbul told the morning breeze this story,
Saying, "What love for the rose's face has done to us, just see.

"It blew aside the rose's veil, the hyacinth's curling hair it ruffled,
"And the knot, holding the rosebud's coat so tightly, it loosened."

On every side that lover, the bulbul, is crying desperately,
In the middle of it all the dawn breeze is laughing joyfully.

The colour of that face my heart's blood was caused to be,
And in the thorns of the rose-bed, that one entangled me.

May the early morning breeze please that one hopefully,
Who for the grief of night-watchers prepared a remedy.

No complaint about strangers will ever again come from me,
For whatever may come to be, it comes from the Friend I see.

If, of the Sultan, I had expectations, the fault was all from me,
If I expected fidelity, the heart-stealer gave me tyranny.

I am a slave of the resolution of one who sincerely,
Does good deeds without pretence or any hypocrisy.

If those eminent city fathers should show any faith in me,
It's the 'father of perfect faith and grace'[1] caused it thus to be.

In the street of the wine-sellers good news announce from me,
Hafiz has made repentance of austerity; yes, and of hypocrisy.


*(W-C 116) The radif here is; "Made".*
[1] *According to Avery this is a reference to Kamaluddin (perfection of faith) Bu'l Vafa who is buried in Shiraz and was held in great respect by Hafiz Saheb.*

Sahar bolbol hekaayat baa sabaa kard
سحر بلبل حکایت با صبا کرد

Ke eshghe rooye gol baa maa chehaa kard
که عشق روی گل با ما چها کرد

Neghaabe gol keshido zolfe sombol
نقاب گل کشید و زلف سنبل

Gereh bande gabaaye ghonche vaa kard
گره بند قبای غنچه وا کرد

Be har soo bolbole aashegh be afghaan
به هر سو بلبل عاشق به افغان

Tana-om az miyaan baade sabaa kard
تنعّم از میان باد صبا کرد

Azaan range rokham khoon dar del andaakht
ازان رنگ رخم خون در دل انداخت

Vazin golshan be khaaram mobtalaa kard
وزین گلشن به خارم مبتلا کرد

Khoshash baad aan nasime sobhgaahi
خوشش باد آن نسیم صبحگاهی

Ke darde shabneshinaan raa davaa kard
که درد شب نشینان را دوا کرد

Man az bigaanegaan digar nanaalam
من از بیگانگان دیگر ننالم

Ke baa man harche kard aan aashenaa kard
که با من هر چه کرد آن آشنا کرد

Gar az soltaan tama kardam khataa bood
گر از سلطان طمع کردم خطا بود

Var az delbar vafaa jostam jafaa kard
ور از دلبر وفا جستم جفا کرد

Gholaame hemmate aan naazaninam
غلام همّت آن نازنینم

Ke kaare kheir bi rooyo riyaa kard
که کار خیر بی روی و ریا کرد

Vafaa az khaajegaane shahr baa man
وفا از خواجگان شهر با من

Kamaale dovlato din bolvafaa kard
کمال دولت و دین بوالوفا کرد

Beshaarat bar be kooye meiforooshaan
بشارت بر به کوی می فروشان

Ke Hafez tovbe az zohde riyaa kard
که حافظ توبه از زهد ریا کرد

A bulbul drank the blood of the liver[1], and thus gained a rose;[2]
In envy, with a hundred heart-hurting thorns, the wind arose.

A parrot's heart was in hope of a piece of sugar it relished,
At once the picture of hope, in a torrent of decay, vanished.

The light of my eye is the memory of that fruit of my heart;
Hard it made my life's work – though it had been easy to depart.

Camel driver, my load has slipped off, help for God's sake!
It was in the hope of being benefitted this litter I chose to take.

Do not be contemptuous of my dusty face and water-filled eye,
Of mixed straw and clay[3], the blue sphere built us a hall of joy.

Such deep grief, that, due to the envious eye of this sphere's moon,
A dwelling in the tomb my crescent eyebrow's moon, has made so soon.

Hafiz, you could have castled and made a mate[4], the chance is gone!
What now can I do? Time's play made me careless and moved on.

<hr>

**(W-C 117) The radif here is; "Made".**
  [1] "..blood of the liver..."See glossary for liver.
  [2] This poem is thought to be about the death of a son of Hafiz.
  [3] "...straw and clay..." Clay and straw are used traditionally in brick making. There may be an association also with the 'children of Israel' who, whilst in captivity in Egypt at the time of prophet Musa, were given the task of making bricks without straw and who suffered with their newborn being murdered.
  [4] A Chess term of course but perhaps saying, about his son, that the chance of seeing him wed has now gone.

Bolboli khoone jegar khordo goli haasel kard
Baade gheirat be sadash khaar parishaan del kard

Toote ee raa be khiyaale shekari del khosh bood
Naagahash seile fanaa naghshe amal baatel kard

Ghorratol-eine man aan miveye del yaadash baad
Ke khod aasaan beshodo kaare maraa moshkel kard

Sarebaan baare man oftaad khodaa raa madadi
Ke omide karamam hamrahe in mahmel kard

Rooye khakiyyo name chashme maraa khaar madaar
Charkhe firooze tarab khaane az in kahgel kard

Aaho faryaad ke az chashme hasoode mahe charkh
Dar lahad maahe kamaan abrooye man manzel kard

Nazadi shaahe rokho fovt shod emkaan Hafez
Che konam baaziye ayyam maraa ghaafel kard

بلبلی خون جگر خورد و گلی حاصل کرد
باد غیرت به صدش خار پریشان دل کرد

طوطیی را به خیال شکری دل خوش بود
ناگهش سیل فنا نقش امل باطل کرد

قرّه العین من آن میوه دل یادش باد
که خود آسان بشد و کار مرا مشکل کرد

ساربان بار من افتاد خدا را مددی
که امید کرمم همره این محمل کرد

روی خاکیّ و نم چشم مرا خوار مدار
چرخ فیروزه طربخانه از این کهگل کرد

آه و فریاد که از چشم حسود مه چرخ
در لحد ماه کمان ابروی من منزل کرد

نزدی شاه رخ و فوت شد امکان حافظ
چه کنم بازی ایّام مرا غافل کرد

That celestial tyrant Turk, the tray of fasting plundered! Come!
A crescent moon suggests time to pass around the cup has come.

The reward of the fast and an accepted Hajj[1] is given,
To one whose pilgrimage is to the dust of love's tavern.

Our real home, in the corner of the tavern is to be found,
May God bless the builder who made this building sound.

Performed in the eyebrow's prayer arch is the ritual prayer,
By one whose wudhu[2], is taken in the blood of the liver[3].

The price of the ruby red wine is just the jewel of reason;
Come on, what a profitable deal it is for the right person.

Oh dear, today the deceitful eye of the chief of the city elders,
Cast a glance, filled with contempt, at the dreg drinkers.

Hear love's true story from Hafiz, not the one admonishing;
Whatever skill that one may have in the art of speechifying.

---

*(W-C 118) The radif here is; "Made".*
   [1] *Hajj (pilgrimage to Mecca at an appointed time) is associated with one Eid – the fasting at Ramadan with another. A pilgrimage like the fast is essentially an offering and has to be accepted to be considered valid.*
   [2] *"...wudhu..." This is the ritual ablution before prayer.*
   [3] *"...blood of the liver..." See the glossary in this volume.*

Biyaa ke torke falak khaane rooze ghaarat kard

بیا که ترک فلک خوان روزه غارت کرد

Helaale eid be dovre ghadah eshaarat kard

هلال عید به دور قدح اشارت کرد

Savaabe roozevo hajje ghabool aan kas bord

ثواب روزه و حجّ قبول آن کس برد

Ke khaake meikadeye eshgh raa ziyaarat kard

که خاک میکده عشق را زیارت کرد

Maghaame asliye maa goosheye kharaabaat ast

مقام اصلی ما گوشه خرابات است

Khodaash kheir dehaad aanke in emaarat kard

خداش خیر دهاد آن که این عمارت کرد

Namaaz dar khame aan abrovaane mehraabi

نماز در خم آن ابروان محرابی

Kasi konad ke be khoone jegar tahaarat kard

کسی کند که به خون جگر طهارت کرد

Bahaaye baadeye chon la-l chist jovhare aghl

بهای باده چون لعل چیست جوهر عقل

Biaa ke sood kasi bord kin tejaarat kard

بیا که سود کسی برد کاین تجارت کرد

Faghaan ke nargese jammashe sheikhe shahr emrooz

فغان که نرگس جمّاش شیخ شهر امروز

Nazar be dord keshaan az sare heghaarat kard

نظر به دردکشان از سر حقارت کرد

Hadise eshgh ze Hafez sheno na az vaaez

حدیث عشق ز حافظ شنو نه از واعظ

Agarche san-ate besyaar dar ebaarat kard

اگر چه صنعت بسیار در عبارت کرد

A knowing one made ablution in the wine's liquid luminosity,
On a visit to the tavern he made one morning, very early.

As soon as the golden cup of the sun from our view parted,
The new moon's crescent[1] hinted at the goblet, and Eid started.

Well received is the prayer and supplication of one who from hurt,
Has made his ritual ablution in tears of the blood of the heart.

Look upon the beloved's face with the eye of appreciation,
For the experienced one has gained insight into every situation.

My heart purchased with my very life your ringlet's frenzy,
In an exchange like this what profit was made, if any?

If the prayer leader should happen to be inquiring,
Inform him that Hafiz with wine has made his cleansing.

*(W-C 119) The radif is "Made".*
   [1]*The thin crescent shaped new moon rising, marking the start of Eid festival also reminding of the shape of the goblet of wine.*

Be aabe rovshane mey aarefi tahaarat kard
Alas sabaah ke meikhaane raa ziyaarat kard

به آب روشن می عارفی طهارت کرد
علی الصّباح که میخانه را زیارت کرد

Hamaan ke saaghare zarrine khor nahaan gardid
Helaale eid be dovre ghadah eshaarat kard

همان که ساغر زرّین خور نهان گردید
هلال عید به دور قدح اشارت کرد

Khoshaa namaazo niyaaze kasi ke az sare dard
Be aabe didevo khoone jegar tahaarat kard

خوشا نماز و نیاز کسی که از سر درد
به آب دیده و خون جگر طهارت کرد

Be rooye yaar nazar kon zed ide mennat daar
Ke kaar dide hame az sare besaarat kard

به روی یار نظر کن ز دیده منّت دار
که کاردیده همه از سر بصارت کرد

Delam be halgheye zolfash be jaan kharid aashoob
Che sood did nadanam ke in tejaarat kard

دلم به حلقه زلفش به جان خرید آشوب
چه سود دید ندانم که این تجارت کرد

Agar emaame jamaa-at talab konad emrooz
Khabar dahid ke Hafez be mey tahaarat kard

اگر امام جماعت طلب کند امروز
خبر دهید که حافظ به می طهارت کرد

Resolved! Like a breath of breeze I will go to your lane,
From your fine scent, musky perfume my breath will gain.

Every droplet of esteem I acquired from knowledge and religion,
I mean to shake on the dust of the path your feet have trodden.

Without wine and you, beloved, my life passed in folly,
That was laziness! From now on hard at work I will be.

Where is the breeze? This life, like the rose, is with blood suffused,
I intend to sacrifice it, for the scent the beloved one's hair diffused.

My morning is lit up like a candle by the sun of your loving kindness,
To dedicate my life to your work, my purpose now is only this.

In memory of that eye of yours, of myself a ruin I mean to make,
The foundations of the ancient covenant[1] stronger I mean to make.

Hafiz! The heart is not made pure by deceit and hypocrisy,
I am resolved to choose the path of love and a Rend[2] to be.

---

**(W-C 120) The radif is "I will make".**
  [1] See under 'Alast' in glossary.
  [2] "...Rend..." Profligate (in the way of God).
  "The theme, clear from the first word, is making a resolve – but the resolve is not for outer activity but the work of love.

Cho baad azme sare kooye yaar khaaham kard
Nafas be booye khoshash moshk baar khaaham kard

چو باد عزم سر کوی یار خواهم کرد
نفس به بوی خوشش مشکبار خواهم کرد

Har aabe rooy ke andookhtam ze daanesh o din
Nesaare khaake rahe aan negaar khaaham kard

هر آبروی که اندوختم ز دانش و دین
نثار خاک ره آن نگار خواهم کرد

Be harze bi meyo mashoogh omr migozarad
Betaalatam bas az emrooz kaar khaaham kard

به هرزه بی می و معشوق عمر می‌گذرد
بطالتم بس از امروز کار خواهم کرد

Sabaa kojaast ke in jaane khoon gerefte cho gol
Fadaaye nak-hate gisooye yaar khaaham kard

صبا کجاست که این جان خون گرفته چو گل
فدای نکهت گیسوی یار خواهم کرد

Cho sha-m sobh damam shod ze mehre ou rovshan
Ke omr dar sare in kaaro baar khaaham kard

چو شمع صبحدمم شد ز مهر او روشن
که عمر در سر این کار و بار خواهم کرد

Be yaade chashme to khod raa kharaab khaaham saakht
Banaaye ahde ghadim ostovaar khaaham kard

به یاد چشم تو خود را خراب خواهم ساخت
بنای عهد قدیم استوار خواهم کرد

Nefaagh o zargh nabakhshad safaaye del Hafez
Tarighe rendiyo eshgh ekhtiaar khaaham kard

نفاق و زرق نبخشد صفای دل حافظ
طریق رندی و عشق اختیار خواهم کرد

From nothing, into the field of existence, now comes the rose,
At its foot the violet has placed its head, and homage shows.

Drink the morning wine while the drum and harp are playing,
To the sound of lyre and reed, the chin[1] of the Saki be kissing.

It's the rose season; let wine, a lovely one, and harp, be present,
Its life lasts no more than a week, like time it is not permanent.[2]

Sweet smelling herbs make the abode of the earth as bright,
As heavenly mansions where auspicious stars shine at night.

Drink wine from the hand of a delicate faced, beloved beauty,
Of Jesus' breath: no more the tale of Aad and Thamud[2] let it be.

The world is a paradise when the lily and rose are blooming,
But what value has that in which permanence is not residing.[3]

When the rose rises up in the air as Prophet Solomon[4] did,
And the bird sings at dawn the psalms of Prophet David -

In the garden renew faith in Zoroaster's fire-worshipping,
As the red tulip has flamed up, like Nimrod's[5] fire rising.

Ask that the morning cup be brimful, and to our age's Asaf drink,
To our own advisor of Solomon, Imamuddin Mahmud[6], drink.

Maybe due to patronage of Hafiz's coterie,
Everything will be just as they want it to be.

*(W-C 121)*
    [1] *"...chin..." The chin – (actually double chin is used here) considered as a sign of beauty at the time.*
    [2] *"...in which permanence is not residing..." Probably a reference to Prophet Abraham (Ibrahim) who according to the holy Qur'an saw first the stars, then the moon and finally the sun as possible objects of worship but then, on realising each of them set, at last reached the conclusion that only the One who was permanent (Allah) was worthy of worship.*
    [3] *"...Aad and Thamud..." Peoples mentioned in the holy book as being destroyed by Allah.*
    [4] *"...rises up in the air as Prophet Solomon did..." Prophet Solomon was given control of the winds.*
    [5] *"...Nimrod..." See Avery pp.259. Nimrod is thought to be the ruler who ordered that Prophet Ibrahim be put in the fire. God however made the fire cool for him.*
    [6] *"...Imamuddin Mahmud..." This refers to a minister of one of Hafiz's patrons.*

Konoon ke dar chaman aamad gol az adam be vojood
کنون که در چمن آمد گل از عدم به وجود

Banafshe dar ghadame ou nahaad sar be sojood
بنفشه در قدم او نهاد سر به سجود

Benoosh jaame saboohi be naaleye dafo chang
بنوش جام صبوحی به ناله دف و چنگ

Beboos ghab ghabe saaghi be naghmeye neyo ood
ببوس غبغب ساقی به نغمه نی و عود

Be dovre gol maneshin bi sharaabo shaahedo chang
به دور گل منشین بی شراب و شاهد و چنگ

Ke hamcho dovre baghaa haftei bovad ma-dood
که همچو دوربقا هفته‌ای بود معدود

Shod az boroohje riyaahin cho aasemaan rovshan
شد از بروج ریاحین چو آسمان روشن

Zamin be akhtare meimoono taale-e mas-ood
زمین به اختر میمون و طالع مسعود

Ze daste shaahede naazok ezaare isaa dam
ز دست شاهد نازک عذار عیسی دم

Sharaab noosho rahaa kon hadise aado samood
شراب نوش و رها کن حدیث عاد و ثمود

Jahaan cho kholde barin shod be dovre soosano gol
جهان چو خلد برین شد به دور سوسن و گل

Vali che sood ke dar vey na momken ast kholood
ولی چه سود که در وی نه ممکن است خلود

Cho gol savar shavad bar havaa soleimaan vaar
چو گل سوار شود بر هوا سلیمان وار

Sahar ke morgh dar aayad be naghmeye daavood
سحر که مرغ درآید به نغمه داوود

Be baagh taaze kon aaeene dine zartoshti
به باغ تازه کن آیین دین زردشتی

Konoon ke laale bar afrookht aatashe namrood
کنون که لاله برافروخت آتش نمرود

Bekhaah jaame saboohi be yaade aasafe ahd
بخواه جام صبوحی به یاد آصف عهد

Vazire molke soleimaan emaade din mahmood
وزیر ملک سلیمان عماد دین محمود

Bovad ke majlese Hafez be yomne tarbiatash
بود که مجلس حافظ به یمن تربیتش

Har aanche mi talabad jomle bashadash movjood
هر آن چه می‌طلبد جمله باشدش موجود

The so-called Sufi, opened a box of tricks, in order to ensnare,
A game of sorcery with the deceitful sphere he began to prepare.

The sphere toyed with him, then smashed the egg in his hat,
Because, before one knowing the mysteries, his tricks fell flat.

Saki! The beautiful friend of the Sufis is here, come please!
With great grace that one began to flatter and to please.

Where is this musician from who composed the melody of Irak?[1]
But whose intention was, from the way to Hejaz[2], to turn back.

O heart, come let us go and the shelter of God try to gain,
From the long reach the short-sleeved[3] tricksters maintain.

Avoid trickery, for whoever played love without sincerity,
Love closed the door of true understanding very promptly.

Tomorrow[4], when the entrance hall to truth becomes evident,
Of the illusions he worked, that traveller will be repentant.

O strutting partridge, going where? Best hide your pleasing gait,
Beware the pious pretence of the ascetic's cat, before it's too late.

Hafiz! Do not criticise the profligate, because, you see,
Outside of time, God freed us from hypocritical austerity.


*(W-C 122) The radif is "Made".*
[1] *"...Irak..." This refers to a musical mode.*
[2] *"...Hejaz..." This refers to an area of Arabia containing the holy cities of Mecca and Medina but also here refers to a musical mode. See Avery pp. 176.*
[3] *"...short-sleeved..." False deceiving Sufis.*
[4] *"...Tomorrow..." This refers to The Day of Judgement.*

Soofi nahaad daamo sare hoghe baaz kard

صوفی نهاد دام و سر حقّه باز کرد

Bonyaade makr baa falake hoghebaaz kard

بنیاد مکر با فلک حقّه باز کرد

Baaziyye dahr beshkanadash beize dar kolaah

بازی دهر بشکندش بیضه در کلاه

Ziraa ke arze sho-bade baa ahle raaz kard

زیرا که عرض شعبده با اهل راز کرد

Saaghi biyaa ke shaahede ra-naaye soofiaan

ساقی بیا که شاهد رعنای صوفیان

Digar be jelve aamado aaghaaze naaz kard

دیگر به جلوه آمد و آغاز ناز کرد

In motreb az kojaast ke saaze araagh saakht

این مطرب از کجاست که ساز عراق ساخت

Vaahange baazgasht ze raahe hejaaz kard

وآهنگ بازگشت ز راه حجاز کرد

Ey del biyaa ke maa be panaahe khodaa ravim

ای دل بیا که ما به پناه خدا رویم

Zaanch aastine kootaho daste deraaz kard

زانچ آستین کوته و دست دراز کرد

San-at makon ke har ke mahabbat na paak baakht

صنعت مکن که هر که محبّت نه پاک باخت

Esh ghash be rooye del dare ma-ni faraaz kard

عشقش به روی دل در معنی فراز کرد

Fardaa ke pish gaahe haghighat shavaad padid

فردا که پیشگاه حقیقت شود پدید

Sharmande rahrovi ke amal bar majaaz kard

شرمنده رهروی که عمل بر مجاز کرد

Ey kabke khosh kharaam kojaa miravi be ist

ای کبک خوش خرام کجا میروی بایست

Gharre masho ke gorbeye aabed namaaz kard

غرّه مشو که گربه عابد نماز کرد

Hafez makon malaamate rendaan ke dar azal

حافظ مکن ملامت رندان که در ازل

Ma raa khodaa ze zohde riyaa bi niyaaz kard

ما را خدا ز زهد ریا بی‌نیاز کرد

Many years the heart sought Jamshid's cup[1] - from me!
What it had, it sought from a stranger with earnest plea.

A pearl, not to be found in the shell of time and being,
It sought from those lost beach-combers; shore-hugging!

Last night, from the Magian Pir I sought a solution,
He, who with just a look reveals subtle inspiration.

I saw him, wine-cup in hand, laughing happily,
Reflected in it, a hundred mysteries he could see.

I asked when, the All-wise, gave the world-revealing cup,
He replied, "The day the azure dome, the sky, He put up."

He said: "That friend[2] who raised the gallows' fame so high,
"His crime was that he made known secrets from on high."

If the Holy Spirit's bounty were again to appear,
The Messiah's miracles another could do here."

I asked for what purpose the idol's locks of hair enchained,
He answered, "Of his own mad heart Hafiz has complained."

*(W-C 123) The radif is "Made".*
[1] *"...Jamshid's cup..." See glossary in this volume.*
[2] *"...that friend..." This refers to Mansur al-Hallaj, a great Sufi executed for declaring "ana'l Haqq" (I am the Truth).*

Saalhaa del talabe jaame jam az maa mikard
Aanche khod daasht ze bigaane tamannaa mikard

ساالها دل طلب جام جم از ما می کرد
آنچه خود داشت ز بیگانه تمنّا می کرد

Govhari kaz sadafe kovno makaan biroon ast
Talab az gom shodegaane rahe daryaa mikard

گوهری کز صدف کون و مکان بیرون است
طلب از گمشدگان ره دریا می کرد

Moshkele khish bare pire moghaan bordam doosh
Koo be taeede nazar halle moamma mikard

مشکل خویش بر پیر مغان بردم دوش
کاو به تایید نظر حل معمّا می کرد

Didamash khorramo khoshdel ghadahe baade be dast
Vandar aan aayene sad goone tamaashaa mikard

دیدمش خرّم و خوشدل قدح باده به دست
واندران آینه صد گونه تماشا می کرد

Goftam in jaame jahaan bin be to key daad hakim
Goft aan rooz ke in gombade minaa mikard

گفتم این جام جهان بین به تو کی داد حکیم
گفت آن روز که این گنبد مینا می کرد

Goft aan yaar kaz ou gasht sare daar boland
Jormash in bood ke asraar hoveidaa mikard

گفت آن یار کزاو گشت سر دار بلند
جرمش این بود که اسرار هویدا می کرد

Feize roohol ghodos ar baaz madad farmaayad
Digaraan ham bekonand aanche masihaa mikard

فیض روح القدس ار باز مدد فرماید
دیگران هم بکنند آنچه مسیحا می کرد

Goftamash zolfe cho zanjire botaan az peye chist
Goft Hafez gelei az dele sheidaa mikard

گفتمش زلف چو زنجیر بتان از پی چیست
گفت حافظ گله‌ای از دل شیدا می کرد

Friends! The daughter of the vine has repented of the veil,
She went, and with the stern censor made her case prevail.

From veil to the gathering, she came; wipe away all perspiration,
So she will tell friends why so far removed was her situation.

The bond of union is the appropriate place to be binding,
The intoxicated daughter, who hid beneath all that veiling.

O heart be happy! News of love the maestro's song is giving,
Of intoxication's return; and with this a remedy is bringing.

Our nature, with the breath of the beloved, like the rosebud bloomed,
Became a scented red rose, whose petals the bulbul's song inspired.

Seven washes and a hundred burnings[1]; the colour won't go,
That on the Sufis robe the juice of the grape did bestow.

Hafiz, from the hand don't lose humility, because the envious one;
Plotting against pride, reputation, wealth, heart and faith is that one.

---

*(W-C 124) The radif is "Made".*
[1] *"…seven washes…" One of the interpretations of religious law indicate that impure objects must washed in water seven times (See Avery pp. 184)*

Doostaan dokhtare raz tovbe ze mastoori kard
Shod sooye mohtasebo kaar be dastoori kard

دوستان دختر رز توبه ز مستوری کرد
شد سوی محتسب و کار به دستوری کرد

Aamad az parde be majles araghash paak konid
Taa begooyad be harifaan ke cheraa doori kard

آمد از پرده به مجلس عرقش پاک کنید
تا بگوید به حریفان که چرا دوری کرد

Jaaye aan ast ke dar aghde vesaalash girand
Dokhtari maste chenin kin hame mastoori kard

جای آن است که در عقد وصالش گیرند
دختری مست کاین چنین کاین همه مستوری کرد

Mojdegaani bede ey del ke degar motrebe eshgh
Raahe mastaane zado chaareye makhmoori kard

مژدگانی بده ای دل که دگر مطرب عشق
راه مستانه زد و چاره مخموری کرد

Na shegeft ar gole tabaam ze nasimash beshkoft
Morghe shab khan tarabaz barge gole soori kard

نه شگفت ار گل طبعم ز نسیمش بشکفت
مرغ شبخوان طرب از برگ گل سوری کرد

Na be haft aab ke rangash be sad aataash naravad
Anche baa khergheye zaahed meye angoori kard

نه به هفت آب که رنگش به صد آتش نرود
آنچه با خرقه زاهد می انگوری کرد

Hafez oftaadegi az dast made zaanke hasood
Erzo maalo delo din dar sare maghroori kard

حافظ افتادگی از دست مده زانکه حسود
عرض و مال و دل و دین در سر مغروری کرد

The mystery Jamshid's cup[1] reveals can come in your eye,
When eye-salve of the tavern's dust to your eyes you apply.

Don't sit without wine and singer under the overarching sky,
If you will let it, away on a melody the heart's grief will fly.

The rose you desire so deeply, on its own will be unveiling,
When, as the dawn breeze does, service you are offering.

Take another step towards the stage of Love, yes do,
For if this journey you will make, it will benefit you.

Come! For delight, the sense of Presence, and order maintained;
From the bounty of the men of vision, this remedy is obtained.

Not screened or veiled from view the beautiful beloved is,
When removed from your eyes the dust of your life's path is.

If, from the house of your own nature, you do not depart,
How to the street of Tariqat[2] the journey can you start.

To be a beggar in the tavern is the elixir of wonder,
Do this and stones into gold you will be able to render.

O heart, if you gain the knowledge of austerity's light,
Like the laughing candle you can abandon life's plight.

But while desire for the lovely lip, and wine to sip, is yours,
You will not think of anything else you can do, of course.

O Hafiz! If you hear this royal counsel truly,
Passage to the realm of Haqiqat[3] is a possibility.

**(W-C 125) The radif is "You can make".**
   [1] "...Jamshid's cup..." See glossary in this volume.
   2 "...Tariqat..." See commentary to (W-C 28) above.
   3 "...Haqiqat..." See commentary to (W-C 28) above.

Be serre jaame jaam aangah nazar tavaani kard

به سرّ جام جم آنگه نظر توانی کرد

Ke khaake meikade kohle basar tavaani kard

که خاک میکده کحل بصر توانی کرد

Mabaash bi meyo motreb ke zire taaghe sepehr

مباش بی می و مطرب که زیر طاق سپهر

Be in taraane gham az del bedar tavaani kard

به این ترانه غم از دل بدر توانی کرد

Gole moraade to aangah neghaab bog shaayad

گل مراد تو آن که نقاب بگشاید

Ke khedmatash cho nasime sahar tavaani kard

که خدمتش چو نسیم سحر توانی کرد

Be azme marhaleye eshgh pish neh ghadami

به عزم مرحله عشق پیش نه قدمی

Ke sood haa koni ar in safar tavaani kard

که سودها کنی ار این سفر توانی کرد

Biyaa ke chaareye zovghe hozooro nazme omoor

بیا که چاره ذوق حضور و نظم امور

Be feize bakh sheshe ahle nazar tavaani kard

به فیض بخشش اهل نظر توانی کرد

Jamaale yaar nadaarad neghaabo parde vali

جمال یار ندارد نقاب و پرده ولی

Ghobaare rah beneshaan taa nazar tavaani kard

غبار ره بنشان تا نظر توانی کرد

To kaz saraaye tabiat nemiravi biroon

تو کز سرای طبیعت نمی‌روی بیرون

Kojaa be kooye tarighat gozar tavaani kard

کجا به کوی طریقت گذر توانی کرد

Gedaaee ye dare meikhaane torfe eksirist

گدایی در میخانه طرفه اکسیریست

Gar in amal bekoni khaak zar tavaani kard

گر این عمل بکنی خاک زر توانی کرد

Delaa ze noore riyaazat gar aagahi yaabi

دلا ز نور ریاضت گر آگهی یابی

Cho sha-m khande zanaan tarke sar tavaani kard

چو شمع خنده زنان ترک سر توانی کرد

Vali to taa labe mashoogho jaame mey khaahi

ولی تو تا لب معشوق و جام می خواهی

Ta-ma madaar ke kaare degar tavaani kard

طمع مدار که کار دگر توانی کرد

Gar in nasihate shaahaane beshnavi Hafez

گر این نصیحت شاهانه بشنوی حافظ

Be shaah raahe haghighat safar tavaani kard

به شاهراه حقیقت سفر توانی کرد

Henceforth my hand holds to the gown of that lofty cypress,
Who uprooted me fully, with movements elegant and gracious.

No need of a musician or of wine, just the veil be removing,
Your fiery face makes me dance wildly, like rue-seed burning.

No face mirrors the face good fortune reveals, except of course,
That face that's been rubbed on the hoof of the beloved's horse.

I said this, "To whatever is the secret of your grief, I just say be."
I have no more patience than this. What to do? How long will it be?

O my musk-bearing deer do not attempt to kill, O hunter,
See the look in that dark eye, feel shame, don't try to capture.

I am the dust of this doorstep and cannot rise from this place,
How can I aspire to kiss the lip, of the door of that high palace?

Night and day for this lover who lost his heart, these words utter,
"No injury may your upright stature from time's vagaries suffer."

Hafiz hears ghazals so fresh and so heart warming,
If they are not perfect, to Khujand1 he is not sending.

Excepting your hair locks Hafiz heart not any other inclination,
Sadly this heart has no wise words due to a hundred temptations.

Hafiz! Withdraw not your heart from that musky hair,
Because the crazy one is best when he is bound there.


*(W-C 126) See appendix.*

Ba-daz in daste mano daamane aan sarve boland
Ke be baalaaye chamaan az bono bikham barkand

Haajate motrebo mey nist to borgha bog shaa
Ke be raghs aavaradam aatashe rooyat cho sepand

Hich rooee nashavad aayeneye hejleye bakht
Magar aan rooy ke maaland dar aan somme samand

Goftam asraare ghamat harche bovad goo mibaash
Sabr az in bish nadaaram che konam taa keyo chand

Makosh aan aahooye moshkine maraa ey sayyaad
Sharm az aan chashme siah daaro mabandash be kamand

Mane khaaki ke az in dar natavaanam barkhaast
Az kojaa boose zanam bar labe aan ghasre boland

Baaz mastaan del az aan gisooye moshkin Hafez
Zaanke divaane hamaan beh ke bovad andar band

بعد از این دست من و دامن آن سرو بلند
که به بالای چمان از بن و بیخم برکند

حاجت مطرب و می نیست تو برقع بگشا
که برقص آوردم آتش رویت چو سپند

هیچ رویی نشود آینه حجله بخت
مگر آن روی که مالند در آن سمّ سمند

گفتم اسرار غمت هر چه بود گو می‌باش
صبر از این بیش ندارم چه کنم تا کی و چند

مکش آن آهوی مشکین مرا ای صیاد
شرم از آن چشم سیه دار و مبندش به کمند

من خاکی که از این در نتوانم برخاست
از کجا بوسه زنم بر لب آن قصر بلند

باز مستان دل از آن گیسوی مشکین حافظ
زان که دیوانه همان به که بود اندر بند

Enter that spiralling lock of hair; this the hand cannot do,
Rely upon the dawn wind, or your pact; one cannot do.

Whatever effort is required I make it in search of you,
But despite this, to change what fate decrees, I cannot do.

With so much of heart's blood; into my hand your robe I drew,
To release it now, whatever the enemy may say, this I cannot do.

Comparing your cheek to the moon in the sky? It's just not true.
A simile to what has neither head nor foot, that just won't do.

The moment, upright cypress, when the the Sama[1] you came to,
What's the importance of life's robe that tearing it[2] one cannot do?

To see the beloved's face requires one of vision, clear and true,
Except for pure ones, to look into that mirror, one just cannot do.

For apprehending love's difficulty our limited thoughts will not do,
To open up this subtle matter, nothing so erroneous will do.

I became jealous because of the world's attraction to you,
To fight with all God's creatures day and night I cannot do.

How should I put it? The gentle delicate nature shown by you,
Is such, that a measured reverential prayer one cannot do.

Except your eyebrow, in Hafiz's heart no other prayer arch will do,
In our Order, except to you, no act of devotion is possible to do.

**(W-C 127)**
   [1] *"...Sama..." Literally this means 'audition' (of the spiritual realities), but it is used often to mean the music concerts that the Sufis attend. Audition also involves vision and other faculties – hence the reference in other verses to vision.*
   [2] *"...Tearing it..." At the music concerts the Sufis who go into a state of spiritual ecstasy would sometimes tear their clothes.*

Dast dar halgheye aan zolfe do taa natvaan kard

Tekye bar ahde tovo baade sabaa natvaan kard

Aanche sa-y ast man andar talabat benmaayam

In ghadar hast ke tagh yire ghazaa natvaan kard

Daamane doost be sad khoone del oftaad be dast

Be fosoosi ke konad khasm rahaa natvaan kard

Aarezash raa be masal maahe falak natvaan goft

Nesbate yaar be har bi saro paa natvaan kard

Sarv baalaaye man aangah ke dar aayad be samaa

Che mahal jaameye jaan raa ke ghabaa natvaan kard

Moshkele eshgh na dar hov seleye daaneshe maast

Halle in nokte bedin fekre khataa natvaan kard

Che begooyam ke to raa nazokiye tab-e latif

Taa be haddist ke aaheste doaa natvaan kard

Nazare paak tavaanad rokhe jaanaan didan

Ke dar aaeene nazar joz be safaa natvaan kard

Gheiratam kosht ke mahboobe jahaani liken

Roozo shab arbade baa khalghe khodaa natvaan kard

Bejoz abrooye to mehraabe dele Hafez nist

Taa-ate gheire to dar mazhabe maa natvaan kard

دست در حلقه آن زلف دوتا نتوان کرد

تکیه بر عهد تو و باد صبا نتوان کرد

آن چه سعی است من اندر طلبت بنمایم

این قدر هست که تغییر قضا نتوان کرد

دامن دوست به صد خون دل افتاد به دست

به فسوسی که کند خصم رها نتوان کرد

عارضش را به مثل ماه فلک نتوان گفت

نسبت یار به هر بی سر و پا نتوان کرد

سرو بالای من آن گه که درآید به سماع

چه محل جامه جان را که قبا نتوان کرد

مشکل عشق نه در حوصله دانش ماست

حلّ این نکته بدین فکر خطا نتوان کرد

چه بگویم که ترا نازکی طبع لطیف

تا به حدّیست که آهسته دعا نتوان کرد

نظر پاک تواند رخ جانان دیدن

که در آئینه نظر جز به صفا نتوان کرد

غیرتم کشت که محبوب جهانی لیکن

روز و شب عربده با خلق خدا نتوان کرد

بجز ابروی تو محراب دل حافظ نیست

طاعت غیر تو در مذهب ما نتوان کرد

That beloved took my heart, then face concealed from view,
For God's sake! A game like this can anyone else bear as I do?

The solitude at the night's end, made plans to take my life away,
But thought of that one's endless kindness, bade me stay.

Why should my heart not be bloody as a tulip can be,
Since from that narcissus eye only disdain I can see.

With whom can I consult about this life-burning agony,
The physician seeks to take the life of my soul from me.

The way a candle consumed itself, the beloved consumed me,
So the wine jug wept and the lute-strings complained loudly.

If you have a remedy, O wind, now's the time to say,
For the pain of longing plans to take my life away.

To the kind-hearted caring ones, what can I really say?
That the beloved said such a thing, organised it this way?

Even the enemy plotting against the life of Hafiz would not do,
What your eyebrow's bow, loosing the eye's arrow, would do.

*(W-C 128) The radif is "Made".*

Del az man bordo rooy az man nahaan kard
دل از من برد و روی از من نهان کرد

Khodaa raa baa ke in baazi tavaan kard
خدا را با که این بازی توان کرد

Sahar tanhaaeeyam dar ghasde jaan bood
سحر تنهای ام در قصد جان بود

Khiyaalash lotf haaye bikaraan kard
خیالش لطف‌های بیکران کرد

Cheraa chon laale khoonin del nabaasham
چرا چون لاله خونین دل نباشم

Ke baa maa nargese ou sar geraan kard
که با ما نرگس او سرگران کرد

Kojaa gooyam ke baa in darde jaan sooz
کجا گویم که با این درد جانسوز

Tabibam ghasde jaane naa tavaan kard
طبیبم قصد جان ناتوان کرد

Baraan saan sookht chon sham-am ke bar man
بران سان سوخت چون شمعم که بر من

Soraahi geryevo barbat faghaan kard
صراحی گریه و بربط فغان کرد

Sabaa gar chaare daari vaghte vaght ast
صبا گر چاره داری وقت وقت است

Ke darde eshtiyaagham ghasde jaan kard
که درد اشتیاقم قصد جان کرد

Miyaane mehrabaanaan key tavaan goft
میان مهربانان کی توان گفت

Ke yaare maa chonin gofto chonaan kard
که یار ما چنین گفت و چنان کرد

Adoo baa jaane Hafez aan nakardi
عدو با جان حافظ آن نکردی

Ke tire chashme aan abroo kamaan kard
که تیر چشم آن ابروکمان کرد

Remember one, who when travelling, recalled us not,
To lift us with the joy of a fond farewell, that one forgot.

That young man whose new job was writing words that free,
I don't know why he forgot to release a poor old slave like me.

That paper garment[1], wash in tears of blood, we would,
The sphere did not guide me to a justice true and good.

The heart, in hope that a loud echoing cry would reach to you,
Made more wailing in this mountains than even Farhad[2] could do![1]

Since from the meadow you withdrew your shadow, see,
The dawn bird does not nest in the curls of the box tree.

It's appropriate, if the messenger wind learns its trade from you,
For movements swifter than you even the wind cannot do.

The beauty bestowing reed-pen draws not to the desire of him,
Who has not recognised that nature's beauty is drawn by Him.

O musician change key, strike the notes of the path of Irak[3],
For this path the beloved trod, not recalling us nor looking back.

The ghazals of Irak are the songs of Hafiz,
Heart-rending! No one heard without tears.

---

**(W-C 129) The radif is "Made not".**
[1] "...That paper garment..." According to Avery those persons seeking redress from the rulers would appear at court in papery type of clothes.

[2] "...Farhad..." See the glossary in this volume.

[3] "...Irak..." This refers to a musical mode.

Yaad baad aanke ze maa vaghte safar yaad nakard
Be vedaaee dele gham dideye maa shaad nakard

Aan javaan bakht ke mizad raghame kheiro ghabool
Bandeye pir nadaanam ze che aazaad nakard

Kaaghazin jaame be khoonaab beshooyam ke falak
Rahnomoonim be paaye alame daad nakard

Del be ommide sedaaee ke magar dar to rasad
Naalehaa kard dar in kooh ke farhaad nakard

Saaye taa baaz gerefti ze chaman morghe sahar
Aashiaan dar shekane torreye shem shaad nakard

Shaayad ar peike sabaa az to biaamoozad kaar
Zaanke chaalaak tar az in harakat baad nakard

Kelke mashaateye son-ash nakeshad nagh-she moraad
Harke eghraar bedaan hosne khodaadaad nakard

Motrebaa parde begardaan o bezan raahe hejaaz
Ke bedin raah beshod yaaro ze maa yaad nakard

Ghazaliyyate araaghist soroode Hafez
Ke shanid in rahe delsooz ke faryaad nakard

یاد باد آنکه ز ما وقت سفر یاد نکرد
به وداعی دل غمدیده ما شاد نکرد

آن جوانبخت که می‌زد رقم خیر و قبول
بنده پیر ندانم ز چه آزاد نکرد

کاغذین جامه به خوناب بشویم که فلک
رهنمونیم به پای علم داد نکرد

دل به امّید صدایی که مگر در تو رسد
ناله‌ها کرد در این کوه که فرهاد نکرد

سایه تا بازگرفتی ز چمن مرغ سحر
آشیان در شکن طرّه شمشاد نکرد

شاید ار پیک صبا از تو بیاموزد کار
زانکه چالاکتر از این حرکت باد نکرد

کلک مشاطّه صنعش نکشد نقش مراد
هر که اقرار بدان حسن خداداد نکرد

مطربا پرده بگردان و بزن راه حجاز
که به این راه بشد یار و ز ما یاد نکرد

غزلیّات عراقیست سرود حافظ
که شنید این ره دلسوز که فریاد نکرد

You left, but to the heart you had stolen no hint made,
Did not recall the friend of the stay, nor on the journey made.

Either it was my misfortune to have left love's way,
Or else you simply did not pass along Tariqat's way[1].

I said, 'Maybe my crying will make your heart soften,
But rain on hard stone does not make any impression.

Grief has broken my heart, both 'wing and feather',
But my head is like a frenzied bird, trapped, in being a lover.

Everyone, upon seeing your face in my eye, kissed it,
My eye and what was seen, was not unappreciated was it!

Like the candle I stand consuming my life for you,
The morning breeze did not pass by, and nor did you.

O Hafiz, how sweet and heart affecting must be your story,
For the pleasure it gives, who is there that does not try to keep it safely.

*(W-C 130) The radif is "Made not".*
  1 *"...Tariqat's way..." See commentary to (W-C 28) above.*

Delbar berafto delshodegaan raa khabar nakard
Yaade harife shahr o rafighe safar nakard

دلبر برفت و دلشدگان را خبر نکرد
یاد حریف شهر و رفیق سفر نکرد

Yaa bakhte man tarighe morovvat foroo gozaasht
Yaa ou be shaah raahe tarighat gozar nakard

یا بخت من طریق مرّوت فروگذاشت
یا او به شاهراه طریقت گذر نکرد

Man istaade taa konamash jaan fadaa cho sha-m
Ou khod gozar be maa cho nasime sahar nakard

من ایستاده تا کنمش جان فدا چو شمع
او خود گذر به ما چو نسیم سحر نکرد

Goftam magar be gerye delash mehrabaan konam
Dar naghshe sang ghatreye baaraan asar nakard

گفتم مگر به گریه دلش مهربان کنم
درنقش سنگ قطره باران اثر نکرد

Del raa agar che baalo par az gham shekaste shod
Sovdaaye daame aasheghi az sar be dar nakard

دل را اگرچه بال و پر از غم شکسته شد
سودای دام عاشقی از سر به درنکرد

Harkas ke did rooye to boosid chashme man
Kaari ke kard dideye maa bi nazar nakard

هر کس که دید روی تو بوسید چشم من
کاری که کرد دیده ما بی نظر نکرد

I pressed my face into the beloved's path but that one didn't come by,
A hundred kindnesses I sought, but got no glance from that one's eye.

Rancour in that heart was unaffected by many a tear,
For on hard stone the raindrop made no impression I fear.

May the good Lord keep from harm this bold young charmer,
Who is heedless of arrows in the sighs of quiet ones in the corner.

Last night both fish and fowl my sobs kept from sleeping,
But that saucy eyed one's head from the pillow was not stirring.

Like a consumed candle at the feet of that beloved I desired to die,
But, unlike the morning breeze that beloved was not passing by.

O beloved! How can anyone so narrow and so hard hearted be?
They would not shield themselves from your blade's injury?

In the gathering, split the tongue of the reed pen of Hafiz,
He did not speak of secrets, unless his head was no more his[1].

*(W-C 131) The radif is "Made not".*
  *"...his head was no more his..." In other words unless he was directly inspired.*

Roo bar rahash nahaadamo bar man gozar nakard

Sad lotf chashm daashtam ou yek nazar nakard

رو بر رهش نهادم و بر من گذر نکرد

صد لطف چشم داشتم او یک نظر نکرد

Seile sereshke maa ze delash kin bedar nabord

Dar sange khaare ghatreye baaraan asar nakard

سیل سرشک ما ز دلش کین بدرنبرد

در سنگ خاره قطره باران اثر نکرد

Yaa rab to in javaane delaavar negaah daar

Kaz tire aahe gooshe neshinaan hazar nakard

یا رب تو این جوان دلاور نگاه دار

کز تیر آه گوشه نشینان حذر نکرد

Mahiyyo morgh doosh nakhoft az faghaane man

Vaan shookh dide bin ke sar az khaab bar nakard

ماهیّ و مرغ دوش نخفت از فغان من

وان شوخ دیده بین که سر از خواب برنکرد

Mikhaastam ke miramash andar ghadam cho sham

Ou khod gozar be maa cho nasime sahar nakard

می‌خواستم که میرمش اندر قدم چو شمع

او خود گذر به ما چو نسیم سحر نکرد

Jaanaa kodaam sang dele bi kefaayat ast

Koo pishe zakhme tighe to jaan raa separ nakard

جانا کدام سنگدل بی‌کفایت است

کاو پیش زخم تیغ تو جان را سپر نکرد

Kelke zabaan keshideye Hafez dar anjoman

Baa kas nagoft raaze to taa tarke sar nakard

کلک زبان کشیده حافظ در انجمن

با کس نگفت راز تو تا ترک سر نکرد

Those who scold from the pulpit and prayer arch, so grand they are,
In their private quarters engaged quite differently they are.

My question is, why, when from the pulpit the elders speaking are,
They demand repentance and yet not repenting themselves they are?

One guesses, belief in the Day of Judgement from them must be far,
Because in the Just Judge's name into fraud and deceit they are.

I am the slave of that Spiritual Guide whose Dervishes always are,
Putting dust on the head of worldly wealth, so free they are.

O Lord! Make it that these nouveau riche riding their own asses are,
Because of having a Turkish slave and an ass, so arrogant they are.

O angel recite the rosary when at the door of love's tavern you are,
For inside, engaged in making dough from Adam's clay, they are.

Countless lovers, by your infinite beauty, destroyed they are,
Countless others, from non-existence, coming for love's sake are.

Beggar at the monastery get up! In the Magian's place they are,
Making hearts strong! Giving the thirsty a drink they are.

Empty your house if to be the King's abode your wishes are,
The lustful making heart and soul a home for soldiers are.

At dawn in the heavens a great roar arose! Wisdom's words are:-
"Those holy songsters, it seems learning Hafiz's ghazals they are."

*(W-C 132) The radif is "Make".*

Vaaezaan kin jelve dar mehraabo mambar mikonand
Chon be khalvat miravand aan kaare digar mikonand
واعظان کاین جلوه در محراب و منبر می کنند
چون به خلوت می روند آن کار دیگر می کنند

Moshkeli daaram ze daaneshmande majles baaz pors
Tovbe farmaayaan cheraa khod tovbe kamtar mikonand
مشکلی دارم ز دانشمند مجلس باز پرس
توبه فرمایان چرا خود توبه کمتر می کنند

Gooeeyaa baavar nemidaarand rooze daavari
Kin hame ghalbo daghal dar kaare daavar mikonand
گوئیا باور نمی‌دارند روز داوری
کاین همه قلب و دغل در کار داور می کنند

Bandeye pire kharaabaatam ke darvishaane ou
Ganj raa az bi niyaazi khaak bar sar mikonand
بنده پیر خراباتم که درویشان او
گنج را از بی نیازی خاک بر سر می کنند

Yaa rab in nov dovlataan raa baa khare khod shaan neshaan
Kin hame naaz az gholaame torko astar mikonand
یا رب این نودولتان را با خر خودشان نشان
کاین همه ناز از غلام ترک و استر می کنند

Bar dare meikhaaneye eshgh ey malak tasbih gooy
Kandar aanjaa tinate aadam mokhammar mikonand
بر در میخانه عشق ای ملک تسبیح گوی
کاندر آنجا طینت آدم مخمّر می کنند

Hosne bi paayaane ou chandaan ke aashegh mikoshad
Zomre ee digar be eshgh az gheib sar bar mikonand
حسن بی‌پایان او چندان که عاشق می کشد
زمره ای دیگر به عشق از غیب سر بر می کنند

Ey gedaaye khaaneghah barjah ke dar deire moghaan
Midahand aabiyyo  delhaa raa tavaan gar mikonand
ای گدای خانقه برجه که در دیر مغان
می‌دهند آبی و دل‌ها را توانگر می کنند

Khaane khaali kon delaa taa manzele soltaan shavad
Kin havas naakaan delo jaan jaaye lashkar mikonand
خانه خالی کن دلا تا منزل سلطان شود
کاین هوسناکان دل و جان جای لشکر می کنند

Vaghte sobh az arsh miaamad khorooshi aghl goft
Ghodsiaan gooee ke shere Hafez az bar mikonand
وقت صبح از عرش می‌آمد خروشی عقل گفت
قدسیان گوئی که شعر حافظ از بر می کنند

Do you know what the Harp and Lyre are saying, really?
"Drink wine, but to be accepted, try to do so secretly."

They say; "Dont speak of, or hear from others, love's mystery."
What they speak glibly about is a story full of difficulty.

From love and the lover they withhold honour and dignity,
The elders they disapprove of, the young they scold openly.

What they give to us outside the door are deceptions only.
Let us see within the veil what they practice deceitfully.

They cost the Pir[1] of the Magians, time and trouble truly,
See what a nuisance these followers are to the Pir, actually.

One can buy a hundred honours with half a glance only,
The beautiful ones do not care to take this opportunity.

Union with the beloved from effort was sought by one party,
But another thought that reliance on fate they needed only.

Better not rely at all on Time's constancy, to put it briefly;
This world is only a workshop for change, to say truly.

Drink wine! For preacher, teacher, lawyer, and Hafiz actually,
All practise fraud, if you look closely enough, and see clearly.


*(W-C 133) The radif is "Make".*
   [1] *"...Pir..." See the glossary in this volume.*

Daani ke chango ood che taghrir mikonand
Penhaan khorid baade ke takfir mikonand

دانی که چنگ و عود چه تقریر می‌کنند
پنهان خورید باده که تکفیر می‌کنند

Gooyand ramze eshgh magooeedo mashnavid
Moshkel hekaayatist ke taghrir mikonand

گویند رمز عشق مگوئید و مشنوید
مشکل حکایتیست که تقریر می‌کنند

Naamoose eshgho rovnaghe oshaagh mibarand
Man-e javaano sarzaneshe pir mikonand

ناموس عشق و رونق عشّاق می‌برند
منع جوان و سرزنش پیر می‌کنند

Maa az boroone dar shode maghroore sad farib
Taa khod daroone parde che tadbir mikonand

ما از برون در شده مغرور صد فریب
تا خود درون پرده چه تدبیر می‌کنند

Tashvishe vaghte pire moghaan midahand baaz
In saalekaan negar ke che ba pir mikonand

تشویش وقت پیر مغان می‌دهند باز
این سالکان نگر که چه با پیر می‌کنند

Sad aabe roo be nim nazar mitavaan kharid
Khoobaan dar in moaamele tagh sir mikonand

صد آب رو به نیم نظر می‌توان خرید
خوبان درین معامله تقصیر می‌کنند

Ghovmi be jeddo jahd nahaadand vasle doost
Ghovmi degar havaale be taghdir mikonand

قومی به جدّ و جهد نهادند وصل دوست
قومی دگر حواله به تقدیر می‌کنند

Fel jomle etemaad makon bar sabaate dahr
Kin kaar khaaneist ke taghyir mikonand

فی الجمله اعتماد مکن بر ثبات دهر
کاین کارخانه‌ایست که تغییر می‌کنند

Mey deh ke sheikho Hafezo moftiyyo mohtaseb
Chon nik bengari hame tazvir mikonand

می ده که شیخ وحافظ ومفتیّ ومحتسب
چون نیک بنگری همه تزویر می‌کنند

Those masters, whose glances, for our dust, are an alchemy,
Perhaps from the corner of the eye, towards us they will see?

Best hide my pain from those who claim to be doctors, falsely,
Perhaps from the hidden treasure house they will give remedy.

Since the veil of the face that beloved one is not removing,
Why are there so many myths and such vain imagining?

Our final ease is not in the hand of profligacy, nor austerity,
It is best to abandon hope from these and seek Divine remedy.

In love's great auction without Divine Knowledge[1] do not be,
From the friend a bargain can be had by those who can see.

Drink wine! For in the veil a hundred crimes strangers are committing,
Are better than one devotion made with hypocritical pretending.

That shirt, which to me the scent of beloved Yusuf is giving,
I fear that those proud brothers intend to be tearing[2].

Within the veil so many kinds of disturbances are happening,
Let's see, when the curtain is drawn back, what it's concealing.

Do not wonder if the stone, on hearing this story, is moaning,
For those who are heart owners such a beautiful tale are telling.

O Hafiz, union with the beloved is not long enduring!
Kings very rarely their attention to a beggar are giving.

*(W-C 134) The radif is "Make".*
[1] *"...Divine Knowledge..." Knowledge of the spiritual realities gained by direct perception and not by conventional learning. The Sufis say Hazrat Ali is the gateway to such a kind of knowledge.*
[2] *This verse refers to the story of Prophet Yusuf (Joseph) and his envious brothers who pretended he had been eaten by a wolf and presented his shirt as evidence to his father.*

Aanaan ke khaak raa be nazar kimiyaa konand
Ayaa bovad ke goosheye chashmi be maa konand

آنان که خاک را به نظر کیمیا کنند
آیا بود که گوشه چشمی به ما کنند

Dardam nahofte beh ze tabibaane moddaee
Baashad ke az khazaaneye gheibash davaa konand

دردم نهفته به ز طبیبان مدّعی
باشد که از خزانه غیبش دوا کنند

Mashooghe chon neghaab ze rokh bar nemikeshad
Harkas hekaayati be tasavvor cheraa konand

معشوقه چون نقاب ز رخ بر نمی کشد
هر کس حکایتی به تصوّر چرا کنند

Chon hosne aaghebat na be rendiyyo zaahedist
Aan beh ke kaare khod be enaayat rahaa konand

چون حسن عاقبت نه به رندئ و زاهدیست
آن به که کار خود به عنایت رها کنند

Bi marefat mabash ke dar man yazide eshgh
Ahle nazar moaamele baa aashenaa konand

بی معرفت مباش که در من یزید عشق
اهل نظر معامله با آشنا کنند

Mey khor ke sad gonaah ze aghyaar dar hejaab
Behtar ze taa-ati ke be rooyo riyaa konand

می خور که صد گناه ز اغیاردرحجاب
بهتر ز طاعتی که به روی و ریا کنند

Piraahani ke aayad az ou booye yoosofam
Tarsam baraadaraane ghayoorash ghabaa konand

پیراهنی که آید از او بوی یوسفم
ترسم برادران غیورش قبا کنند

Haali daroone parde basi fetneh miravad
Taa aan zamaan ke pardeh bar oftad chehaa konand

حالی درون پرده بسی فتنه می رود
تا آن زمان که پرده برافتد چها کنند

Gar sang az in hadis benaalad ajab madaar
Saahebdelaan hekaayate del khosh adaa konand

گرسنگ از این حدیث بنالد عجب مدار
صاحبدلان حکایت دل خوش ادا کنند

Hafez davaame vasl moyassar nemishavad
Shaahaan kam eltefaat be haale gedaa konand

حافظ دوام وصل میسّر نمی شود
شاهان کم التفات به حال گدا کنند

If those lovely heart-stealers this way continue to be,
A breach in the piety preacher's faith there will be.

When, from the stalk, that narcissus flowering we see,
A vase for it, the eye of the rosy-cheeked ones will be.

When the start of Sama[2] by our beloved master we see,
Hand-waving, in glee, dwellers in the ninth heaven will be.

Whilst you have cypress-stature, youth, hit the ball firmly;
Before time causes that stature, curved like a chaugan[2] to be.

Without control over their own head, lovers must be,
They obey the beloved, whatever the command may be.

Blood-soaked my eye's pupil became, you can easily see,
Their tyranny against man! Where else like this can it be.

Barely a drop in my eye their tales appear to be,
Those stories of that great flood[3] do not impress me.

When is your cheek's 'Eid of Sacrifice'?[4] So that lovers may be,
Sacrificed, life and soul, and faithful they will be shown to be.

Mystery knowing hearts, though in grief, still they remain happy,
For in the crucible of separation, cause for much joy there can be.

Hafiz! From the midnight sigh don't withdraw your head swiftly,
So that the heart's mirror, morning-bright they can make it to be.

---

**(W-C 135) The radif is "Make".**

[1] *"...Sama..." See glossary in this volume. Hand waving and 'dancing' is part of the activity associated with the music concerts that facilitate Sama.*

[2] *"...chaugan..." A kind of polo stick having a curved receptacle at one end in which the ball can be caught.*

[3] *"...great flood..." This refers to the flood of Noah.*

[4] *"...the Eid of sacrifice." This refers to the festival at the end of the Hajj pilgrimage. It is associated with the sacrifice of an animal as a substitute for Prophet Ibrahim sacrificing his son.*

Shaahedaan gar delbari zin saan konand
Zaahedaan raa rekhne dar imaan konand

شاهدان گر دلبری زین سان کنند
زاهدان را رخنه در ایمان کنند

Har kojaa aan shaakhe narges besh kofad
Gol rokhaanash dide nargesdaan konand

هر کجا آن شاخ نرگس بشکفد
گلرخانش دیده نرگسدان کنند

Yaare maa chon saazad aaghaaze samaa
Ghod siyaan bar arsh dast afshaan konand

یار ما چون سازد آغاز سماع
قدسیان بر عرش دست افشان کنند

Ey javaane sarv ghad gooee bezan
Pish az aan kaz ghaamatat chov gaan konand

ای جوان سروقد گویی بزن
پیش از آن کز قامتت چوگان کنند

Aasheghaan raa bar sare khod hokm nist
Harche farmaane to baashad aan konand

عاشقان را بر سر خود حکم نیست
هر چه فرمان تو باشد آن کنند

Mardome chashmam be khoon aagheshte shod
Dar kojaa in zolm bar ensaan konand

مردم چشمم به خون آغشته شد
در کجا این ظلم بر انسان کنند

Pishe chashmam kamtar ast az ghatrei
Aan hekaayat haa ke az toofaan konand

پیش چشمم کمتر است از قطره‌ای
آن حکایت‌ها که از طوفان کنند

Eide rokhsaare to koo taa aasheghaan
Dar vafaayat jaane khod ghorbaan konand

عید رخسار تو کو تا عاشقان
در وفایت جان خود قربان کنند

Khosh baraa baa ghosse ey del kahle raaz
Eyshe khod dar booteye hejraan konand

خوش برآ با غصّه‌ای دل کاهل راز
عیش خود در بوته هجران کنند

Sar makesh Hafez ze aahe nim shab
Taa cho sobhat aayeney rakhshaan konand

سر مکش حافظ ز آه نیم شب
تا چو صبحت آینه رخشان کنند

I said, "When will your mouth and your lip make me prosper?"[1]
You said, "Chashm[2], whatever you ask for, they will offer."

I said "Your sweet lip, from Egypt, tribute is demanding."
You said, "In this affair any less would be loss incurring."

I said, "To the dot of your mouth who is it that is travelling?"
You said, "Only to one knowing fine points this they are telling."

I said "Do not worship idols. Sit with the folk of Eternity."
You said, "On love's street, both this and that they do we see."

I said, "The desire for the tavern, the heart's grief is easing."
You said, "Happy are those who even one heart is pleasing."

I said, "Not part of religion's rituals is wine and khirqa.[3]"
You said, "These are the practises of the Magian's order."

I said, "From the sweet ruby lips how does the elder profit?"
You said, "From one sweet kiss renewed youth is the benefit."

I said, "When does the Khwaja retire to the pleasure chamber?"
You said, "At the time when Jupiter and the Moon lie together."

I said, "Prayer for that one's welfare in the early morning I proffer."
You said, "This prayer angels of the seventh heaven offer."

---

**(W-C 136) The radif is "Make".**
  [1] Here there is possibly a dialogue with the minister of one of Hafiz's royal patrons, whose name was
  Qavamuddin Muhammed. He is referred to here as Khwaja (elder). Possibly Hafiz is referring to a
  forthcoming marriage of the Khwaja (see Avery pp. 253). As ever Hafiz finds the eternal in the transitory.
  . [2] "...Chashm..." This means literally "on my eye"; meaning, 'certainly, sure, ok'.
  [3] "...Khirqa..." This refers to a patched robe worn by Sufis.

Gotam keyam dahaano labat kaamraan konand
Goftaa be chashm harche to gooee chonaan konand

گفتم کی‌ام دهان و لبت کامران کنند
گفتا به چشم هر چه تو گوئی چنان کنند

Goftam kharaaje mesr talab mikonad labat
Goftaa dar in moaamele kamtar ziyaan konand

گفتم خراج مصر طلب می‌کند لبت
گفتا درین معامله کمتر زیان کنند

Goftam be noghteye dahanat khod ke bord raah
Goft in hekaayatist ke baa nokte daan konand

گفتم به نقطه دهنت خود که برد راه
گفت این حکایتیست که با نکته دان کنند

Goftam sanam parast masho baa samad neshin
Goftaa be kooye eshgh hamino hamaan konand

گفتم صنم پرست مشو با صمد نشین
گفتا به کوی عشق هم این و هم آن کنند

Goftam havaaye meikade gham mibarad ze del
Goftaa khosh aan kasaan ke deli shaad maan konand

گفتم هوای میکده غم می‌برد ز دل
گفتا خوش آن کسان که دلی شادمان کنند

Goftam sharaabo kherghe na aaeene mazhab ast
Goft in amal be maz habe pire moghaan konand

گفتم شراب و خرقه نه آیین مذهبست
گفت این عمل به مذهب پیر مغان کنند

Goftam ze la-le noosh labaan pir raa che sood
Goftaa be booseye shekarinash javaan konand

گفتم ز لعل نوش لبان پیر را چه سود
گفتا به بوسه شکرینش جوان کنند

Goftam ke khaaje key be sare hejle miravad
Goft aan zamaan ke moshtariyo mah gheraan konand

گفتم که خواجه کی به سر حجله می‌رود
گفت آن زمان که مشتری و مه قران کنند

Goftam doaaye dovlate ou verde Hafez ast
Goft in doaa malaaeke haft aasemaan konand

گفتم دعای دولت او ورد حافظ است
گفت این دعا ملایک هفت آسمان کنند

Crowned-heads are slaves of your intoxicated eyes,
Drunk on your ruby lip's wine, even the sober and wise.

The Saba wind[1] gave news of you; the water of my tears, of me,
Otherwise keeping their secret, the lover and beloved would be.

When you pass by, under your lovely hair-braids, see,
On right and left how they long for you restlessly.

Like the wind, blow across the violet bed and so see,
From the tyranny of your hair how they suffer grievously.

O you who hope to see God, go! For paradise awaits us,
For deserving of Mercy you see are the sinners, like us.

Your rose cheek is wooed in song by many another,
Not just me; on every side a thousand bulbuls gather.

O Khizr thy blessed feet let my hand hold on to,
For on foot I go, whilst companions ride, they do.

Go to the tavern and with red wine make your cheeks glow,
To the prayer-place where dark deed's doers still reside dont go.

O from the curling locks of your hair release not Hafiz,
For being caught in them is felicity, and true freedom it is!

*(W-C 137) The radif is "Are".*
  [1] *"...Saba wind..." See the glossary in this volume.*

Gholaame nargese maste to taaj daaraanand

Kharaabe baadeye la-le to hooshyaaraanand

غلام نرگس مست تو تاجدارانند

خراب باده لعل تو هوشیارانند

To raa sabaavo maraa aabe dide shod ghammaz

Vagarna aashegho mashoogh raaz daaraanand

تو را صبا و مرا آب دیده شد غمّاز

وگر نه عاشق و معشوق رازدارانند

Ze zire zolfe dotaa chon gozar koni bengar

Ke az yamino yasaarat che bigharaaraanand

ز زیر زلف دوتا چون گذر کنی بنگر

که از یمین و یسارت چه بیقرارانند

Gozaar kon cho sabaa bar banafshe zaaro bebin

Ke az tataavole zolfat che soog vaaraanand

گذار کن چو صبا بر بنفشه زار و ببین

که از تطاول زلفت چه سوگوارانند

Nasibe maast behesht ey khodaa shenaas boro

Ke mostahaghe keraamat gonaah kaaraanand

نصیب ماست بهشت ای خداشناس برو

که مستحقّ کرامت گناهکارانند

Na man bar aan gole aarez ghazal soraayamo bas

Ke andalibe to az har taraf hezaaraanand

نه من بر آن گل عارض غزل سرایم و بس

که عندلیب تو از هر طرف هزارانند

To dastgir sho ey khezre pey khojaste ke man

Piyaade miravamo hamrahaan savaaraanand

تو دستگیرشوای خضری خجسته که من

پیاده می‌روم و همرهان سوارانند

Biyaa be meikadevo chehre arghavaani kon

Maro be sovme-e kaanjaa siyaah kaaraanand

بیا به میکده و چهره ارغوانی کن

مرو به صومعه کانجا سیاه کارانند

Khalaase Hafez az aan zolfe taab daar mabaad

Ke bastegaane kamande to rastegaaraanand

خلاص حافظ از آن زلف تابدار مباد

که بستگان کمند تو رستگارانند

When those jasmine-scented ones settle, so does the dust of grieving,
Those Pari-faced ones[1] can rob us of patience if they are striving.

With the saddle-strap of tyranny our hearts tightly they are binding,
From the ambergris of hair, both scent and souls they're scattering.

Pomegranate-like rubies from my eye rains, when they're laughing,
Hidden mysteries in my face they read, when at me they're looking.

In a lifetime they sit only briefly with us, then are quickly rising,
But they plant the seedling of desire in our heart, when they're rising.

If in the corner of the recluse's eyes, tears like pearls they're finding;
From love of dawn-riser's they turn not away, if they are knowing.

Like Mansur[2] on the gallows, from extreme need to the gallows they go,
When they summon Hafiz to this high place he is simply told to go.

When to Presence desire brings their plea, disdainfully they are acting,[3]
To this high place they call him only when Hafiz's life they are ending.

**(W-C 138)**
[1] *"...Pari-faced..." See glossary in this volume.*
[2] *"...Mansur..." Mansur al-Hallaj. See glossary.*
[3] *These lines are problematic – the last line could read - "Because if they are looking for a cure, in pain they are remaining."*

Saman booyaan ghobaare gham cho benshinand ben shaanand

سمن بویان غبار غم چو بنشینند بنشانند

Pari rooyaan gharaare del cho bes tizand bes taanand

پری رویان قرار دل چو بستیزند بستانند

Be fetraake jafaa delhaa cho bar bandand bar bandand

به فتراک جفا دلها چو بربندند بربندند

Ze zolfe ambarin jaanhaa cho bog shaayand bef shaanand

ز زلف عنبرین جانها چو بگشایند بفشانند

Ze chashmam la-le rommaani cho mikhandand mibaarand

ز چشمم لعل رمّانی چو می‌خندند می‌بارند

Ze rooyam raaze penhaani cho mibinand mikhaanand

ز رویم راز پنهانی چو می‌بینند می‌خوانند

Be omri yek nafas baa maa cho ben shinand bar khizand

به عمری یک نفس با ما چو بنشینند برخیزند

Nahaale shovgh dar khaater cho bar khizand ben shaanand

نهال شوق در خاطر چو برخیزند بنشانند

Sereshke gooshe giraan raa cho dar yaaband dor yaaband

سرشک گوشه گیران را چو دریابند در یابند

Rokhe mehr az sahar khizaan nagardaanand agar daanand

رخ مهر از سحرخیزان نگردانند اگر دانند

Cho Mansoor az moraad aanaan ke bar daarand bar daarand

چو منصور از مراد آنان که بردارند بردارند

Bedin dargaah Hafez raa cho mi khaanand mi raanand

بدین درگاه حافظ را چو می‌خوانند می‌رانند

Dar in hazrat cho moshtaaghaan niyaaz aarand naaz aarand

در این حضرت چو مشتاقان نیاز آرند نازآرند

Ke ba in dard agar dar bande dar maanand dar maanand

که با این درد اگر در بند درمانند در مانند

Unmixed pure wine and a goodly Saki, are two traps on the way,
To escape this noose, even wise ones of the world, find no way.

I am a Rend, and drunken lover whose book is blackened; still,
That the city's friends are pure; give God many thanks, I will.

Place no foot on the tavern floor without respect and care,
Even the door-keepers are the king's companions in there.

Tyranny is not the mode of the Dervish[1] or traveller on the Way,
Bring wine! These harsh travellers are not men of the Way.

Do not hold in contempt the beggars found in love's way,
These beltless kings; rulers whose crowns they don't display.

Do not act in such a way that love's glory falls apart,
With servants running off and slaves leaping up to depart.

Slave of the determination of one-coloured dreg-drinkers I am,
Not one of that blue-garmented[2] but black-hearted crowd I am.

Beware! When the wind of self-dependence puffs you up this way,
For a thousand pious harvests, a grain you won't get in pay.

Hafiz, the rank of love is high, so show real resolution,
For lovers don't accept those with no determination.


*(W-C 139)*
   [1] *"...Dervish..." See glossary in this volume.*
   [2] *"...blue-garmented..." Dress associated with a sect of Sufis.*

Sharaabe bi ghasho saaghiyye khosh do daame rahand
Ke zirakaane jahaan az kamandeshaan narahand

شراب بی‌غش و ساقیّ خوش دو دام رهند
که زیرکان جهان از کمندشان نرهند

Man ar che aasheghamo rendo masto naame siaah
Hezaar shokr ke yaaraane shahr bi gonahand

من ار چه عاشقم و رند و مست و نامه سیاه
هزار شکر که یاران شهر بی گنهند

Ghadam maneh be kharaabaat joz be sharte adab
Ke saakenaane darash mahramaane paad shahand

قدم منه به خرابات جز به شرط ادب
که ساکنان درش محرمان پادشهند

Jafaa na pisheye darvishi asto raah rovi
Biyaar baade ke in saalekaan na marde rahand

جفا نه پیشه درویشیست و راهروی
بیار باده که این سالکان نه مرد رهند

Mabin haghir gedaayaane eshgh raa kin ghovm
Shahaane bi kamaro khosrovaane bi kolahand

مبین حقیر گدایان عشق را کاین قوم
شهان بی کمر و خسروان بی کلهند

Makon ke kovkabeye delbari shekaste shaved
Cho bandegaan begorizando chaakeraan bejahand

مکن که کوکبه دلبری شکسته شود
چو بندگان بگریزند و چاکران بجهند

Gholaame hemmate dordi keshaane yek rangam
Na aan gorooh ke azragh lebaaso del siyahand

غلام همّت دردی کشان یکرنگم
نه آن گروه که ازرق لباس و دل سیهند

Behoosh baash ke hengaame baade esteghnaa
Hezaar kharmane taa-at be nim jov nanahand

بهوش باش که هنگام باد استغنا
هزار خرمن طاعت به نیم جو ننهند

Jenaabe eshgh boland ast hemmati Hafez
Ke aasheghaan rahe bi hemmataan be khod nadahand

جناب عشق بلند است همّتی حافظ
که عاشقان ره بی‌همّتان به خود ندهند

I know not what the intoxication is that to us, its face now shows,
Who the wine-bearer was, or, from where came the wine he brought.

This knowing musician, what is the mystery he knows,
That into the midst of a ghazal talk of the friend he brought.

Take the wine-cup in hand and go towards the meadows,
You will hear the sweet song, the sweet song-bird has brought.

A joyous welcome there is here for both rose and rambling rose,
The violet - happiness and beauty; the lily - purity, has brought.

The hoopoe of Solomon[1] is the breeze that good news blows,
Just as from the garden of Saba, joyful tidings were brought.

O heart, fortune closed like a rosebud may be, but who knows,
For with the dawn came a breeze that an opening up brought.

The saucy smile of the Saki is the only remedy our feeble heart knows;
Be prepared, the doctor has come and the treatment has brought.

O elder worry not if this one to the Magian's Pir as disciple goes,
What you promised one day, to me, here and now he has brought.

I boast of the narrow eyes of the warrior who one purpose shows;
And on poor me, owning but one coat, an attack has brought.

Now the heavens submit, and as Hafiz wishes, so everything goes,
Because to your fortunate door his need for protection he brought.

*(W-C 140) The radif is "brought".*
    [1] *"...The hoopoe of Solomon..." See the glossary in this volume.*

Che masti yast nadaanam ke rah be maa aavard
Ke bood saaghiyo in baade az kojaa aavard
چه مستی است ندانم که ره به ما آورد
که بود ساقی و این باده از کجا آورد

Che raah mizanad in motrebe maghaam shenaas
Ke dar miyaane ghazal ghovle aashnaa aavard
چه راه می زند این مطرب مقام شناس
که در میان غزل قول آشنا آورد

To niz baade be chang aaro raahe sahraa gir
Ke morghe naghme saraa saaze khosh navaa aavard
تو نیز باده به چنگ آر و راه صحرا گیر
که مرغ نغمه سرا ساز خوش نوا آورد

Residane golo nasrin be kheiro khoobi baad
Banafshe shado gash aamad saman safaa aavard
رسیدن گل و نسرین به خیر و خوبی باد
بنفشه شاد و گش آمد سمن صفا آورد

Sabaa be khosh khabari hod hode soleimaan ast
Ke moj deye tarab az golshane sabaa aavard
صبا به خوش خبری هدهد سلیمان است
که مژده طرب از گلشن سبا آورد

Delaa cho ghonche shekaayat ze kaare baste makon
Ke baade sobh nasime gereh goshaa aavard
دلا چو غنچه شکایت ز کار بسته مکن
که باد صبح نسیم گره گشا آورد

Alaaje za-fe dele maa kereshmeye saaghist
Bar aar sar ke tabib aamado davaa aavard
علاج ضعف دل ما کرشمه ساقیست
برآر سر که طبیب آمد و دوا آورد

Moride pire moghaanam ze man maranj ey sheikh
Cheraa ke va-de to kardiyyo ou be jaa aavard
مرید پیر مغانم ز من مرنج ای شیخ
چرا که وعده تو کردیّ و او به جا آورد

Be tang chashmiye aan torke lashkari naazam
Ke hamle bar mane darvishe yek ghabaa aavard
به تنگ چشمی آن ترک لشکری نازم
که حمله بر من درویش یک قبا آورد

Falak gholaamiye Hafez konoon be to-v konad
Ke eltejaa be dare dovlate shomaa aavard
فلک غلامی حافظ کنون به طوع کند
که التجا به در دولت شما آورد

You haven't written for a long time telling us how you do,
I need someone I can trust so I can get a message to you.

We cannot possibly reach up to that high state anyhow,
Unless you kindly help us to move forward somehow.

From the jug the glass is filled, and the rose is unveiling,
So take this chance for the heart's ease and wine drinking.

Rose conserved with sugar, our sick heart won't cure,
Kisses, mixed with abusive swearing, is more sure.

O pietist to be safe flee the circle of profligacy,
Or risk ruin by consorting with those of infamy.

You have spoken of the faults of wine; tell its virtue too,
Don't deny wisdom for the sake of the hearts of a few.

Oh you beggars at the tavern, God alone is your Friend,
Look for no favours then that a gang of 'animals' might send.

To his dregs-drinkers, spoke the tavern keeper, very wisely -
"To immature minds, of the heart's states, no talk let there be."

Burning desire for your shining love-lit face consumed Hafiz,
In your satisfied state look kindly at one who unfulfilled is.


*(W-C 141) The radif is "some time" or variants such as "some message", "some cups" & etc.*

Hasbe haali naneveshtiyyo shod ayyaami chand
Mahrami koo ke ferestam be to peighaami chand

حسب حالی ننوشتیّ و شد ایّامی چند
محرمی کو که فرستم به تو پیغامی چند

Maa be aan maghsade alaa natavaanim rasid
Ham magar pish nahad lotfe shomaa gaami chand

ما به آن مقصد اعلی نتوانیم رسید
هم مگر پیش نهد لطف شما گامی چند

Chon mey az khom be saboo rafto gol afkand neghaab
Forsate eish negah daaro bezan jaami chand

چون می از خم به سبو رفت و گل افکند نقاب
فرصت عیش نگه دار و بزن جامی چند

Ghande aamikhte baa gol na alaaje dele mast
Boosei chand bar aamiz be doshnaami chand

قند آمیخته با گل نه علاج دل ماست
بوسه ای چند بر آمیز به دشنامی چند

Zaahed az koocheye rendaan be salaamat begozar
Taa kharaabat nakonad sohbate bad naami chand

زاهد از کوچه رندان به سلامت بگذر
تا خرابت نکند صحبت بدنامی چند

Eibe mey jomle cho gofti honarash niz begoo
Nafye hekmat makon az bahre dele aami chand

عیب می جمله چو گفتی هنرش نیز بگو
نفی حکمت مکن از بهر دل عامی چند

Ey gedaayaane kharaabaat khodaa yaare shomaast
Chashme en aam madaarid ze an aami chand

ای گدایان خرابات خدا یار شماست
چشم انعام مدارید ز انعامی چند

Pire meykhaane che khosh goft be dordi keshe khish
Ke magoo haale dele sookhte baa khaami chand

پیر میخانه چه خوش گفت به دردی کش خویش
که مگو حال دل سوخته با خامی چند

Hafez az shovghe rokhe mehr forooghe to besookht
Kaamgaaraa nazari kon sooye naakaami chand

حافظ از شوق رخ مهرفروغ تو بسوخت
کامگارا نظری کن سوی ناکامی چند

The whole world is not worth even a moment's sadness,[1]
For wine sell our worthless Dervish dress. Its value is less!

Wine-merchants won't take the prayer carpet for a cup of wine,
All that piety then,  and worth less than a single cup of wine!

My rival scolded me; urged me from this door to turn away;
So my head is not worth the doorstep's dust, you say!

Fear of assassination makes the Sultan's crown worthless,
The gorgeous hat is of no worth, if you become headless.

At first the profitable hardships of the ocean seemed easy to me,[1]
Error! Those many jewels were made worthless by a stormy sea.

Better conceal your face from those eager, longing eyes,
The joy of world conquest is not worth its armies' cries!

Better let the mean world pass by, and like Hafiz be content,
To be in debt to the miserly for one grain is not his intent.

*(W-C 142) The radif is "Is not worth"*
   [1] *This ghazal was written on the occasion Hafiz was due to set sail from Hormuz at the invitation of the King of an Indian state. Whilst the boat was still in the harbour a storm arose and Hafiz decided not to continue his journey. Hafiz knew well how to read the signs that Allah sends through natural events.*

Dami ba gham be sar bordan jahaan yek sar nemiarzad
Be mey befroosh dalghe maa kazin behtar nemiarzad

Be kuye meyforushanash be jaami bar nemigirand
Zehi sajjaadeye taghvaa ke yek saaghar nemiarzad

Raghibam sarzanesh haa kard kaz in baab rokh bartaab
Che oftaad in sare maa raa ke khaake dar nemiarzad

Shokuhe taaje soltaani ke bime jaan daroo darj ast
Kolaahi delkash ast ammaa be tarke sar nemiarzad

Bas aasaan minomud avval ghame daryaa be buye sood
Ghalat goftam ke in toofaan be sad govhar nemiarzad

To raa aan beh ke ruye khod ze moshtaaghaan bepushaani
Ke shadiyye jahaangiri ghame lashgar nemiarzad

Cho Hafiz dar ghanaat koosho az donyaaye doon bogzar
Ke yek jov mennate doonaan do sad man zar nemi arzad

دمی با غم به سر بردن جهان یکسر نمی‌ارزد
به می بفروش دلق ما کزین بهتر نمی‌ارزد

به کوی می فروشانش به جامی بر نمی‌گیرند
زهی سجّاده‌ی تقوا که یک ساغر نمی‌ارزد

رقیبم سرزنش‌ها کرد کز این باب رخ برتاب
چه افتاد این سر ما را که خاک در نمی‌ارزد

شکوه تاج سلطانی که بیم جان در او درج است
کلاهی دلکش است اما به ترک سر نمی‌ارزد

بس آسان می‌نمود اوّل غم دریا به بوی سود
غلط گفتم که این طوفان به صد گوهر نمی‌ارزد

ترا آن به که روی خود ز مشتاقان بپوشانی
که شادی‌ جهانگیری غم لشکر نمی‌ارزد

چو حافظ در قناعت کوش و از دنیای دون بگذر
که یک جو منّت دونان دو صد من زر نمی‌ارزد

My heart goes only to faces where the moon's beauty shines,[1]
In my heart is wiser counsel, but to follow this it never inclines.

Counsellor, for God's sake, talk of the line of down[2] of the Saki,
A more beautiful image than this in our mind there cannot be.

Secretly, I take the goblet of wine, though it looks like a book,
Strange if this hypocrisy does not one day ignite the book.

One day I will burn this false, gold-seeming, Dervish garment,
For it the wine-selling Pir will give not a single glass in payment.

Those whose play is purity find it in the wine, because,
In its ruby reflections only the picture of truth ever was.

The reveller's critic, who is really at war with God's decree,
Perhaps he takes no wine for he looks really miserable to me.

Laughter within tears; like the candle I am weeping,
But my fiery tongue does not light up this gathering.

If Alexander's mirror[3] should come at last into my hand,
Its refraction will in time ignite all, me too, understand.

What a drunken eye that happily took my heart for its prey,
For amongst the wild birds one cannot find a better prey!

We talk of our need, but the beloved nothing ever needed,
Heart, why try your charms, when the beloved is unaffected.

For God's sake, to this Dervish some kindnesses display;
He, who knows not any other door - nor any other way.

Why doesn't the King of Kings, for verse as sweet as this,
Not take, to be covered in gold from head to foot, our Hafiz.

**(W-C 143) The radif is "Takes not".**
  [1] "...where the moon's beauty shines..." As the moon is often associated with the holy Prophet here the implication can be that it refers to those persons whose faces reflect their love of him. One may also take it to mean the faces that shine with spiritual splendour.
  [2] "...the line of down..." See glossary in this volume.
  [3] "...Alexander's mirror..." See the glossary in this volume.

Delam joz mehre mah rooyaan tarighi bar nemigirad

دلم جز مهر مه‌رویان طریقی بر نمی‌گیرد

Ze har dar midaham pandash valikan dar nemigirad

ز هر در می‌دهم پندش ولیکن در نمی‌گیرد

Khodaa raa ey nasihat goo hadis az khatte saaghi goo

خدا را ای نصیحت‌گو حدیث از خطّ ساقی گو

Ke naghshi dar khiyaale maa az in khosh tar nemigirad

که نقشی در خیال ما ازین خوش‌تر نمی‌گیرد

Soraahi mikesham pen haano mardom daftar engaarand

صراحی می‌کشم پنهان و مردم دفتر انگارند

Ajab gar aatashe in zargh dar daftar nemigirad

عجب گر آتش این زرق در دفتر نمی‌گیرد

Man in dalghe mollama raa bekhaaham sookh tan roozi

من این دلق ملمّع را بخواهم سوختن روزی

Ke pire mey forooshaanash be jaami bar nemigirad

که پیر می فروشانش به جامی بر نمی‌گیرد

Az aan rooyast yaaraan raa safaahaa baa meye la-lat

از آن روی است یاران را صفاها با می لعلت

Ke gheir az raasti naghshi dar in jovhar nemigirad

که غیر از راستی نقشی درین جوهر نمی‌گیرد

Nasihat gooye rendaan raa ke baa hokme ghazaa jang ast

نصیحت‌گوی رندان را که با حکم قضا جنگ است

Delash bas tang mibinam magar saaghar nemigirad

دلش بس تنگ می‌بینم مگر ساغر نمی‌گیرد

Miyaane gereye mikhandam ke chon sha-m andar in majles

میان گریه می‌خندم که چون شمع اندرین مجلس

Zabaane aatashinam hast liken dar nemigirad

زبان آتشینم هست لیکن در نمی‌گیرد

Man aan aaeene raa roozi be dast aaram sekandar vaar

من آن آئینه را روزی به دست آرم سکندروار

Agar migirad in aatash zamaani var nemigirad

اگر می‌گیرد این آتش زمانی ور نمی‌گیرد

Che khosh seyde delam kardi benaazam chashme mastat raa

چه خوش صید دلم کردی بنازم چشم مست را

Ke kas morghaane vahshi raa az in khosh tar nemigirad

که کس مرغان وحشی را ازین خوش‌تر نمی‌گیرد

Sokhan dar ehtiaaje maavo esteghnaaye mashoogh ast

سخن در احتیاج ما و استغنای معشوق است

Che sood afsoon gari ey del cho dar delbar nemigirad

چه سود افسونگری ای دل چو در دلبر نمی‌گیرد

Khodaa raa rahmi ey monem ke darvishe sare kooyat

خدا را رحمی ای منعم که درویش سر کویت

Dari digar nemidaanad rahi digar nemigirad

دری دیگر نمی‌داند رهی دیگر نمی‌گیرد

Bedin shere tare shirin ze shaahan shah ajab daaram

بدین شعر تر شیرین ز شاهنشه عجب دارم

Ke sar taa paaye Hafez raa cheraa dar zar nemigirad

که سر تا پای حافظ را چرا در زر نمی‌گیرد

My idol's face, a rose, framed by hyacinth curls, seems to be,
A line in the Arghavan's blood the spring of that cheek seems to be.

O Lord! The sun of that face, hidden by the dust of that line is,
Give enduring life to that one whose beauty everlasting is.

When I became a lover I said, "The jewel I sought, has come to me,"
Little knowing how wild the waves in a blood-filled sea would be.

From that eye I cannot withdraw the soul. Whichever direction I go,
The eye corner I see waiting in ambush; arrow poised in the bow.

Don't exclude my eye from your heart-breaking cypress-like stature,
Plant it near the eye's spring, pleasing water springs up from there.

If you strap me to your saddle, for God's sake take your prey now,
In delay there are troubles for the earnest seeker - or loss anyhow.

When the beloved made a snare for the lovers by loosening the hair,
To the wind's gossip that one said – "O wind keeps secret this affair".

Bulbul[1], when the rose laughs in your face, avoid that cunning snare,
Don't rely on the rose, albeit the world's charms can be found there.

From fear of separation make me safe - if you have hope of this,
Say, "From the envious eye of ill-thinkers, in God, safety there is."

On dust sprinkle wine; see the state of the people of worldly fame,
A myriad tales of Jamshid and Kai Khusreau[2], that dust can claim.

O watchman of the gathering, for the sake of God, justice for me,
With others the beloved drank wine, but just a weight put on me.

What excuse to my fortune! That trouble-maker of the city,
Has killed Hafiz with bitterness, but in that mouth sugar one can see.

*(W-C 144) The radif is "Has".*
[1] *"...bulbul..." See the glossary in this volume.*
[2] *"...Jamshid and Kai Khusrau..." See glossary in this volume.*

Boti daaram ke gerde gol ze sombol saaye baan daarad

Bahaare aarezash khatti be khoone arghavaan daarad

Ghobaare khat bepooshaanid khorshide rokhash yaa rab

Baghaaye jaav-daanash deh ke hosne jaavdaan daarad

Cho aashegh mishodam goftam ke bordam govhare maghsood

Nadaanestam ke in daryaa che movje khoon feshaan daarad

Ze chashmat jaan nashaayad bord kaz har soo ke mibinam

Kamin az gooshei kardasto tir andar kamaan daarad

Ze sarve ghadde del jooyat makon mahroom chashmam raa

Bedin sar cheshmeash ben shaan ke khosh aabi ravaan daarad

Be fetraak ar hami bandi khodaa raa zood seidam kon

Ke aafat haast dar ta-khiro taaleb raa ziyaan daarad

Cho daame torre afshaanad ze garde khaatere oshaagh

Be ghammaaze sabaa gooyad ke raaze maa nahaan daarad

Cho dar rooyat bekhandad gol masho dar daamash ey bolbol

Ke bar gol etemaadi nist gar hosne jahaan daarad

Ze khovfe hejram imen kon agar ommide aan daari

Ke az chashme bad andishaan khodaayat dar amaan daarad

Biyafshaan jorei bar khaako haale ahle shovkat pors

Ke az jamshido key khosro faraavaan daastaan daarad

Khodaa raa daade man bestaan az ou ey shahneye majles

Ke mey baa digari khordasto baa man sar geraan daarad

Che ozre bakhte khod gooyam ke aan ayyare shahr aashoob

Be talkhi kosht Hafez raavo shekkar dar dahaan daarad

For the heart that shows inner secrets and has Jamshid's chalice,[1]
Over the temporary loss of a seal ring, a reason for grief there is?

Do not give the heart's treasure to down or mole of a beggarly one,
You should give it to the hand that knows its worth, a kingly one.

Not every tree can endure the onslaught of autumn's cruelty,
I am impressed by the determined cypress - foot planted so firmly.

The joyful season is here; let whoever has them place six coins thus,
Round the base of the goblet, like petals of the drunk narcissus.

Do not hold back gold but pay for the wine, like the rose;
For in Divine Reason a hundred grounds for suspicion arose.

My heart, that used to be proud of solitude, is now busy talking,
With the morning breeze, about the scent your hair is giving.

Who will give the heart's desire? There is no beloved so lovely,
As to combine both visual splendour and a generous tendency.

No one knows that Hidden Secret, so don't discuss it here,
The way into that sacred place, is known to what heart-seer?

What profit from the pocket of the patched robe of Hafiz?
We are seeking the Eternal, but he with his idol eternally is.

*(W-C 145) The radif is "Has".*
  [1] *"...Jamshid's chalice..." See glossary in this volume.*

Deli ke gheib nomaayasto jaame jam daarad
Ze khaatami ke dami gom shaved che gham daarad

دلی که غیب نمای است و جام جم دارد
ز خاتمی که دمی گم شود چه غم دارد

Be khatto khaale gedaayaan made khazineye del
Be daste shaah vashi deh ke mohtaram daarad

به خطّ و خال گدایان مده خزینه دل
به دست شاه وشی ده که محترم دارد

Na har derakht tahammol konad jafaaye khazaan
Gholaame hemmate sarvam ke in ghadam darad

نه هر درخت تحمّل کند جفای خزان
غلام همّت سروم که این قدم دارد

Resid movseme aan kaz tarab cho nargese mast
Nahad be paaye ghadah hark e shesh deram daarad

رسید موسم آن کز طرب چو نرگس مست
نهد به پای قدح هر که شش درم دارد

Zar az bahaaye mey aknoon cho gol darigh madaar
Ke aghle kol be sadat eib mottaham daarad

زر از بهای می اکنون چو گل دریغ مدار
که عقل کل به صدت عیب متّهم دارد

Delam ke laafe tajarrod zadi konoon sad shoghl
Be booye zolfe to baa baade sobhdam daarad

دلم که لاف تجرّد زدی کنون صد شغل
به بوی زلف تو با باد صبحدم دارد

Moraade del ze ke jooyam cho nist deldaari
Ke jelveye nazaro shiveye karam daarad

مراد دل ز که جویم چو نیست دلداری
که جلوه نظر و شیوه کرم دارد

Ze serre gheib kas aagaah nist ghesse makhaan
Kodaam mahrame del rah dar in haram daarad

ز سرّ غیب کس آگاه نیست قصّه مخوان
کدام محرم دل ره درین حرم دارد

Ze jeibe khergheye Hafez che tarf betvaan bast
Ke maa samad talabidimo ou sanam daarad

ز جیب خرقه حافظ چه طرف بتوان بست
که ما صمد طلبیدیم و او صنم دارد

Everyone who regards with due, deep respect, the true men,
God preserves them from calamities, every where and when.

If you desire that the beloved will always keep good faith with you,
Respectfully keep your end of the cord, so that loved one will too.

Except to the friend, I don't talk of the pain of the friend,
What the friend has to say is preserved only by the friend.

I would give gold, head, heart and soul, for that one gladly,
Who preserves the right of the company and pact of loyalty.

Breeze, if you should see my heart on the tip of that lock of hair,
It would be a kindness if you tell it to preserve its place there.

O heart live in such a way that should you lose your footing,
You will be preserved by an angel with both hands supplicating.

That one did not take our heart and for suffering had no consideration,
Saying, "What comes from the slaves hand is in God's observation.

Where is the dust blowing from your path, so for Hafiz it may be,
A keepsake, to preserve the breeze's work, in a fragrant memory?

*(W-C 146) The radif is "Preserves".*

Har aanke jaanebe ahle vafaa negah daarad

Khodaash dar hame haal az balaa negah daarad

هر آن که جانب اهل وفا نگه دارد

خداش در همه حال از بلا نگه دارد

Garat havaast ke mashoogh nagsalad peimaan

Negaah daar sare reshte taa negah daarad

گرت هواست که معشوق نگسلد پیمان

نگاه دار سر رشته تا نگه دارد

Ze dared doost nagooyam hadis joz baa doost

Ke aashenaa sokhane aashenaa negah daarad

ز درد دوست نگویم حدیث جزبا دوست

که آشنا سخن آشنا نگه دارد

Saro zaro delo jaanam fadaaye aan mahboob

Ke haghe sohbato ahde vafaa negah daarad

سر و زر و دل و جانم فدای آن محبوب

که حق صحبت و عهد وفا نگه دارد

Sabaa dar aan sare zolf ar dele maraa bini

Ze rooye lotf begooyash ke jaa negah daarad

صبا دران سر زلف ار دل مرا بینی

ز روی لطف بگویش که جا نگه دارد

Delaa ma-aash chenaan kon ke gar belaghzad paay

Fereshteat be do daste doaa negah daarad

دلا معاش چنان کن که گر بلغزد پای

فرشته‌ات به دو دست دعا نگه دارد

Negah nadaasht dele maavo jaaye ranjesh nist

Ze daste bande che khizad khodaa negah daarad

نگه نداشت دل ما و جای رنجش نیست

ز دست بنده چه خیزد خدا نگه دارد

Ghobaare raahe gozaarat kojaast taa Hafez

Be yaadegaare nasime sabaa negah daarad

غبار راهگذارت کجاست تا حافظ

به یادگار نسیم صبا نگه دارد

Not from hair nor waist comes the beauty of the beloved one,
Be enslaved by the beauty that has a quality beyond anyone.

No doubt the style of Peri and Huri[1] can be an attractive one,
But unique in grace and beauty is that special beloved one.

O rose, so alive with laughter, seek my eye's fountain,
From longing for you a sweet torrent it can't restrain.

In the art of shooting arrows from a bow, do you see how,
Every one yields their bow to the curve of your eyebrow.

To wrest the ball of beauty from you, there is not any one,
A rider to grab your reins? Even the sun is not such a one.

You found my speech agreeable, now it sits in the heart of everyone,
Yes, yes, truly, love's words are a sign deeply impressed on one.

In the mystery of Love's way complete surety is given to none,
It appears differently according to the understanding of each one.

To the regulars of the tavern, don't boast of grace's gifts,
Each word has its time and somewhere each subtlety fits.

The wise bird doesn't go to the meadow singing loudly,
For in every spring season an autumn follows closely.

O claimant! Your wit and skill don't try selling to Hafiz,
The tongue of clear explanation our reed pen certainly is.

*(W-C 147) The radif is "Has".*
  [1] *"..Peri and Huri..." See glossary in this volume.*

Shaahed aan nist ke mooeeyo miyaani daarad
شاهد آن نیست که موئی و میانی دارد

Bandeye tal-ate aan baash ke aani daarad
بنده طلعت آن باش که آنی دارد

Shiveye hooro pari garche latif ast vali
شیوه حور و پری گرچه لطیف است ولی

Khoobi aan asto letaafat ke folaani daarad
خوبی آن است و لطافت که فلانی دارد

Cheshmeye chashme maraa ey gole khandaan daryaab
چشمه چشم مرا ای گل خندان دریاب

Ke be ommide to khosh aabe ravaani daarad
که به امّید تو خوش آب روانی دارد

Khame abrooye to dar san-ate tir andaazi
خم ابروی تو در صنعت تیراندازی

Bestad az daste har aan kas ke kamaani daarad
بستد از دست هر آن کس که کمانی دارد

Gooye khoobi ke barad az to ke khorshid aanjaa
گوی خوبی که برد از تو که خورشید آنجا

Na savaarist ke dar dast anaani daarad
نه سواریست که در دست عنانی دارد

Del neshaan shod sokhanam taa to ghaboolash kardi
دلنشان شد سخنم تا تو قبولش کردی

Aari aari sokhane eshgh neshaani daarad
آری آری سخن عشق نشانی دارد

Dar rahe eshgh nashod kas be yaghin mahrame raaz
در ره عشق نشد کس به یقین محرم راز

Har kasi bar hasabe fekr gamaani daarad
هر کسی بر حسب فکر گمانی دارد

Baa kharaabaat neshinaan ze keraamaat malaaf
با خرابات نشینان ز کرامات ملاف

Har sokhan vaghtiyo har nokte makaani daarad
هر سخن وقتیّ و هر نکته مکانی دارد

Morghe zirak nashavad dar chamanash naghme soraay
مرغ زیرک نشود در چمنش نغمه سرای

Har bahaari ke ze dombaale khazaani daarad
هر بهاری که ز دنباله خزانی دارد

Moddaaee goo loghozo nokte be Hafez maforoosh
مدّعی گو لغز و نکته به حافظ مفروش

Kelke maa niz bayaniyyo zabani daarad
کلک ما نیز بیانیّ و زبانی دارد

From our eye, with the heart's blood our face is covered,
What is happening on our face, I really can't well explain it.

Within the heart is great desire, which we have concealed,
If it becomes a wind, that blows away our heart's seat, so be it.

Our face on the dust of the friend's path we gladly placed,
Dust on the face is permitted, if the friend's foot treads on it.

The water of our eye flows in a torrent; whosoever it passed -
However stony hearted, could not help but be moved by it.

With our tears we sat in special closed session and discussed,
Why tears go to your street. Day and night we tried to solve it.

From envy the rising sun its garments would have shredded,
If my sun-loving moon had got a robe and tried to show it.

To the tavern's street Hafiz went often and with the sincerity,
That the pure Sufi would exhibit in the place for piety.

**(W-C 148) The radif is "Goes".**

Az dide khoone del hame bar rooye maa ravad
از دیده خون دل همه بر روی ما رود

Bar rooye maa ze dide nabini chehaa ravad
بر روی ما ز دیده  نبینی چها رود

Maa dar daroone sine havaaee nahofteim
ما در درون سینه هوائی نهفته‌ایم

Bar baad agar ravad dele maa zaan havaa ravad
بر باد اگر رود دل ما زان هوا رود

Bar khaake raahe yaar nahaadim rooye khish
بر خاک راه یار نهادیم روی خویش

Bar rooye maa ravaast agar aashenaa ravad
بر روی ما رواست اگر آشنا رود

Seil ast aabe didevo bar har ke bogzarad
سیل است آب دیده وبرهر که بگذرد

Garche delash ze sang bovad ham ze jaa ravad
گرچه دلش ز سنگ بود هم ز جا رود

Maa raa be aabe dide shabo rooz maajaraast
ما را به آب دیده شب و روز ماجراست

Zaan rahgozar ke bar sare kooyash cheraa ravad
زان رهگذر که بر سر کویش چرا رود

Khorshide khaavari konad az rashk jaame chaak
خورشید خاوری کند از رشک جامه چاک

Gar maahe mehr parvare man dar ghabaa ravad
گر ماه مهرپرور من در قبا رود

Hafez be kooye meikade daaem be sed ghe del
حافظ به کوی میکده دایم به صدق دل

Chon soofiyaane sovme-e daar az safaa ravad
چون صوفیان صومعه دار از صفا رود

When my hand touches that hair tip, angrily off you go;
If I seek agreement, you become highly critical, and depart.

Like a new moon, when the raised corner of your eyebrow you show,
The hapless observers you seduce, and then into the veil depart.

On a wine-filled night you get me legless, but to sleep I can't go,
And if I complain of this the next day, into sleep you depart.

O heart in the way of love, much disturbance you will know,
One is heading for a fall on this journey, if in haste you depart.

When the wind of pride in the wine's bubble upward makes it go,
On the surface of the wine its sovereign dignity has to depart.

For the empire of the world let not begging at the beloved's door go,
Into that sun from the shade of this door, would any wish to depart?

O heart, in age, pride in beauty and eloquence don't try to show,
For only in the world of youth from modesty can you depart.

When it's time to close that book of youthful black hair, know,
However many white hairs you pluck, whiteness will not depart.

Hafiz you yourself are the veil of the path, so out from 'self' go,
Happy is one on this path who from the veil of 'self' can depart.

*(W-C 149) The radif is "Goes".*

Cho dast bar sare zolfash zaman be taab ravad

Var aashti talabam baa sar etaab ravad

Cho maahe nov rahe nazzaaregaane bi chaare

Zanad be goosheye abroovo dar neghaab ravad

Shabe sharaab kharaabam konad be bidaari

Vagar be rooz shekaayat konam be khaab ravad

Tarighe eshgh por aashoobo fetne ast ey del

Biyoftad aanke dar in raah baa shetaab ravad

Hobaab raa cho fetad baade nekhvat andar sar

Kolaah daariyash andar sare sharaab ravad

Gedaaeeye dare jaanaan be saltanat maforoosh

Kasi ze saayeye in dar be aaftaab ravad

Delaa cho pir shodi hosno naazoki maforoosh

Ke in moaamele dar aalame shabaab ravad

Savaad naameye mooye siyaah chon tey shod

Bayaaz kam nashavad gar sad entekhaab ravad

Hejaabe raah toee Hafez az miyaan barkhiz

Khoshaa kasi ke dar in parde bi hejaab ravad

چو دست بر سر زلفش زنم به تاب رود

ور آشتی طلبم با سر عتاب رود

چو ماه نو ره نظّارگان بیچاره

زند به گوشه ابرو و در نقاب رود

شب شراب خرابم کند به بیداری

وگر به روز شکایت کنم به خواب رود

طریق عشق پرآشوب و آفت است ای دل

بیفتد آنکه درین راه با شتاب رود

حباب را چو فتد باد نخوت اندر سر

کلاه داری اش اندر سر شراب رود

گدائی در جانان به سلطنت مفروش

کسی ز سایه این در به آفتاب رود

دلا چو پیر شدی حسن و نازکی مفروش

که این معامله در عالم شباب رود

سواد نامه موی سیاه چون طی شد

بیاض کم نشود گر صد انتخاب رود

حجاب راه توئی حافظ از میان برخیز

خوشا کسی که درین پرده بی حجاب رود

O Muslims, once I had a heart of such a kind,
That I could confide to it any problems on my mind.

If to fall into a whirlpool my grief ever led me,
In its words hope of the shore there would be.

In every untoward circumstance, however bad,
A true, hard working and capable friend I had.

In the beloved's street that heart was lost by me,
Lord! What a skirt-seizing, stop-over it turned out to be.

What requires skill, risks disappointment, inevitably,
But did any beggar ever such disappointment see?

On the poor disturbed life of this soul have some mercy,
Once a skilled, experienced, worker my heart was you see.

Whilst, to me, such very fine utterances, love was teaching,
The fine points of my words were famous at every gathering.

But don't speak anymore of the finer points of Hafiz,
For now stands revealed just how great his folly is.

*(W-C 150) The radif is "Was".*

Mosalmaanaan maraa vaghti del i bood
Ke baa vey goftami gar moshkel i bood

مسلمانان مرا وقتی دلی بود
که با او گفتمی گر مشکلی بود

Be gerdaabi cho moiftaadam az gham
Be tadbirash omide saahel i bood

به گردابی چو می افتادم از غم
به تدبیرش امید ساحلی بود

Deli ham dardo yaari maslahat bin
Ke estezhaare har ahle deli bood

دلی همدرد و یاری مصلحت بین
که استظهار هر اهل دلی بود

Ze man zaaye shod andar kooye jaanaan
Che daamangir yaa rab manzeli bood

ز من ضایع شد اندر کوی جانان
چه دامنگیر یا رب منزلی بود

Honar bi eybe hermaan nist liken
Ze man mahroomtar key saaeli bood

هنر بی عیب حرمان نیست لیکن
ز من محرومتر کی سائلی بود

Bar in jaane parishaan rahmat aarid
Ke vaghti kaardaani kaameli bood

برین جان پریشان رحمت آرید
که وقتی کاردانی کاملی بود

Maraa taa eshgh talime sokhan kard
Hadisam nokteye har mahfel i bood

مرا تا عشق تعلیم سخن کرد
حدیثم نکته هر محفلی بود

Magoo digar ke Hafez nokte daan ast
Ke maa didimo mohkam ghaafeli bood

مگو دیگر که حافظ نکته دانست
که ما دیدیم و محکم غافلی بود

When that beloved of mine takes the wine-cup in hand,
The market for fair idols suffers complete loss of demand.

In great grief at those beloved feet I have fallen,
Hoping that by the beloved's hand I am taken.

Into that ocean I have fallen and like a fish I live there,
So that me the beloved one, on a hook, may ensnare.

Exclaimed everyone who caught that one's look,
'Where is the night-watch, bring this drunkard to book.

Joyful of heart is the one who, like Hafiz,
Drinking wine from the cup of Alast[1] is.

*(W-C 151)  **The radif is "Takes".***
   [1] *"...Alast..." See glossary in this volume.*

Yaaram cho ghadah be dast girad
یارم چو قدح به دست گیرد

Baazaare botaan shekast girad
بازار بتان شکست گیرد

Dar paash fetaadeam be zaari
در پاش فتاده‌ام به زاری

Aayaa bovad aanke dast girad
آیا بود آن که دست گیرد

Dar bahr fetaadeam cho maahi
در بحر فتاده‌ام چو ماهی

Taa yaar ma raa be shast girad
تا یار مرا به شست گیرد

Har kas ke bedid chashme ou goft
هر کس که بدید چشم او گفت

Koo mohtasebi ke mast girad
کو محتسبی که مست گیرد

Khorram dele ou ke hamcho Hafez
خرّم دل او که همچو حافظ

Jaami ze meye alast girad
جامی ز می الست گیرد

If the Saki[1] pours wine into the cup in this special way,
All the knowing-ones, wine drinkers, will forever stay.

If mole, like a grain[2], beneath beloved's tress is displayed,
Many a wise old bird by that bait will soon be ensnared.

Sublime the state of the drunk who, at the feet of that one,
Would cast either head or turban, but is not sure which one.

By day seek to acquire skills: for those who drink by day,
The bright heart's mirror they cast into darkness that way.

Know the time of the wine of morning's splendour, has arrived,
When a veil on the tent of the horizon, evening has bestowed.

The puritan remains raw, unseasoned, whilst in denial he stays,
Into maturity he goes, when on the wine cup he casts his gaze.

Be careful not to drink with the guardian of morals in the city,
He drinks your wine, but only a stone thrown by him will there be.

*(W-C 153) The radif is "Cast".*
[1] *"..Saki..." See the glossary in this volume.*
[2] *"..like a grain..." This is probably a reference to the grain of wheat that in Muslim belief was the object that tempted Adam to his fall from grace.*

Saaghi ar baade az in dast be jaam andaazad
Aarefaan raa hame dar shorbe modaam anndaazad

Var chonin zire khame zolf nahad daaneye khaal
Ey basaa morghe kherad raa ke be daam andaazad

Ey khoshaa haalate aan mast ke dar paaye harif
Saro dastaar nadaanad ke kodaam andaazad

Aan zamaan vaghte meye sobh foroogh ast ke shab
Gerde khargaahe ofogh pardeye shaam andaazad

Zaahede khaam ke enkaare meyo jaam konad
Pokhte gardad cho nazar bar meye khaam andaazad

Baade baa mohtasebe shahr nanooshi zenhaar
Bekhorad baade ato sang be jaam andaazad

ساقی ار باده ازین دست به جام اندازد
عارفان را همه در شرب مدام اندازد

ور چنین زیر خم زلف نهد دانه خال
ای بسا مرغ خرد را که به دام اندازد

ای خوشا حالت آن مست که در پای حریف
سر و دستار نداند که کدام اندازد

روز در کسب هنر کوش که می خوردن روز
دل چون آینه در زنگ ظلام اندازد

آن زمان وقت می صبح فروغ است که شب
گرد خرگاه افق پرده شام اندازد

زاهد خام که انکار می و جام کند
پخته گردد چو نظر بر می خام اندازد

باده با محتسب شهر ننوشی حافظ
بخورد باده‌ات و سنگ به جام اندازد

O my heart! Good news! The morning breeze came back,
From Saba's land. With good news, that hoopoe[1] came back.

O morning bird, pray prolong the sweet song of David[2],
From air, the rose of Solomon, came back, by wind carried.

On the breath of morning, sweet wine the tulip scented,
In hope of that remedy, she came back with heart tainted.

Where is a wise-man who knows the language of the lily?
So about her going and coming back, we can make inquiry.

God given fortune showed that human kindness it did not lack,
When for God's sake, that stone-hearted idol it brought back.

On the road of the caravan, I looked long and hard after,
As back into my heart's ear came the bells of departure[3].

It beat the door of offence, when a vow was broken by Hafiz,
What grace! In peace the beloved coming back from the door is.

---

**(W-C 154) The radif is "Has come back".**

[1] *"...that hoopoe..."* See the glossary in this volume.
[2] *"..David..."* This refers to Prophet David one of whose blessings was a sweet voice. He was the father of Prophet Solomon who was given control over the winds.
[3] *"...bells of departure..."* Bells in the caravans of camels would mark the time for departure.

Mojde ey del ke degar baade sabaa baaz aamad

مژده ای دل که دگر باد صبا باز آمد

Hod hode khosh khabar az tarfe sabaa baaz aamad

هدهد خوش خبر از طرف صبا بازآمد

Bar kash ey morghe sahar nagh meye davoodi baaz

برکش ای مرغ سحر نغمه داوودی باز

Ke soleimaane gol az baade havaa baaz aamad

که سلیمان گل از باد هوا بازآمد

Laale booye meye nooshin beshenid az dame sobh

لاله بوی می نوشین بشنید از دم صبح

Daagh del bood be omide davaa baaz aamad

داغ دل بود به امید دوا بازآمد

Aarefi koo ke konad fahme zabaane soosan

عارفی کو که کند فهم زبان سوسن

Taa beporsad ke cheraa rafto cheraa baaz aamad

تا بپرسد که چرا رفت و چرا بازآمد

Mardomi kardo karam lotfe khodaa daad be man

مردمی کرد و کرم بخت خداداد به من

Kaan bote sangdel az raahe vafaa baaz aamad

کان بت سنگدل از راه وفا بازآمد

Chashme man dar rahe in ghaafeleye raah bemaand

چشم من در ره این قافله راه بماند

Taa be gooshe delam aavaaze daraa baaz aamad

تا به گوش دلم آواز درا بازآمد

Garche Hafez dare ranjesh zado peimaan beshekast

گر چه حافظ در رنجش زد و پیمان بشکست

Lotfe ou bin ke be lotf az dare maa baaz aamad

لطف او بین که به صلح از در ما بازآمد

Without the beloved's face the rose has no value,
Without wine the spring season is without virtue.

The border of the meadow and the garden's air,
Without that tulip cheek, there is no charm there.

The dance motion of the cypress and the rose's bliss,
Without the nightingale's notes, no pleasure is in this.

The beloved's sugar-sweet lip and rose-like body,
Without kissing and embracing only makes us sorry.

Rose, garden, and wine, very good they may be,
But without your society are not pleasing to me.

Every picture that reason has drawn with heavy hand,
Except of the lovely idol, no pleasure does command.

The life is a coin of no worth at all to Hafiz;
To scatter it before the beloved, not nice it is.

*(W-C 155) The radif is "Is not pleasant".*

Gol bi rokhe yaar khosh nabaa shad     گل بی رخ یار خوش نباشد
Bi baade bahaar khosh nabaa shad     بی باده بهار خوش نباشد

Tarfe chamano tavaafe bostaan     طرف چمن و طواف بستان
Bi laale ezaar khosh nabaa shad     بی لاله عذار خوش نباشد

Raghsidane sarvo haalate gol     رقصیدن سرو و حالت گل
Bi sovte hazaar khosh nabaa shad     بی صوت هزار خوش نباشد

Baa yaare shekar labe khosh andaam     با یار شکرلب خوش اندام
Bi booso kenaar khosh nabaa shad     بی بوس و کنار خوش نباشد

Baaghe golo mol khosh ast liken     باغ گل و مل خوش است لیکن
Bi sohbate yaar khosh nabaa shad     بی صحبت یار خوش نباشد

Har naghsh ke daste aghl bandad     هر نقش که دست عقل بندد
Joz naghshe negaar khosh nabaa shad     جز نقش نگار خوش نباشد

Jaan naghde mohagh gharast Hafez     جان نقد محقّر است حافظ
Az bahre nesaar khosh nabaashad     از بهر نثار خوش نباشد

Last night the wind gave news of the beloved on a journey,
So my heart I gave to the wind too! What is to be will be.

My work reached such intensity that I am now confiding,
With the evening lightning and the wind of the morning.

In your spiral of hair my unprotected heart forgot to tell,
My memory, 'Carry me to the residence that I know well.'

Today appreciation of the counsel of dear ones came to me,
O Lord, full of joy may the souls of my advisers ever be.

My heart bled when in the meadow I remembered you,
The rose bud's collar became loosened by the wind too.

My feeble existence slipped away; in my hand it didn't remain;
With the perfume of your hair the wind gave me life back again.

Hafiz! A good disposition will bring you what it is you desire
Souls offer themselves, for the well disposed man they admire.

*(W-C 156) The radif is "Be".*

Doosh aagahi ze yaare safar karde daad baad

Man niz del be baad daham har che baad baad

دوش آگهی ز یار سفرکرده داد باد

من نیز دل به باد دهم هر چه باد باد

Kaaram bedaan rasid ke ham raaze khod konam

Har sham barghe laame o har baam daad baad

کارم بدان رسید که همراز خود کنم

هر شام برق لامع و هر بامداد باد

Dar chine torreye to dele bi hefaaze man

Hargez nagoft mas-kane ma-loof yaad baad

در چین طرّه تو دل بی حفاظ من

هرگز نگفت مسکن مالوف یاد باد

Emrooz ghadre pande azizaan shenaakhtam

Yaa rab ravaane naasehe maa az to shad baad

امروز قدر پند عزیزان شناختم

یا رب روان ناصح ما از تو شاد باد

Khoon shod delam be yaade to har gah ke dar chaman

Bande ghabaaye ghoncheye gol migoshaad baad

خون شد دلم به یاد تو هر گه که در چمن

بند قبای غنچه گل می گشاد باد

Az dast rafte bood vojoode zaeefe man

Sobham be booye vasle to jaan baaz daad baad

از دست رفته بود وجود ضعیف من

صبحم به بوی وصل تو جان بازداد باد

Hafez nahaade nike to kaamat bar aavarad

Jaanhaa fadaaye mardome nikoo nahaad baad

حافظ نهاد نیک تو کامت برآورد

جان‌ها فدای مردم نیکونهاد باد

O Majesty, may the heavens but a ball in your chaugan's curve[1] be;
May existence in time and space your wide playing field be.

Attached to your flag, like tassels, the flowing locks of Lady Victory,
The lover of your galloping charges may the timeless eye ever be.

You, whose grandeur the writings of Mercury[2] do declare,
May Reason itself be the seal of the book of your record fair.

Your upright cypress-like stature shames even the Tuba tree[3],
The width of your hall fills the expanse of paradise with envy.

Not only stones and vegetation and animals should be,
Under your command, but the ordered universe should be.

---

**(W-C 157) The radif is "Of yours be".**
  [1] "...chaugan's curve..." See the glossary in this volume.
  [2] "...Mercury..." The planet associated with writing. See Avery pp. 148.
  [3] "...Tuba tree..." See the glossary in this volume.

Khos rovaa gooye falak dar khame chov gaane to baad
Saahate kovno makaan arseye meidaane to baad

خسروا گوی فلک در خم چوگان تو باد
ساحت کون و مکان عرصه میدان تو باد

Zolfe khaatoone zafar shifteye par chame tost
Dideye fathe abad aasheghe jovlaane to baad

زلف خاتون ظفر شیفته پرچم توست
دیده فتح ابد عاشق جولان تو باد

Ey ke enshaaye otaared sefate shovkate tost
Aghle kol chaakere toghraa keshe divaane to baad

ای که انشای عطارد صفت شوکت توست
عقل کل چاکر طغرا کش دیوان تو باد

Teyreye jelveye toobaa ghade chon sarve to shod
Gheirate kholde barin saahate eyvaane to baad

طیره جلوه طوبی قد چون سرو تو شد
غیرت خلدبرین ساحت ایوان تو باد

Na be tanhaa hayavaanaato nabaataato jamaad
Harche dar aalame amr ast be farmaane to baad

نه به تنها حیوانات و جمادات و نبات
هر چه در عالم امر است به فرمان تو باد

Saki![1] The story of the rose, tulip and cypress departed,
Three cups of wine[2] washed away a dispute now completed.

Drink wine! The meadow's bride has perfect beauty,
No need of any intermediate to conclude this story.

The parrots of Hindustan[3] are smitten with the taste of sugar,
On account of the Farsi sweets that to Bengal we deliver.

See the journey of these verses in place and in time,
The child of one night; but one year to deliver the rhyme.

That eye of magic that fascinated the devotee,
Behind it see trailing the long caravan of sorcery.

Do not leave the Way, for that old hag of worldly deceit,
Cheats when she sits, and is a strumpet when on her feet.

The beloved's sweat, in moving proudly; makes shamefaced,
The sweat of night-dew on the white rose's face displayed.

The spring wind passes over the garden of the king,
And in the tulip's bowl, wine from dew is going.

Your love for the assembly of Ghyas-ud-din, O Hafiz,
Express openly! Due to his weeping, your work going is.

---

**(W-C 158) The radif is "Goes".**
[1] *"...Saki..." See the glossary in this volume.*
[2] *"...three cups of wine..." traditionally drunk in the morning to clean the body of bad humors. (W-C pp.310).*
*The dispute referred to is described by W-C in the same commentary. At all events it would appear the poem*
*was written for a King of Bengal (Ghiyas-ud-din) in northern India and sent to him.*
[3] *"...parrots of Hindusthan..." This refers to the poets of India.*

Saaghi hadise sarvo golo laale miravad
ساقی حدیث سرو و گل و لاله می‌رود

Vin bahs baa salaaseye ghassale miravad
وین بحث با ثلاثه غسّاله می‌رود

Mey deh ke nov aroose sokhan hadde hosn yaaft
می ده که نوعروس سخن حدّ حسن یافت

Kar in zaman ze san-ate dallale miravad
کار این زمان ز صنعت دلّاله می‌رود

Shekkar shekan shavand hame tootiyaane hend
شگرشکن شوند همه طوطیان هند

Zin ghande paarsi ke be bangaale miravad
زین قند پارسی که به بنگاله می رود

Teye makaan bebino zamaan dar solooke sher
طی مکان ببین و زمان در سلوک شعر

Kin tefl yekshabe rahe yek saale miravad
کاین طفل یک شبه ره یک ساله می‌رود

Aan chashme jaa dovaaneye aabed farib bin
آن چشم جادوانه عابدفریب بین

Kesh kaarvaane sehr ze dombaale miravad
کش کاروان سحر ز دنباله می‌رود

Az rah maro be eshveye donyaa ke in ajooz
از ره مرو به عشوه دنیا که این عجوز

Makkare mi neshinado mohtaale miravad
مکّاره می‌نشیند و محتاله می‌رود

Khey karde mikharaamado bar aareze saman
خوی کرده می خرامد و بر عارض سمن

Az sharme rooye ou aragh az jaale miravad
از شرم روی او عرق از ژاله می رود

Baade bahaar mivazad az golsetaane shaah
باد بهار می‌وزد از گلستان شاه

Vaz jaale baade dar ghadahe laale miravad
و از ژاله باده در قدح لاله می‌رود

Hafez ze shovghe majlese soltaan ghiyaase din
حافظ ز شوق مجلس سلطان غیاث دین

Khaamosh masho ke kaare to az naale miravad
خامش مشو که کار تو از ناله می‌رود

My desire is for that which, if it were given from my hand,
The ending of sorrows will be the work done by that hand.

That plain we see within the heart is not a conflict zone,
When the demon departs the angels make it their own.

The society of the ruler is the darkness of night,
If you ask the sun, maybe it will give you light.

At the door of the world's powerful, those who lack masculinity,
How long will you wait, O Khwaja, to become an invitee?

Abandon not begging, in case treasure you may be receiving,
From the exchange of looks with a traveller who is passing.

Salih[1] and Talah[2] showed obedience to the Divinity,
The one who gets accepted, in our sight may we see.

O bulbul, you lover, all you need ask for is life, for you can assume,
The garden gets green and the red rose in the heart will bloom.

In this vestibule[3] it is no surprise to see Hafiz carefree,
Whoever visits the tavern, senseless that one will be.

*(W-C 159) The radif is "Come".*
[1] *"...Salih..." A Prophet sent to the Thamud. See Qur'an 7:74 and 12: 61-68.*
[2] *"...Talah..." According to W-C he was a warrior for the faith (W-C pp 312).*
[3] *"...this vestibule..." This refers to the present life.*

Bar sare aanam ke gar ze dast bar aayad
Dast be kaari zanam ke ghosse sar aayad

بر سر آنم که گر ز دست برآید
دست به کاری زنم که غصّه سر آید

Manzare del nist jaaye sohbate azdaad
Div cho biroon ravad fereshte dar aayad

منظر دل نیست جای صحبت اضداد
دیو چو بیرون رود فرشته درآید

Sohbate hokkam zolmate shabe yaldaast
Noor ze khorshid khaah boo ke bar aayad

صحبت حکّام ظلمت شب یلداست
نور ز خورشید خواه بو که برآید

Bar dare arbaabe bi morovvate donyaa
Chand neshini ke khaaje key be dar aayad

بر در ارباب بی‌مروّت دنیا
چند نشینی که خواجه کی بدرآید

Tarke gedaaee makon ke ganj biyaabi
Az nazare rahrovi ke dar gozar aayad

ترک گدائی مکن که گنج بیابی
از نظر رهروی که در گذر آید

Saaleho taaleh mataae khish nomoodand
Taa ke ghabool oftado che dar nazar aayad

صالح و طالح متاع خویش نمودند
تا که قبول افتد و چه در نظر آید

Bolbole aashegh to omr khaah ke aakher
Baagh shaved sabzo shaakhe gol be bar aayad

بلبل عاشق تو عمر خواه که آخر
باغ شود سبز و شاخ گل به بر آید

Gheflate Hafez dar in saraache ajab nist
Harke be mey khaane raft bikhabar aayad

غفلت حافظ درین سراچه عجب نیست
هر که به میخانه رفت بی‌خبر آید

The sun of all seeing - may your beauty be,
May beauty's beauty be exceeded by your face's beauty.

So like the falcon's long feather, is your  hair. The Huma[1],
In the shade of whose wing is the heart of every worldly ruler.

One, not in fascination drawn to that hair of yours,
Will be tossed in wild abandon, like that hair of yours.

The one whose heart is not your face's lover,
Will be drowned forever in the blood of the liver.[2]

O idol when your glance looses its arrow,
My wounded heart before it I may show.

When that sugar-sweet ruby bestows a kiss,
My life from this, filling with sweetness is.

Each moment brings me a fresh new love for you,
Each hour a splendid new beauty appears in you.

O with all his soul Hafiz desires your face to see,
On the state of the desiring ones may your look be.

*(W-C 160) The radif is "Be".*
  [1] *"...the Huma..." See the glossary in this volume.*
  [2] *"...liver..." The liver is the seat of the body faculty as the brain is of the intellect and the heart muscle of the heart.*

Jamaalash aaftaabe har nazar baad
Ze khoobi rooye khoobash khoobtar baad

جمالش آفتاب هر نظر باد
ز خوبی روی خوبش خوبتر باد

Homaaye zolfe shaahin shahparash raa
Dele shaahaane aalam zire par baad

همای زلف شاهین شهپرش را
دل شاهان عالم زیر پر باد

Kasi koo basteye zolfash nabaashad
Cho zolfash dar hamo ziro zebar baad

کسی کو بسته زلفش نباشد
چو زلفش درهم و زیر و زبر باد

Deli koo aasheghe rooyash nagardad
Hamishe gharghe dar khoone jegar baad

دلی کاو عاشق رویش نگردد
همیشه غرقه در خون جگر باد

Botaa chon ghamzeat naavak feshaanad
Dele maj roohe man pishash separ baad

بتا چون غمزهات ناوک فشاند
دل مجروح من پیشش سپر باد

Cho la-le shekkarinat boose bakhshad
Mezaaghe jaane man zoo por shekar baad

چو لعل شکّرینت بوسه بخشد
مذاق جان من زو پرشکرباد

Maraa az tost har dam taaze eshghi
To raa har saa-ati hosni degar baad

مرا از تست هر دم تازه عشقی
تو را هر ساعتی حسنی دگر باد

Be jaan moshtaaghe rooye tost Hafez
To raa dar haale moshtaaghaan nazar baad

بجان مشتاق روی تست حافظ
تو را در حال مشتاقان نظر باد

Constantly increasing may your beauty ever be,
Tulip-coloured may your cheeks every year be.

The image of your love in the eye of the mind,
There each and every day, increasing, may I find.

May the high and handsome; this world's heart-stealers,
Be low and hollow before you, like the *Nuun*[1] in letters.

In the meadow, rising up tall and erect, every cypress tree,
Bent low in homage to your *Alif*-like[1] stature may they be.

May that eye which is not enamoured of you,
Be blood drenched, and those pearl tears too.

In the fine art of stealing the hearts away,
May your eye make use of every magical way.

Wherever a heart is found that for you is sorrowing,
May it, without patience or peace, be restlessly turning.

May one who from you cannot bear being separated,
From the circle of union with you also be excluded.

Your ruby lip that is the essence of Hafiz, really,
Removed far from it may any mean, sordid lip be.

**(W-C 161) The radif is "Be".**

[1] *"...Nuun...Alif..." Arabic letters: Nuun =* ن *: Alif =* ا

Hosne to hamishe dar fozoon baad
Rooyat hame saale laale goon baad

حسن تو همیشه در فزون باد
رویت همه ساله لاله‌گون باد

Vandar sare maa khiyaale eshghat
Har rooz ke hast dar fozoon baad

وندر سر من خیال عشقت
هر روز که هست در فزون باد

Ghadde hame delbaraane aalam
Dar khedmate ghaamatat negoon baad

قدّ همه دلبران عالم
در خدمت قامتت نگون باد

Har sarv ke dar chaman bar aayad
Pishe alefe ghadat cho noon baad

هر سرو که در چمن براید
پیش الف قدت چو نون باد

Chashmi ke na fetneye to baashad
Az govhare ashk bahre khoon baad

چشمی که نه فتنه تو باشد
از گوهر اشک بحر خون باد

Chashme to ze bahre delrobaaee
Dar kardane sehr zoo fonoon baad

چشم تو ز بهر دلربائی
در کردن سحر ذوفنون باد

Har jaa ke delist az ghame to
Bi sabro gharaaro bi sokoon baad

هر جا که دلیست از غم تو
بی صبر و قرار و بی سکون باد

Hark as ke nabaashadash sare hejr
Az halgheye vasle to boroon baad

هرکس که نباشدش سر هجر
از حلقه وصل تو برون باد

La-le to ke hast jaane Hafez
Door az labe har khasise doon baad

لعل تو که هست جان حافظ
دور از لب هرخسیس دون باد

In need of the physician's tender touch may your body never be,
Nor your delicate existence, be subject to any kind of injury.

Your safety is the safety of everything, as far as the eye can see,
Made sorrowful by any accidents may your person never be.

When autumn falls upon the meadow, intent upon its plundering,
To your upright, elegant, cypress's height, may it never be reaching.

That place where your splendid beauty becomes manifest,
May the power of negative perceptions never infest.

Inner and outer beauty proceeds from your prosperity,
May outward anger and inner disturbance you never see.

Every envious, evil-eyed, one who your moon face may see,
Nothing but rue-seed[1] in your fire may that one's very life be.

From the sugar-sweet words Hafiz scatters, look for recovery,
So there will be no need for any candy and rose-water remedy.

*(W-C 162) The radif is "Be not".*
  [1] *"...rue seed..." See the glossary in this volume.*

Tanat be naaze tabibaan niyaaz mand mabaad
Vojoode naazokat aazordeye gazand mabaad

تنت به ناز طبیبان نیازمند مباد  
وجود نازکت آزرده گزند مباد

Salaamate hame aafaagh dar salaamate tost
Be hich aareze shakhse to dard mand mabaad

سلامت همه آفاق در سلامت توست  
به هیچ عارضه شخص تو دردمند مباد

Bedin chaman cho dar aayad khazaan be yaghmaaee
Rahash be sarve sahi ghaamate boland mabaad

بدین چمن چو در آید خزان به یغمائی  
رهش به سرو سهی قامت بلند مباد

Dar aan basaat ke hosne to jelve aaghaazad
Majaale ta-neye badbino bad pasand mabaad

در آن بساط که حسن تو جلوه آغازد  
مجال طعنه بدبین و بد پسند مباد

Kamaale soorato mani ze amno sehatte tost
Ke zaaherat dojamo baatenat najand mabaad

کمال صورت و معنی ز امن و صحّت تست  
که ظاهرت دژم و باطنت نژند مباد

Har aanke rooye cho maahat be chashme bad binad
Bar aatashe to be joz chashme ou sepand mabaad

هر آنکه روی چو ماهت به چشم بد بیند  
بر آتش تو به جز چشم او سپند مباد

Shafaa ze gofteye shekkar feshaane Hafez jooy
Ke haajatat be alaaje golaabo ghand mabaad

شفا ز گفته شکّر فشان حافظ جوی  
که حاجتت به علاج گلاب و قند مباد

One who holds in the hand the cup revealing divine vision,
Has forever the wine of sovereignty that Jamshid[1] was given.

Khizr[2] found eternal life in that water;
In the tavern's cup seek that life-giver.

Let the thread of life lie within that cup,
That the true pattern of life it may draw up.

Paired with wine we are, as the pious are with piety,
Let's see towards which the beloved's desire may be.

None gathered in life's circle, their desire can have fed,
If from the circle of the Saki's lip they are excluded.

All the drunken ways the narcissus displays,
Are loans from your beautiful eye's gaze.

In my heart remembrance of your face and hair,
Morning and evening, is constant pain there.

For the wounded hearts of the sorrowful,
Of healing saltiness your lip is full.

O life, in the well of your chin two hundred are,
Who, like Hafiz, in slavery to your beauty are.


**(W-C 163) The radif is "Has".**
  *This ghazal is in volume 2 of Khanlari but is in Avery and Saberi.*
  [1] *"...Jamshid..." See glossary in this volume.*
  [2] *"...Khizr..." See glossary in this volume.*

Aan kas ke be dast jaam daarad

آنکس که به دست جام دارد

Soltaaniye jam modaam daarad

سلطانی جم مدام دارد

Aabi ke khezer hayaat azou yaaft

آبی که خضر حیات ازو یافت

Dar meikade joo ke jaam daarad

در میکده جو که جام دارد

Sar reshteye jaan be jaam bogzaar

سر رشته جان به جام بگذار

Kin reshte azou nezaam daarad

کاین رشته ازو نظام دارد

Maavo meyo zaahedaano taghvaa

ما و می و زاهدان و تقوی

Taa yaar sare kodaam daarad

تا یار سر کدام دارد

Biroon ze labe to saaghiyaa nist

بیرون ز لب تو ساقیا نیست

Dar dovr kasi ke kaam daarad

در دور کسی که کام دارد

Narges hame shivehaaye masti

نرگس همه شیوه های مستی

Az chashme khoshat be vaam daarad

از چشم خوشت به وام دارد

Zekre rokho zolfe to delam raa

ذکر رخ و زلف تو دلم را

Verdist ke sobho shaam daarad

وردی ست که صبح و شام دارد

Bar sineye rishe dard mandaan

بر سینه ریش دردمندان

La-lat namaki tamaam daarad

لعلت نمکی تمام دارد

Dar chaahe zanakh cho Hafez ey jaan

در چاه زنخ چو حافظ ای جان

Hosne to do sad gholaam daarad

حسن تو دو صد غلام دارد

One who the beloved's beautiful down keeps viewing,
That one has for sure got great clarity in his seeing.

Like a pen we have laid our head under your written order,
Obediently waiting your blade to remove it from our shoulder.

Granted union is the one who, like a candle, every moment,
Loses his head to your blade, but gains another on the instant.

Worthiness to kiss your feet is in the hand only of one, who,
Has his head permanently laid down like a doorstep for you.

I tire of dry austerity, bring me pure wine,
For its scent ever keeps fresh this brain of mine.

If this wine lacks does nothing else for you, at least,
From the temptation to rationalise[1] for a time you are released.

One who has never set foot outside the door of piety,
So as reach to the tavern now wishes a traveller to be.

To the grave's dust the broken heart of Hafiz will carry,
A love stain that on his liver[2] like the tulip streak will be.

---

**(W-C 164) The radif is "Has" or "Keeps".**
> [1] *"...temptation to rationalise..."* Rational thought, whatever its merits, is responsible for much that is not spiritually beneficial. Spiritual wine inhibits rational thought and opens the heart and mind to another level of experience.
> [2] *"...liver..."* See commentary on (W-C 160) above.

Kasi ke hosne khate doost dar nazar daarad

کسی که حسن خط دوست در نظر دارد

Mohaghaghast ke ou haasele basar daarad

محقق است که او حاصل بصر دارد

Cho khaame bar khate farmaane ou sare taa-at

چو خامه در ره فرمان او سر طاعت

Nahaadeim magar ou be tigh bardaarad

نهاده ایم مگر او به تیغ بردارد

Kasi be vasle to chon sha-m yaaft parvaane

کسی به وصل تو چون شمع یافت پروانه

Ke zire tighe to har dam sari degar daarad

که زیر تیغ تو هر دم سری دگر دارد

Be paay boose to daste kasi resid ke ou

بپایبوس تو دست کسی رسید که او

Cho aastaane bedin dar hamishe sar daarad

چو آستانه بدین در همیشه سر دارد

Ze zohde khoshk maloolam kojaast baadeye naab

ز زهد خشک ملولم کجاست باده ناب

Ke booye baade modaamam demaagh tar daarad

که بوی باده مدامم دماغ تر دارد

Ze baade hichat agar nist in na bas ke to raa

ز باده هیچت اگر نیست این نه بس که تو را

Dami ze vasvaseye aghl bi khabar daarad

دمی ز وسوسه عقل بی خبر دارد

Kasi ke az dare taghvaa ghadam boroon nanahaad

کسی که از ره تقوی قدم برون ننهاد

Be azme meikade aknoon rahe safar daarad

به عزم میکده اکنون ره سفر دارد

Dele shekasteye Hafez be khaak khaahad bord

دل شکسته حافظ به خاک خواهد برد

Cho laale daaghe havaaee ke bar jegar daarad

چو لاله داغ هوایی که بر جگر دارد

One whose hyacinth curls are a torment for the ambergris[1];
To the heart-hurting ones shows disdain and tyranny.

Rushing past your slain victim's head, like the wind that one is
What to do, for that one is life, therefore swift surely is?

Veiled by hair that one's moon reveals the bright sun,
In the same way a cloud screens the intensity of the sun.

If the true water of life the friend's lip possesses,
Then surely what Khizr[2] has are merely mirages.

From all the corners of my eyes these tears copiously flow,
So that, with water, your upright cypress fresh will grow.

Mistakenly your bold gaze sheds this blood of mine,
Let this opportunity come, for this judgement is fine.

Your drunken eye seeks in my heart to burn the liver;
Does that drunken Turk fancy roasted kebab I wonder?

My sick soul has not the wherewithal to ask of you anything,
Happy is the shattered one who the friend is answering.

When will a drunken look come to the hurting heart of Hafiz,
From that drunken eye in whose every corner a ruined one is?

*(W-C 165) The radif is "Has"*
  [1] *"...ambergris..." See the glossary in this volume.*
  [2] *"...Khizr..." See the glossary in this volume.*

Anke az sombole ou ghaaliye taabi daarad
Baaz baa delshodegaan naazo etaabi daarad

آنکه از سنبل او غالیه تابی دارد
باز با دلشدگان ناز و عتابی دارد

Az sare koshteye khod migozarad hamchon baad
Che tavaan kard ke omr asto shetaabi daarad

از سر کشته خود می گذرد همچون باد
چه توان کرد که عمرست و شتابی دارد

Maahe khorshid nomaayash ze pase pardeye zolf
Aaftaabist ke dar pish sahaabi daarad

ماه خورشید نمایش ز پس پرده زلف
آفتابیست که در پیش سحابی دارد

Aabe heivaan agar in ast ke daarad labe doost
Rovshan ast inke khezer bahre saraabi daarad

آب حیوان اگر این است که دارد لب دوست
روشن است اینکه خضر بهره سرابی دارد

Chashme man kard be har gooshe ravaan seile sereshk
Taa sahi sarve to raa taaze be aabi daarad

چشم من کرد بهر گوشه روان سیل سرشک
تا سهی سرو تو را تازه به آبی دارد

Ghamzeye shookhe to khoonam be khataa mirizad
Forsatash baad ke khosh fekre savaabi daarad

غمزه شوخ تو خونم به خطا می ریزد
فرصتش باد که این فکر صوابی دارد

Chashme makhmoore to daarad ze delam ghasde jegar
Torke mast ast magar meile kabaabi daarad

چشم مخمور تو دارد ز دلم قصد جگر
ترک مست است مگر میل کبابی دارد

Jaane bimaare maraa nist ze to rooye soaal
Ey khosh aan khaste ke az doost javaabi daarad

جان بیمار مرا نیست ز تو روی سؤال
ای خوش آن خسته که از دوست جوابی دارد

Key konad sooye dele khasteye Hafez nazari
Chashme mastat ke be har gooshe kharaabi daarad

کی کند سوی دل خسته حافظ نظری
چشم مست که به هر گوشه خرابی دارد

Last night a messenger from high Asaf[1] happy news did impart,
That great Solomon had given to us the signal to let joy start.

Mix with the eye's tears the dust of our existence, to make clay,
For the heart's desolate mansion the time to rebuild is - today.

Hey, you wine soaked cloak, keep my fault hidden,
For one whose garments are pure intends a visitation.

They describe the beauty of your lovely hair, continually,
Only one word out of thousands possible is told openly.

The position of each of the lovely ones is declared this day,
When, enthroned, the court's moon-faced beauty is on display.

On the throne of Jam[2], whose crown is the ladder of the sun,
Look, a low striving ant that, by a look, such elevation is given.

O heart protect your faith from that one's sharp eye,
Because for plunder that magician will let an arrow fly.

Sin stained Hafiz, to the king for his grace apply.
His liberal generosity has come in order to purify.

The king's assembly is an ocean, now it is time for pearl diving!
You who are hit hard by loss, it is time for profitable bartering.

---

*(W-C166) The radif is "Came"*
  [1] *"...Asaf..." See the glossary in this volume.*
  [2] *"...Jam..." See glossary in this volume.*
  *Central to this ghazal are the lines about relative 'positions' followed by one about 'elevation' of the ant
(= man). For an exposition of this see "Fusus al Hikam" of Khawaja Ibn Arabi in the chapter about Prophet
Enoch (Idris).*

Doosh az jenaabe aasaf peike beshaarat aamad
Kaz hazrate soleimaan eshrat eshaarat aamad

دوش از جناب آصف پیک بشارت آمد
کز حضرت سلیمان عشرت اشارت آمد

Khaake vojoode maa raa az aabe baade gel kon
Viraan saraaye del raa gaahe emaarat aamad

خاک وجود ما را از آب باده گل کن
ویران سرای دل را گاه عمارت آمد

Eybam bepoosh zenhaar ey khergheye mey aalood
Kan paak daaman injaa bahre ziaarat aamad

عیبم بپوش زنهار ای خرقه می آلود
کا پاکدامن اینجا بهر زیارت آمد

In sharhe bi nahaayat kaz hosne yaar goftand
Harfist az hezaaraan kandar ebaarat aamad

این شرح بینهایت کز حسن یار گفتند
حرفیست از هزاران کاندر عبارت آمد

Emrooz jaaye har kas peidaa shavad ze khooban
Kaan maahe majles afrooz andar sedaarat aamad

امروز جای هر کس پیدا شود ز خوبان
کان ماه مجلس افروز اندر صدارت آمد

Bar takhte jam ke taajash meraaje aaftaab ast
Hemmat negar ke moori baa aan heghaarat aamad

بر تخت جم که تاجش معراج آفتاب است
همّت نگر که موری با آن حقارت آمد

Az chashme shookhash ey del imaane khod negah daar
Kaan jaadooye kamaan kash bar azme ghaarat aamad

از چشم شوخش ای دل ایمان خود نگه دار
کان جادوی کمانکش بر عزم غارت آمد

Aaloodei cho Hafez feizi ze shaah dar khaah
Kaan onsore samaahat bahre tahaarat aamad

آلوده ای چو حافظ فیضی ز شاه در خواه
کان عنصر سماحت بهر طهارت آمد

Daryaast majlese ou daryaab vaghto dor yaab
Haan ey ziyaan reside vaghte tejaarat aamad

دریاست مجلس او دریاب وقت و در یاب
هان ای زیان رسیده وقت تجارت آمد

Last night the dawn wind brought a breath of news to me,
Saying; "Not for much longer the day of work and woe will be".

To the musicians of the cup of morn, goes our torn garment,
On account of the message that the morning wind has sent.

Yes to Shiraz we will travel with the favour of our friend,
O superb - that one became my fellow traveller in the end.

Come! Come! As a Huri Rizvan[1] has brought you here,
For this poor slave's heart, in this world you appear.

Strive, within the heart for goodness! Our cap of felt,
Many a sovereign's crown its shattering blow has felt.

My heart's moans reached to that royal lunar canopy,
When the glow of the moon brought your cheek to my memory.

Hafiz may cause the Shah's[2] flag of victory to fly sky high,
When his shelter he brings to the court of the king so high.

*(W-C 167) The radif is "Brought"*
  [1] *"...Huri Rizvan..." See glossary in this volume for both words*
  [2] *"...Shah..." This is a reference to Shah Mansur (d. 1393) who aided Hafiz's patron Shah Shuja to return to Shiraz having been exiled. (See Avery pp. 195).*

Nasime baade sabaa doosham aagahi aavard
     نسیم باد صبا دوشم آگهی آورد

Ke rooze mehnato gham roo be kootahi aavard
     که روز محنت و غم رو به کوتهی آورد

Be motrebaane saboohi dahim jaameye chaak
     به مطربان صبوحی دهیم جامه چاک

Bedin navid ke baade sahar gahi aavard
     بدین نوید که باد سحرگهی آورد

Biyaa biyaa ke to hoore behesht raa rezvaan
     بیا بیا که تو حور بهشت را رضوان

Dar in jahaan ze baraaye dele rahi aavard
     در این جهان ز برای دل رهی آورد

Hami ravim be shiraz baa enaayate bakht
     همی رویم به شیراز با عنایت بخت

Zehi rafigh ke bakhtam be hamrahi aavard
     زهی رفیق که بختم به همرهی آورد

Be kheire khaatere maa koosh kin kolaahe namad
     بخیر خاطر ما کوش کاین کلاه نمد

Basaa shekast ke baa afsare shahi aavard
     بسا شکست که با افسر شهی آورد

Che naalehaa ke resid az delam be kharmane maah
     چه ناله ها که رسید از دلم به خرمن ماه

Cho yaade aareze aan maahe khargahi aavard
     چو یاد عارض آن ماه خرگهی آورد

Resaand raayate mansoor bar falak Hafez
     رساند رایت منصور بر فلک حافظ

Ke eltejaa be jenaabe shahanshahi aavard
     که التجا به جناب شهنشهی آورد

One, Who gave your cheek the hue of roses, red and white,
Peace, security and calm will that one give me in my plight?

Who taught those flowing locks their way of plundering,
Justice to poor sad-hearted me that One can surely be giving.

O for Farhad, I had to give up all hope on that same day,
Control of his heart, for Shirin's sweet lip, he gave away.[1]

If not given gold, still the corner of contentment endures;
Who gave kings gold, this gift for the beggar He ensures.

Outwardly a fine bride the world appears to be,
Whoever married her, gave his life as a dowry.

Now on river's bank I stay, cypress' robe in the hand firmly;
Especially since news of February the dawn breeze gave me.

The sorrows of this sad time turned to blood the heart of Hafiz.
O Khwaja Kivamuddin[2] for this parting from your face, justice!

---

**(W-C 168) The radif is "gave".**
  [1] "...Farhad...Shirin..." See under Farhad in the glossary in this volume.
  [2] "...Khwaja Kivamuddin..." This refers to a patron of Hafiz but also meaning "one who supports the faith".

Aanke rokhsaare to raa range golo nasrin daad

Sabro aaraam tavaanad be mane meskin daad

Vaanke gisooye to raa rasme tataavol aamookht

Ham tavaanad karamash daade mane ghamgin daad

Man hamaan rooz ze farhaad tama bobridam

Ke anaane dele sheidaa be labe shirin daad

Ganje zar gar nabovad konje ghanaa-at baaghist

Aanke aan daad be shaahaan be gedaayaan in daad

Khosh aroosist jahaan az rahe soorat liken

Har ke peivast bedoo omre khodash kaavin daad

Bad az in daste mano daamane sarvo labe jooy

Khaase aknoon ke sabaa mojdeye farvardin daad

Dar kafe ghosseye dovraan dele Hafez khoon shod

Dar feraaghe rokhat ey khaaje ghavaamoddin daad

آنکه رخسار تو را رنگ گل و نسرین داد
صبر و آرام تواند به من مسکین داد

وانکه گیسوی تو را رسم تطاول آموخت
هم تواند کرمش داد من غمگین داد

من همان روز ز فرهاد طمع ببریدم
که عنان دل شیدا به لب شیرین داد

گنج زر گر نبود کنج قناعت باقی ست
آنکه آن داد به شاهان به گدایان این داد

خوش عروسیست جهان از ره صورت لیکن
هر که پیوست بدو عمر خودش کاوین داد

بعد از این دست من و دامن سرو و لب جوی
خاصّه اکنون که صبا مژده فروردین داد

در کف غصّه دوران دل حافظ خون شد
در فراق رخت ای خواجه قوام الدّین داد

# Glossary 1 Some Symbols

## Garden

**The cypress tree** – slender, upright, elegant, singular and like the letter Alif (a single vertical line in Farsi). It represents the rectitude of the Sheykh not merely in the moral sense, but in the inner and outer posture. To sit in meditation upright, from within, reflecting perhaps the idea of the Qutub – the spiritual pole or axis around which the universe revolves.

**The rosebud** – the, as yet, not fully realised spiritual potential of the seeker on the way.

**The rose** – the centripetal manifesting power of God, the Beloved, or the human heart. Its scent is spirit; its centre the essence; its petals the manifesting of God or the opening of the human heart. It is an object for practising concentration by the Sufis.

**The bulbul** (nightingale) – the lover of the rose and in some respects the voice of the rose. The rose is silent, appearing aloof, whilst the lover is full of extravagant expressions. It is the manifestation of The Word in words. Inwardly, in meditation, it refers to ideas or thoughts arising in the conscious mind from deep inside.

**The breeze** – consists of intimations or voices from the unseen dimension; or the flow of spiritual energy that inspires the dance in the Sufis. It also carries the connotation of the Nafas ar-Rehman (the Breath of the Merciful) which is referred to in Hadiths.

**The fountain** – the source of purification through tears. Weeping is a recognised state amongst Sufis arising from being in touch with the essence of deep seated emotions such as sorrow. It also indicates the generosity and abundance of Allah.

## The Body

**Head** – in man his highest selfhood which must be abased before the Divinity (submission).

**Hair -** is manifestation of unity into diversity. The curls may refer to the spiralling patterns of the Spirit's energy whose compelling movements the mystic becomes caught up in when 'dancing'..

**Face -** 'Everything perishes but His Face'(Qur'an 28:8); therefore it refers to the Eternal Divinity. The field of Absolute Existence in the most comprehensive sense; on which various features are identified. It could be described as the substance of the spiritual Essence.

**Mole -** Mystically it is the single point of unity encompassing all creation.

**Eye** – if used in the singular we take it to mean perception. Sometimes called the window to the soul. The pupil is said to stand in the same relation to the eye as the perfect man does to God (see Avery pp 109).

**Eyelash** – beauty that wounds the heart.

**Lip** – essence of Divinity. Ecstacy.

**Waist -** the bridge between the higher nature and the lower nature of man.

**Hand -** control. God says in the Qur'an *'I become My servant's hand and foot'* meaning God controls him.

**Feet** – As above, but also the lowest part, therefore to point one's feet towards something sacred is a sign of disrespect. To kiss someone's foot a sign of veneration for that person.

# Glossary 2

Alphabetic reference to terms found in the text of the ghazals.
gh = ghazal number in this edition

**Ad (and Samud);** tribes spoken of in the holy Qur'an who were punished for disbelief and persecution of their Prophets.

**Adab;** good manners – this has a subtle implication indicating that behaviour to others should be refined and spiritually punctilious and pure. For example it would be bad manners to remind someone of a favour given or to sit with one's feet pointing towards Kaaba or the shrine of a saint or to give a thing with ostentation. The demonstration of good manners is considered to reflect the inner state of the person. It can be far more subtle than this – for example the bad thought that a murid might get about the sheikh is poor manners. Extreme refinement of subtle Adab is a preoccupation amongst Sufis. It is also the greeting used to non Muslims rather than asalaam aleikum, which is used between Muslims.

**Allah;** the Arabic word for God. Sometimes this is translated as the Essence or as The (only) God. Allah and God and the Divinity are used as interchangeable words in this volume.

**Allahu Akbar;** gh 35: 'Greatness belongs to God': the first words (repeated four times) of the call to prayer in Islam.

**Alast;** many ghazals: A 'day' described as being outside of phenomenal time and space, in which Allah asks the first-created pure un-embodied souls created from the Nur–i-Muhammed' (Logos) –"Am I not your Lord?" To which the souls reply, 'YES'. It is the distant 'remembrance' of this day by the embodied souls that has been said to be the cause of the ecstasy in Sama (music concert) of the Sufis. (See Quran 7:172).

**Aloes wood;** gh 93: incense obtained from wood resin, thought to have medicinal properties and widely used in religious ceremonies.

**Anka/Anqa;** many ghazals: King of birds – used to symbolise the Beloved or God. Located, according to Fariduddin Attar, on the mysterious Mount Kaf

**Ambergris;** gh 22: a grey sweet smelling substance used for fixing perfumes.

**Arch;** 'The heart of those following the *haqiqa*t, when it is tuned and turned towards the real purpose it is called an arch by the enlightened ones' - Khwaja

Muinuddin Hasan Chishti, in '*Meditations of Khwaja Muinuddin Hasan Chishti.; Sharib Press 1992.*

**Arghavan**; gh16: A purple-pink/reddish flower, also known as 'redbud' (*Cercis Siliquastrum*) or the Judas tree.

**Asaf**; gh 20, 36: advisor (vizier) to Prophet (King) Solomon. He was scolded by an ant for not seeking earnestly enough the great seal ring lost for a while to Solomon. Used as the exemplar of the wise advisor.

**Ashura**; gh 16: tenth night of the Muslim month of Muharrem, and one of particular grieving and melancholy for Muslims marking the martyrdom of the son of Hazrat Ali, Imam Hussein.

**Ayaz**; gh 87: Minister of King Mahmud, the bond of affection between them is famous.

**Babylon**; gh 83: an ancient city associated with magic.

**Beloved**; many ghazals: God, Allah, or the murshid (spiritual guide), or a human beloved (male or female according to context and also used ambiguously as Hafiz writes on many levels at the same time. It is said the Sufis talk outwardly of God or Allah, but inwardly address the Divinity as the Beloved or Friend. The implication in Hafiz will depend on the context and may vary within one ghazal.

**Blue-garmented**; gh 139: outwardly pious (but inwardly black-hearted). Hypocrites.

**Blood Price**; gh 84: Money paid to relatives after a murder of one of the family. This indemnifies those who pay from revenge attacks.

**Bokhara (and Samarqand)**; gh 8: Two prominent Persian cities famed for learning and culture; symbolic here possibly of this world and the next.

**Breeze**; many ghazals: Usually Saba – the soft dawn breeze; a kind of zephyr; the messenger to and from the Beloved; spiritual intuition.

**Bulbul**; gh 30: The nightingale; a bird carrying news of events to the rose (the beloved). The archetype of the lover.

**Chashm**; gh 136: Literally 'by (or on) my eye' meaning to agree to do something.

**Chaugan**: gh 2; a mallet (probably with a hollow curve) used to play a game on horseback – the origin of modern polo. To be the ball in the game may be symbolic of accepting the' back and forth' of destiny. Also refers to the arch of the eyebrow metaphorically, and thus to the prayer arch.

**Cheek**; many ghazals: The divine splendour, beauty or glory. Manifestation of the Divine Essence (Avery).

**Civit**; gh 23: small lithe cat-like animal,

**Clay**; many ghazals: Basic human (animal) nature consisting of savage instincts such as lust, anger, greed etc.

**Corner-sitter**; many ghazals: One who sits in the corner of the tavern – a reclusive mystic. A corner can in this context also refer to a place where mystics meet informally as distinct from the formal Sufi hospices. Zawiya.

**Croesus**; an ancient king fabled for his vast wealth.

**Daughter of the vine**; many ghazals: Wine.

**Day of Awakening**; gh 3; The Last Judgement.

**Day of Alast/Azal**; see under Alast

**Dervish**; many ghazals: generally taken to be synonymous with 'Sufi', but it actually is more properly used to denote a Sufi of high degree and one who has no care for the world whatsoever. Feared and venerated for the power to bless or curse.

**Dimple** (of the chin): gh 2; often seen as a pit or well (connotes also the well of prophet Joseph) into which the lover may fall from desire for the beloved's beauty.

**Down** (Khatt); many ghazals: the fine face hair. Also the newly sprouted hair on an adolescent boy's face presaging the growth of a beard. In many styles of eastern art female beauty may be depicted with a fine shadow to emphasise the roundness of the face. Mystically this can refer to the integration of the spiritual with the material reality. That absolute clarity of detail that takes one beyond imagining. It has the quality of being a border or frame for beauty of the face. The Farsi word can also mean writing.

**Dust on the head of...**; many ghazals: making something worthless.

**Eid-ul-Fitr**; gh 113: literally breaking the soil (as when a plant emerges from the ground). The Islamic day of festivity following the fasting month of Ramadan. It commences with the sighting of the new moon of the month of Shawal.

**Eye** ( on my eye or by my eye); see under 'Chashm'. 'Narcissus eye' – see under narcissus. See under 'Symbols' page 328.

**Farhad**; gh 129: The Persian lover whose love for his beloved Shirin inspired many Farsi poets! Given an impossible task to carve stairs out of hard rock on nearly completing it he was falsely informed she had died. (see also Shirin).

**Fana**; Extinction. The state in which the individuality of the Sufi is merged into a Greater Reality so as to be almost indistinguishable from it. What remains of the individuality forms the basis for another state called Baqa (survival). The classic description of this is of a man attending his own funeral. The corpse is Fana the man attending is Baqa,

**Fatiha**; gh 100: The 'oft- repeated' seven opening verses of the holy Qur'an. It is recited as part of the Muslim ritual prayer. It is recited by pilgrims to sacred tombs and on all other religious occasions.

**Faqir;** gh 139: Poor – it implies Muslim saints of material poverty and great spiritual wealth; wandering Dervishes who depend on alms for living; associated with complete humility.

**Girdle**; gh 69: symbol of Christianity – usually a chain worn round the waist. It is treated as a symbol of disbelief in the religion of Islam.

**Goglet**; gh 93: long necked traditional jug for pouring wine. Symbolically may be the spiritual guide, or the holy Prophet Muhammed.

**Halwa;** many ghazals: Sweetmeats or a sweet dessert.

**Hair** (or tress)/Zulf; many ghazals: may be understood in many ways such as symbolising the many and varied strands or modes of life which have a single underlying unity - the multiplicity of Divine manifestation. Its other functions in the poems include: veiling the beloved's face; guarding the beloved's face; as a rope for the aspiring lover; as darkness of disbelief or as darkness of non-existence.

**Hoopoe**; many ghazals: Lapwing. The small crested bird that carried a message from Solomon to the Queen of Sheba (Bilqis queen of Saba). Sometimes used to symbolise the guide (as in Attar's 'Conference of the Birds'). It is referred to in the holy Qur'an.

**Harut**; gh 83: one of two fallen angel associated with magic in Babylon. (the other is Marut).

**Hajji Khivam**; gh 3: can be understood to be obliquely referring to God; The Murshid; or literally to a minister to Abu Ishaq (d 1353). Hajji is one who has performed the Hajj pilgrimage to Mecca.

**Hejaz** (Hijaz); gh 122: That part of Saudi Arabia in which Mecca and Medina can be found.

**Himmat;** gh 86 ; literally this means 'striving', but can also refer to the spiritually energetic look directed forcefully by a mystic. Austin describes it as directed use of the creative imagination of the Gnostic. Shah Wali Ullah in speaking of the creation of Eve (Huwa) describes it as arising from the concentrated desire Adam taking on actual physical form.

**Hoo, Hu or Ho;**, variants on the Arabic word used to denote the ipseity of the Divinity. Allah being the name of the Essence of God, *Hu* though untranslatable (sometimes He is used), has no gender. Described sometimes as implying the Personality of God. *Ho* is used to denote the Jamali nature of God (Beautiful, Loving, and Compassionate) whereas *Hu* or *Hoo* refers to the Jalali nature of God (Majestic and Powerful).

**Huma;** An auspicious legendary bird – it was said that on whoever the bird's shadow fell would become a king.

**Huri/Houri**; many ghazals: 'Silver-limbed' beautiful females of paradise.

**Idol/idol worship**; many ghazals; Hafiz Saheb uses the term in different ways - most frequently in relations to beauties. These are idols in as much as their beauty apparently attracts one away from the worship of One God, but in fact Hafiz sees beyond this – they are a manifestation of God's Beauty and seen in this way are not really idols. Khawaja Muinuddin Hasan Chishti describes idol worship in this way; "Idol worship is this, that the pilgrims on the way may treat pride and fame as the mark of perfection and the pinnacle of glory." The Sufis generally regard self-worship as the real idolatry.

**Ihram**; gh 68; this is the two unstitched cotton sheets worn by Muslim pilgrims to Mecca whilst performing the circling of the Kaaba.

**Iram;** gh 55: Qur'an 89:6, but in legend a city built to imitate paradise. The builder was destroyed for his presumption.

**Isa/Eesa**; gh22: Lord Jesus. Regarded as a prophet by Muslims.

**Jam/Jamshid**: .a (probably mythical) Persian King associated in mysticism with a goblet in which the whole world can be seen; amongst Sufis thought of as 'the divine mirror'.

**Jesus breath;** many ghazals: health or life giving breath as Lord Jesus was associated with many healing miracles and raising from the dead.

**Jinn;** many ghazals. One of the creatures made of "smokeless fire"; in other words of a non-material substance. Another is the Pari – renowned for their great beauty. Jinns may be well disposed or mischievous. They are mentioned often in the holy Qur'an and linked to man in having some degree of will. See Sura an-Nas. They are popular figures in fairy stories such as Aladdin..

**Kaaba**; gh 33: The House of Allah, found in Mecca, Saudi Arabia; the object of pilgrimage for Muslims at least once in their lifetime if possible. A simple cube shaped building around which circumambulations are performed by pilgrims.

**Kaf;** many ghazals: A mystic mountain and home of the Anka/Anqa.

**Kalandar** (Qalandar); gh 58: A wandering Dervish inclined to ecstatic states and unconventional ways.

**Karun**; gh 36: a man of vast wealth at the time of Moses, he is reported as having been sucked into the sands and it is believed this is in perpetuity.

**Kauther (Kawther)**; gh 55: This refers to a fountain in paradise.

**Kerbala/Karbala**; gh 13: A battle in which Hz. Hussein the grandson of the holy Prophet was martyred. (10th Muharrem AD 680), Kerbala is in present day Iraq. Hz Hussein had refused allegiance to Yazid and was defeated by a much larger force after being denied even water. The event is commemorated with much sorrow to this day.

**Khanqah;** gh 54: the lodge or hospice of the Sufis – at times these could be richly decorated grand buildings.

**Khilvatis**; many ghazals: Reclusive mystics.

**Khirqa;** gh 136: The cloak or coat passed from the Sufi Sheikh to a disciple carrying with it spiritual blessings.

**Khizr**; many ghazals: Possibly a temporary guide of the Prophet Moses (see Qur'an 18:65, where he is not named) and of certain other Prophet's and Saints. A helper in difficulty; a friend of God.

**Kohl**; gh 12, 29: black eye-liner used to beautify and enhance the eyes.

**Lailat-i-Qadr;** see Night of Power.

**Lala;** gh 17: Red poppy-like tulip; appears in spring.

**Layla** (also Laila, Leyla, etc); gh 87: Literally 'Night' but the name of a woman who was the object of the love of the 'madman' Majnun: so also standing for the Beloved.

**Lip**; many ghazals: the attraction of divine love; the essence of the soul.

**Liver/liver's blood**; many ghazals: the liver is the seat of the spiritual faculty governing the body; as such it is associated with grief and difficulty arising from the bodies needs and desires. The drinking of the liver's blood means taking on difficulties that result in spiritual gain, eventually.

**Magian(s)**; many ghazals: The name is associated with the Zoroastrian religion, whose followers were fire-worshippers. The Pir of the Magians is the spiritual master of mystics of that sect.

**Majnun**; gh 22: literally 'madman' or' lunatic', refers to the lover of Laila/ Layla in many tales of the Middle East, and in particular in Sufi literature. Used widely as a model for the crazed lover of God. He is used in Sufi literature to demonstrate various aspects of love. For example he once appeared as a beggar when Laila was distributing water to a queue of beggars. When it came to his turn she refused water. He went away happy. Someone asked why. "Because she singled me out for different treatment from the rest," was his reply.

**Mansur** (al-Hallaj); gh 138: Sufi martyr, executed for declaring 'I am the Truth.'

**Marwah** (or Marwa); gh 91: A small hill adjacent to the Kaaba in Mecca. (see also Safa).

**Marut**; gh 83: one of two fallen angel associated with magic in Babylon. (see also Harut)

**Messiah;** literally 'the anointed one'. Usually this is referring to Lord Jesus.

**Mole;** many ghazals: in Hafiz referring to a mole or blemish on the face but regarded as a sign of beauty. Mystically it is the single point of unity encompassing all creation.

**Mihrab;** gh 83, 86, 102 and many others: usually an arch enabling the worshipper to face in the direction of Mecca. Compared frequently to the eyebrow by Hafiz. See also under *Arch.*

**Mirror;** the mystics mirror enables him or her to see events in the unseen; also events can be seen in the physical world in the mirror of the heart. The mirror of the intellect sees different levels of the inner life.

**Moon;** many ghazals: may refer to a beauty (human or divine); also associated with the holy Prophet Muhammed.

**Murid;** Disciple of a spiritual guide.

**Murshid;** gh 102: The seeker's spiritual guide in the Sufi way of mysticism.

**Musk;** perfume of exceptional quality found in a gland in the naval of a musk-deer. Symbolically something of great rarity- spiritual essence.

**Mustapha;** gh 54: The chosen one, the holy Prophet Muhammed.

**Narcissus;** variant of daffodil used by Hafiz to symbolise the drunken eye of the beloved. The colour may be associated with sickness – in the sense of being love-sick. The yellow cup of the flower set against the white petals gives the appearance of an eye.

**Night of Power;** gh 26,113: A night in which divine blessings descend; frequently associated with certain nights towards the end of Ramadan, the fasting month: the night is called Laylat-i-Qadr in Arabic and is described in the holy Quran as a special mystical night of Peace in which many blessings descend on the one fortunate enough to receive this – until dawn. See the Qur'an sura called by the same name.

**Nimrod;** gh 121: A worldly ruler of ill repute who put Prophet Ibrahim (Abraham) into the fire, but Allah made it experienced as coolness for him.

**Parvis;** several ghazals. In literature an ancient king who became part of a complex love triangle with Shirin and Farhad.

**Peri;** many ghazals: Beautiful spirit being from the realm of 'creatures made of smokeless fire'; below the rank of angel; inhabitant of the lowest level of heaven.

**Pine-cone;** many ghazals: the heart was seen as shaped like a pine cone.

**Pir;** many ghazals: Sometimes used as synonymous with Sufi elder or Murshid, at other times to indicate a Sufi of higher attainment.

**Pir of the Magians;** originally the title of pre-Islamic spiritual teacher – according to some this became degraded to meaning the keeper of a tavern – in a derogatory sense – but later regained some credibility as in Hafiz poetry.

**Qibla** (also Kibla); gh 10, 36: the direction of prayer, often marked by a Mihrab or arch, enabling the Muslim to pray in the direction of Mecca.

**Ramadan;** many ghazals; the month of fasting between dawn and sunset for Muslims. The word itself means 'consuming fire' (Avery).

**Rebab;** gh 18, 48: bowed string instrument probably predecessor of the modern violin.

**Redbud;** many ghazals: see 'Arghavan' above.

**Rend/Rind;** many ghazals. Usually translated as profligacy; shameless dissoluteness; reckless extravagance; great abundance. Referring to those Sufis who tend towards enthusiasm and extravagance in their devotion to the Beloved (God).

**Rizwan;** gh 19, 36: Gate keeper of the paradise gardens.

**Ruknabad;** many ghazals: A river in Shiraz.

**Rose;** many ghazals; May symbolise the divine or human beloved or the spiritual guide according to context.

**Ruby;** many ghazals: precious stone thought to have gained its purity from the effect of the sun on stone. A symbol of spiritual transformation.

**Saba/Sheba;** many ghazals, see also under Solomon. Saba is the state ruled by Bilqis, 'Queen of Sheba'.

**Saba breeze/wind;** many ghazals: Saba is a breeze that blows at dawn from the east. It is a breeze to which lovers confide their secrets and which, according to Abdul-Razzagh Kashani, is "the Clement Waft" Nafahaat-e-Rahmaaniyeh") that blows from the Spiritual East. Saba takes on many roles in Hafez's poems and is a harbinger that carries good news between lover and beloved. Saba Wind blows slowly and brings the scent of the beloved to Hafez so that he will not stay alone. *(Kia , Ali Asghara and Saghe'i-Saeed) see bibliography.*

**Safa;** gh 91: One of two small hills (the second is called Marwa) adjacent to the site of the Kaaba in Mecca. Running, or walking urgently, between the two, seven times, forms part of the Hajj pilgrimage. It commemorates the frantic search for water by Abraham's wife that culminated in disclosure of the sacred Zamzam spring. Safa also has the meaning of purity. See also Marwa above.

**Salam/asalam aleikum;** Salam is usually translated as peace however the word has a broader connotation in Arabic implying both peace and security or safety. Salaam aleikum (peace be upon you) is the initial greeting of Muslims meeting each other and is supposed to precede any other conversation. As-salaam is one of Allah's 99 Beautiful names.

**Saki;**many ghazals.The Saki is traditionally a young boy who would serve wine at a party, but it can also be the spiritual guide who gives inspiration. Hazrat Abdul Qadir al-Jillani mentions the holy Prophet saying –"I have seen my Lord in the shape of a most beautiful youth." He goes on to say: "As Allah is beyond all shape and form .... it is interpreted as the manifestation of the Lord's beautiful attributes reflected on the mirror of the pure soul..... this is called the child of the heart.....this reflected image is also a connection between the servant and his Lord."(See also our introduction in this volume).

**Sama/Sema;** gh 127: literally – audition. A state the Sufi may enter during listening to special music under particular conditions – the music concert is often called Sama, but in fact Sama as a state does not actually require formal music. Mevlana Rumi is said to have got this state on hearing the beating of the goldsmith's hammering. Sama need not only involve hearing but other senses such as sight and smell and touch.

**Samiri;** gh 123: One of those who escaped Egypt with Prophet Moses. He had the golden calf made whilst Prophet Moses was away receiving the Ten Commandments and was punished severely. It is assumed he used some form of magic to get the idol to make a sound.

**Shariat**; gh 92: Religious laws derived from the holy Qur'an and Hadiths (accounts of the sayings and actions of the holy Prophet Muhammed).

**Sidhra** tree; gh 88: It is a very large Tree beyond the seventh heaven. It is named the Sidrat al-Muntahā because there terminates at it whatever ascends from the earth and whatever descends [from heaven] including what comes down from God, (and) waḥy (divine inspiration) and other things besides. *(As-Saʿdi, Tafsir, 819) courtesy of Wikipedia.*

**Solomon** (Sulaiman); gh 26: Prophet and king, associated with wisdom and linked to the Queen of Sheba. Many Qur'anic and biblical references.

**Sikander;** Alexander the Great. Sikander's mirror was a mirror in which could be seen all the events going on in the world – sought by Alexander. See also Jamshid.

**Silver-limbed**; many ghazals: refers usually to a houri/huri – one of the handmaidens of paradise (see many references in holy Qur'an).

**Tariqat**; gh 28: A stage intermediary between the outward following of divine law (Shariat), and the stage of Truth (Haqiqat). In Shariat one pays the customary charity of 2.5%, in Tariqat one pays 97.5% and keeps only the residue. In Haqiqat everything is given and nothing is reserved (see Meditation of Khwaja Muinuddin Hasan Chishti: Sharib Press 1992). Hafiz summarises Tariqat as "Whatever comes my way is best". It is also called the Way. In it there is deep moral and spiritual struggle; the inner or greater Jihad. It is to pass from form (shariat) to essence, whilst haqiqat can perhaps be described as passing from essence to the substance of essence.

**Tasbih**; gh 132: String of beads that are counted when reciting one of the names of God or some other formulae of remembrance of God. A rosary.

**Tavern**; many ghazals: can be referring to the Khanqah or hospice where Zikr or hearing music for spiritual purposes or spiritual teaching takes place. May also refer to an inner place experienced in meditation. Khwaja Muinuddin Hasan Chishti says: The real tavern is in the heart. But without the guidance of the perfect spiritual guide the absorbed traveller on the way cannot understand it. The tavern means and implies that in the gambling house of love you may lose your wealth, position, garden, land, and whatever is destined in the universe and in both the worlds. (*From the Meditations of Khwaja Muinuddin Hasan Chishti – Sharib Press 1992, Southampton*)

**Temple**; many ghazals; "The implication of 'the temple and the place of idol worship' is wide enough to cover even the slightest thought of both the worlds occupying your heart." (*from the Meditations of Khwaja Muinuddin Hasan Chishti – Sharib Press 1992, Southampton*)

**Tuba tree**; gh 19, 22: A tree in Paradise, whose width is a hundred years, and the clothes of the people of Paradise are taken from its bark (Hadith). A place of good return after this life. [www.qtafsir.com]

**Turk**; many ghazals: varied usage – can refer to the *beloved;* also to a powerful force.

**Venus**; gh 9: acc to W-C. - Venus (Zuhra) is female singer in the fourth heaven in which the Messiah, Jesus, lives. A propitious planet.

**Way, the**; many ghazals: Can mean the straightway described in the holy Qur'an, also of course path or road. The Sufi Way – the path on which the Sufi travels to the Beloved (God).The progression through mystical stages of awakening. In English, of course, there is a double meaning since we talk of the 'way' we do something as distinct from *what* we do. This expresses an aspect of what the Way means amongst Sufis – in some respects it is not what is done but the *way* in which it is done that counts.

**Wheat**; gh 24: used in the Qur'an (rather than apple as in bible) as the means of Adam's seduction and fall.

**Wine**: The real wine in a clear heart is the sign and symbol of moving about in Allah, and refers to the virtues and qualities and to the way of life to be moulded according to the attributes of Allah. The pure and purifying wine is this; that the divine grace may descend upon the heart of the faithful witness of the truth. (*from the Meditations of Khwaja Muinuddin Hasan Chishti – Sharib Press 1992, Southampton*)

**Wudhu;** gh 27,118: the ritual ablution preceding the Muslim ritual prayer.

**Yemen prayer**; 100: A prayer taught by the holy Prophet to his son-in-law Hz Ali, when he sent him to Yemen as envoy.

**Yemen, (breath coming from)**; gh 66: probably a reference to a comment of the holy Prophet who speaks of a breath of divine mercy coming from Yemen, and possibly meaning from Uwais Qarni a man whose love of the Prophet, who he did not get to meet physically, caused him to remove his own teeth in sympathy for the hurt done to a tooth of the holy prophet in battle.

**Yusuf**; many ghazals: Prophet Joseph (see Qur'an - Sura Yusuf, and Biblical accounts).Key features to his story include his ability to interpret dreams, his great physical beauty, his being put down a well by his brothers, his rescue and being sold into slavery, the attempted seduction by Zuleika, the love his father Prophet Yaqub (Jacob) had for him, that caused prophet Yaqub to go blind, the sending of a shirt of Prophet Yusuf that cured the older man of blindness.

**Zoroaster/Zarathustra;** gh 121: Founder of the ancient Zoroastrian religion of Persia in which fire worship is the main feature.

**Zuleika (Zuleikha);** See holy Qur'an (Sura Yusuf). The wife of the purchaser of Prophet Joseph (Yusuf) when he was enslaved first in Egypt. She fell in love with Yusuf and tried to seduce him – he refused, and was sent to prison falsely accused of assault. Many stories are told in Persian literature of her continued devotion to the Prophet – she therefore is used to represent 'the faithful lover'.

# Bibliography

## Primary English Sources;

**Avery**, P.; The Collected Lyrics of Hafiz of Shiraz; Archetype; 2007; ISBN 1-901383-09-1.
**Wilberforce-Clarke**, H; The Divan. Volumes 1 and 2, The Octagon Press Ltd, London. 1974. SBN 90086018 9.
**Sharib**, Z H.;The Rubaiyat of Hafiz; Sharib Press; Southampton, 1993; ISBN 0-9508926-5-3.
**Smith**, P; Divan of Hafiz; New Humanity Books; 1983; ISBN 0-949-191-00-0.

## Secondary English Sources

*Anon;* Selection of Rubaiyat and Odes; Watkins. Nd.
*Arberry*, A.J.; Shiraz, Persian City of Saints and Poets; Norman University of Oaklahoma Press; 1960; no ISBN.
*Alston;* In Search of Hafiz; Shanti Sadan: 1996: 0 854244 045 4
*Avery P., and J. Heath-Stubbs, Hafiz of Shiraz,* London, 1952.
*Bell*, G.; Teachings of Hafiz; Octagon Press, London; 1979; ISBN 90086063 4
*Gray, E. T.* (1995). The Green Sea of Heaven. Ashland: White Cloud Press.
*Idem, Fifty Poems of Hafiz, Text and Translations,* Cambridge, 1947.
*Jamshidipur*, Y.; Selected Poems of Hafiz; Tehran; 1963.
*Ladinski*, D.; The Gift,;Arkana 1999; ISBN 0 14 01.9581 5
*Loloi, P.;*Hafiz, Master of Persian Poetry; I.B.Taurus; New York; 2004.
*MacCarthy, Ghazels from the Divan of Hafiz done into English,* London, 1893.
*Nicholson*, R.A; Translations of Eastern Poetry and Prose; Curzon Press Ltd., London. 1987. ISBN 0 70070196 6.
*Saberi, R,;*The Divan of Hafiz; A Bilingual text, Persian-English.. UPA. Lanham/ New York/ Oxford. 2002. ISBN 0-7618-2246-1.
*Sahlepour*, S. Divan of Hafiz; Booteh Press, Tehran; 1998. ISBN 964-90021-5-4.

*Salami,* I,; The Divan of Hafiz; Tehran, 2013.ISBN 978-964-8741-55-1.
*Smith, P.;* Tongue of the Hidden; New Humanity Books;. 1974: 0 949191 05 1
*Smith, P;* Introduction to Divan of Hafiz; New Humanity Books: 1986: 0
949 191 00 0
*Smith, P.;* Loves Perfect Gift; New Humanity Books. 1988: 0 949191 04 3

## On-line English sources

Zahuri Sufi Web Site – www.zahuri.org – see Persian Pages
http://www.hafizonlove.com/bio/
http://www.iranonline.com/literature/hafez/one.html
http://www.majzooban.org/en/articles/3178-shams-al-din-hafez-shirazi-
great-poet-of-persia.html
http://en.wikipedia.org/wiki/Hafez
http://www.thesongsofhafiz.com/life.htm Primary Farsi Sources;
http://www.iranicaonline.org/articles/hafez-x
http://www.academicjournals.org/article/article1379490294_Bahrami.pdf
https://coursewikis.fas.harvard.edu/aiu18/Hafez
http://islam.uga.edu/sufipoetry.html

## Farsi Resources

Khoramshahi ,B.:Hafez Name;Tehran 2011.ISBN 978-964-445-175-1
Shojaeeadib,Sh,;The Divan of Hafiz; Khatere majmoo;2003,ISBN 964-7020-
10-4
Divan-e Khajeh Shamseddin Mohammad Hafiz-e Shirazi, *by Mohammad
Ghazvini and Dr. Ghasem Ghani (in Persian)*
Divan-e Hafiz-e Shirazi, *by Dr. Seyyed Mohammad Reza Jalaly Nayeenii (in
Persian)*
Divan-e Khajeh Shamseddin Mohammad Hafiz-e Shirazi, *compiled by
Mohammad Jaafar Mahjoobi (in Persian)*
Divan-e Khajeh Shamseddin Mohammad Hafiz-e Shirazi (revised and
elucidated); Dr.Parviz Natel Khanlari.

## On-line Farsi Resources

http://ganjoor.net/hafez/
http://hafezdivan.blogpars.com/
http://www.1doost.com/hafez/omen/

# Some books related to Sufism

*Akhtar/Taher*; Sufi Saints; Anmol Publications; 1998: 81 7488 939 6*Atta Illah/Danner;* Sufi Aphorisms (Kitab al-Hikam); E.J.Brill. Leiden; 1973: 90 04 07168 7

*Atta Illah/Danner;* Book of Wisdom: SPK (La).

*Arabi/Bursevi* Kernel of Kernels   Beshara. nd.

*Arabi/Austin;* The Sufis of Andalusia ; Beshara ;1971; 0 904 975 13 4

*Arabi/Austin;* The Bezels of Wisdom; Paulist Press; 1980    0 8091 2331 2 (pr) 0 8091 0313 3 (cl)

*Arabi/Weir ;* Whosoever Knoweth Himself; Beshara;1976;  0 904975 06 1

Arberry. ;Kalabadhi/y ;The Doctrine of the Sufis Muhammad Ashraf   1966

*Arabi/Burkhardt ;* Hisbul-l-Wiqayah   Ibn Arabi Society ; Beshara; 1977 ;  0 904975 09 6

Arberry, A.Classical Persian Literature; Curzon   1994       0 7007 0276 8

*Attar/Darbandi;* Conference of the Birds; Penguin: 1988: 0-14-044434-3

*Attar/Arberry:* Muslim Saints and Mystics; Arkana: 1990: 0 14 019264 6

*Babajan/Shepherd ;* A Sufi Matriarch; Anthropographia Publications, Camb: 1985: 0 9508680 1 9

*Baldick,;* Mystical islam: I. B. Tauris;1989   1 85043 137 X  :  1 85043 140 X

*Bistami/Sells ;* Early Islamic Mysticism ; Paulist Press ; 1996       0-8091-0477-6 (cloth)

*Brown, E.G.:* The Dervishes: Frank Cass & Co.  1968

*Chittick ,W.;* Sufi Path of Knowledge; S. Univ. N.York: 1989:   0 88706 885 5 (p) 0 88706 884 7

*Danner/Kingsley;* Quest for Red Sulphur;  Islamic Text Soc. 1993;    0 946621 45 4 )p) 0 946621 4 4 6 cl

*Ernst, C.:* Words of Ecstasy in Sufism ; SUNY; 1985; 0 87395-917-5

*Ernst, C;* Eternal Garden; SUNY Press 1992; 0-7914-0883-30-7 914-0884-1(pbk)

*Ernst, C.;*Shambala Guide to Sufism;Shambala: 1997: 1 57062 180 2

*Ernst, C.* Ruzbihan Baqli - Rhetoric of Sainthood in Persian Sufism; Curzon Press;1996; 0 7007 0342 X

*Fadiman/Frager;* Essential Sufism; Harper; San Fransisco ; 1997; 0 06 251474 1 (cl) 0 06 251475 x (pb)

*Harris ;* Journey to the Lord of Power; Inner Traditions Int.; 1980; 089281 024 6

*Hujwiri/Nicholson;* Kashf al-Mahjub ; Luzac & Co.;1976 ; 0 7189 0203 3

*Husaini;* Pantheistic Monotheism of Ibn Arabi; Ashraf ..

*Lawrence;* Notes from a Distant Flute Coombe Springs Press. 1978. 0 9508926 9 6.

*Lewishon;* The Heritage of Sufism Vol 2; One World: 1992: 1-85168-189-2

*Lewis;* Rumi - Past and Present, East and West One World (Oxford); 2000 ISBN. 1 85168 214 7.

*Lings, M.;* What is Sufism; 1975.

*Nicholson R.A.;* Personality in Sufism; Adam Publishers: 1998: 81 7435 142 6

*Nicholson R.A.;*Studies in Islamic Mysticism; Cambridge Uni. Press 1989 . ISBN 0 521 29546 7

*Nizami;* Life & Times of Nasiruddin Chirag; Idarah-i-Adabyat-i-Delli: 1991:

*Rastogi;* Islamic Mysticism Sufism; East West: 1982: 0 856 92 096 7

*Rumi/Nicholson;* The Masnavi (6 bks in 3 vols);Gibb Memorial Trust;1990: 0 906094 10 0 (3rd vol).

*Schimmel A.;* Deciphering the Signs of God; SUNY: 1994: 0 7914 1982 7

*Schimmel A.;*As Through a Veil:Mystical Poetry in Islam; New York 1982.

*Sells,;* Early Islamic Mysticism; Paulist Press: 1996.

*Sharib  Z.H.*;Reflections of the Mystics of Islam;  Sharib Press; 1995;  0 9508926 9 6

*Sharib Z.H.;*Ghous-ul-Azam Piran-e-Pir ;Asma;  1961

*Sharib Z.H.;* The Culture of the Sufis; Sharib Press; Southampton; 1999. 0 9531517 1 9

*Sharib:* The Sufi Saints of the Indian Subcontinent; Munshiram Manoharlal; Delhi. 2006. ISBN: 81-215-1052-X.

*Sharib, Z.H.;* Khwaja Gharib Nawaz;Muhammad Ashraf: 1990: none

*Sharib Z.H.;*Ghous-ul-Azam Piran-e-Pir; Asma: 1961:

*Sharib Z.H.* Reflections of the Mystics of Islam   Sharib Press; 1995;  0 9508926 9 6.

as-Sulami/Cornell; Early Sufi Women; Fons Vitae: 1999: 1-887752 06 4

Sushud/Holland; The Masters of Wisdom of C. Asia; Coombe Springs Press; 1983:  0 900306 93 9

*Syed Ali Reza* Najul Bhalaga (Peak of Eloquence)   Tahrika ;Tarsil Qur'an, Inc ;1985:   0 940368 43 9     0 940368 42 0

*Trimingham;* The Sufi Orders in Islam; OU Press 1971

*Troll (ed)* Muslim Shrines in India; Oxford Uni. Press : 1989 :

*Waliullah/Baljon;* Mystical Interpretation of Prophetic Tales; Brill - Leiden:  1973:  90 04 03833 7

*Waliullah/Jalbani;* The Lamahat and Sata'at; Octagon Press:  1980:  9008 6081 2
*Waliullah/Jalbani;*The Sacred Knowledge; Octagon Press:  1982:  90086093 6

Publications by **Sharib Press** of books by Dr Zahurul Hasan Sharib available at www.zahuri.org
The Psalm of Life/The Psalm of Love/ The Psalm of Light/ The Meditations of Khwaja Moinuddin Hasan Chishti/Abu Said Abi'l Khair and his Rubaiyat/ Hafiz and his Rubaiyat/Sarmad and his Rubaiyat/The Culture of the Sufis/Reflection of the Mystics of Islam/Qur'anic Prayers/Qur'anic Precepts/Qur'anic Parables.

# Appendix

*Re-wording from English to English of ghazals given by Mr Wilberforce-Clarke in his translation, but where no Farsi version could be located or where there appears to be doubts of authenticity. In some cases this is just one or two verses from a ghazal; in others the whole ghazal is given here. We have usually followed the order and number of lines in Khanlari and Avery. For rendering the English we have also consulted Avery and Saberi.*
*We have not included these lines or ghazals in Farsi.*

(W-C 7)
In those long, flowing, locks what intention is there?
Again you have mussed up that musk-scented hair.

(W-C 9)
In gratitude for the good fortune of a glorious company,
Extend sympathy to desert wanderers, with generosity.

(W-C 11)
My heart was turned into blood by your eye's sorcery,
Beloved, see what I mean - how you have murdered me!

What is this doomsday scenario shown to many a lover?
Show your face! Our heart and life in sacrifice we offer.

The heart of unhappy Hafiz bleeds, from separation,
O beloved what if it had known a moment of union?

(W-C 17)
The right of salt[1], your ruby lip commands,
Against the roasted heart's wounds demands.

O pious preacher drink wine as drunkards do,
O wise friends, fear God as you ought to.

If it is the water of eternal life you want to find,

Seek it in wine, and the sound of music refined.

If you seek the essence of life, like Alexander,
To the beloveds ruby red lip, just surrender.

To the nymph like cheek that the Saki does display,
Drink, like Hafiz, in the rose season, without delay.

Hafiz, grieve not! The beloved is good fortune,
And will remove the veil later on, if not soon.

(W-C 15)
When lovers were invited to union with you by your beauty
With heart and life for mole and hair they fell into calamity.

What the very life of the lovers suffer in separation from you,
None in the world knows other than Karbala's martyred few.

My dear if that bold Turk gets drunk and behaves as a Rend,
From the start it's appropriate if chastity and piety you end.

The happy time, the season of joy and wine and roses,
Regard as a treasure these five days of joyfulness.

Hafiz, if the king's feet you should succeed in kissing,
Great honours and high status both worlds will be giving.

(W-C 16)
Again I spoke, "O my moon, that rose-hued cheek veil not;
For, if you do, surely distress and angst is this stranger's lot."

(W-C 17)
A quiet haven, secure; and goodly company that is pleasing,
O Lord – what I see, am I awake or am I really sleeping?

(W-C 19) *(Khanlari attributes this ghazal to Salman Saavaji)*
Even Rizwan's garden originates in *your* garden of union;
Hell-fire's torment is tormented by the fire of separation.
Shelter in your stature and cheek's beauty, they are seeking,

Paradise and tuba; a good place of sure return* they're wanting

All night the rivers of paradise see, as my eye sees,
In sleep, the sight of your intoxicated eye sees.

To every season spring describes your great beauty;
Each book opened in paradise mentions your bounty.

My heart is eaten up, my soul did not satisfy the heart's desire;
My eyes would not have wept blood if the heart had its desire.

Don't think in the circle of your lovers is just the drunkard,
To the intoxication of the pious fanatic you give no regard.

On seeing the red circle of your lips, on *your* radiant face,
I understood that the ruby jewel is from the sun's grace.

Draw the veil aside! How long do you plan to hide?
In this veil only modesty is the benefit on your side.

The rose saw your face and then burst into flame;
Rose-water caught your scent, and ashamed became.

Hafiz says that love of *your* face in troubles submerged him.
See how he is dying! For once please come and help him.

Hafiz do not let life slip by in idle foolishness,
Work hard, and on yourself the value of life impress.

*\*Qur'an reference – paradise with the Tuba Tree is described as a place of good return – but here they are themselves seeking a place of good return with the Beloved (God).*

(W-C 21)
Strive for Truth, that from your soul the sun will rise today,
Due to falseness the first dawn a black face will display.

(W-C 22)
May the vista of my eye be never devoid of that one's presence,

Because in its corner is the quiet chamber of remembrance.

Every rose becoming decoration for the green of the meadows,
Colour and perfume from converse with the beloved shows.

If my heart and I are sacrificed for the beloved, no fear,
My beloved's welfare and safety is my sole object here.

Anything but the beloved may your eye never try to see,
For it's in that corner of the chamber, the beloved will be.

(W-C 26)
In the procession, when they saddle up the wind, for him to mount,
How will I ride with great Solomon, when my steed is the little ant?

(W-C 29)
We, the threshold of love, and a head that is needy,
Let us see who, in the bosom of the Friend, sleeps sweetly.

(W-C 35)
Come back quickly, my eye seeks your coming as eagerly,
As the faster's ear listens for 'Allah Ho Akbar' greedily.

(W-C 36)
Kings are the Qibla the whole world turn to for help in need,
Because to serve the majesty of the Dervishes, they give heed.

(W- 37)
Like the candle I burn up my own existence, all night till morning,
Consumed like a moth I am; only during the day am I sitting.

W-C 38)
Your mouth, the fountain of the water of life's essence it is,
But that chin dimple, your lip's pit edge; not without purpose it is.

W-C 41
O Lord, this liberality of yours, from where is it derived?
Is it from the similarity of stars to my tears, it arrived?

(W-C 42)
For me to be a beggar of yours is better than sovereignty,
Submission to your tyranny and infidelity is glory and honour for me.

(W-C 45)
The master of wisdom, who saw through this magic affair,
Shut up his own shop, and closed the door of speaking there.

(W-C 46)
Even in a single day, from your scent, the heart's expansion I see,
Like the rosebud, in the heart of one in whom desire for you there be.

O breeze of union an altogether other life was found in you,
See the error of the heart's hoping for fidelity from you.

(W-C 47)
All creation tends towards inevitable deterioration,
Excepting only love alone - secure in its foundation.

Eternal decree made that camel's face blacken,
Proverbially, no scrubbing will make it whiten.

(W-C 48)
So richly green are the plain and valley - so leave them not!
Don't ignore the water just because the world is reflected in it.

(W-C 50)
It is grace indeed if you graciously should call us,
And no complaint can we make if you reject us.

No book can describe you; to try would be in vain,
So far exceeding description you will ever remain.

The beloved is seen by sight that penetrates to the unseen only,
The light in that lover's eye goes from Kaf and back instantly.
O heart's beloved, upright cypress; stone hard you are,
The fountains that flow from our face, say that you are.

Without equal! You value Paradise's wealth as nought,

From all this it seems me to limbo you have brought.

In the Book of the beloved's face, read a sign of revelation,
For of Khashf e Khashf's high stations it is an explanation.

The enemy who wants to compete with Hafiz in poetry,
Is a low-flying swallow that an Anqa vainly tries to be.

(W-C 53)
Though untouched by me, from that ruby wine I got intoxication;
With whom is it ensconced; whose cup is its constant companion?

(W-C 54)
Basra's Hasan*, Syria's Suhaib, Habsh's Bilal, for faith came far,
Abu Jahal, in Mecca's dust, stayed an infidel - things amazing are.
O sir, a thousand rationales and good manners I did possess,
Now I'm a drunk, ruined by one who is completely manner-less.

*Khwaja Hasan Basri was a famous early Sufi. Shuhaib and Bilal : were
companions of the holy Prophet Muhammad. Abu Jahl and Abu Lahab were
both reviled enemies of the holy Prophet

(W-C 58)
The tyranny of the friend became of such an extreme intensity,
I feared that, were it to end, aversion might rise up instantly.

If you have closed the door of repenting, wake and open it now!
When the rose season comes the lover can't use it anyhow.

(W-C 59)
But don't rely on your own deeds, for on the timeless Day,
Do you know what the record of creation's pen had to say?

Pleasant indeed is paradise's garden, but be very wary,
Regard as plunder too the field's edge and willow so shady,
(W-C 61)
O pious fanatic, go! Leave off this inviting me to Paradise,
For on that day, before time was, God determined otherwise.

Not a single grain can one harvest from being existent,
If the seed was not sown in God's Way, by self effacement.

Yours: the rosary, prayer mat, austerity and chastity:
My bell, path, cell and prayer place is the tavern only.

O Sufi forbid me not wine, for the All-wise Ones sake,
Who in Eternity my clay to mix with pure wine did make.

A true Sufi is not fit for paradise, unless, like me, he does incline,
To sell the cloak of religion in order to purchase the tavern's wine.

The pleasures of paradise and the Houri's lips will seem bland,
To one who lets the garment of the *beloved* slip from the hand.

O Hafiz! If God's grace he does generously bestow,
Concern for hell or paradise you need not ever show.

(W-C 62)
The grievous pain of the lover is due to separation from you,
 But you never ask "Where is my consumed lover, do you?

My heart is fed up with the cave of the sheikh and his place of prayer,
The young Christian friend - where? The vintner's house – where?

(W-C 63)
Last night, drunk, I strolled past the garden's banqueting place,
Likeness to your mouth in the rose-bud I thought I could trace.

O All-high! My dire state is the result of that face enhancing line,
What reed pen did ever such heart-enticing picture design?

(W-C 67)
Give wine in a gold cup because the cup that dawn risers are drinking,
Takes the whole world, like the sword of a gold scattering king.

As the tulip jauntily slants his hat, each heart that is stained,
The cup of wine, that is the colour of the red arghavan, drained.

(W-C 69)
Our supplication and entreaty don't have an effect on that beauty;
Happy indeed is he who from the lovely ones gained prosperity.

The wise seeker who reached the state of non-existence,
Was held in intoxication by those mysteries' existence.

(W-C 70)
Happy days for the drunken rend² for both worlds caring not,
Gave them away; gave up that sorrow and cared not a jot.

(W-C 76)
Bring out the red wine! In the tavern just last night the Pir spoke,
He talked of God's kindness, His Mercy and Compassion did invoke.

(W-C 83)
You spilled my blood and so from heart grief released me,
I am proffering thanks for that dagger in your look I see.

I cry, and from the rain of tears, my hope must be,
That the seed of love may be planted in you by me.

Be graceful and allow me with burning heart to draw near,
So I can hold your foot and there rain jewels. Each one a tear.

If my eye and heart have shown desires for another,
That heart I burn up and the eye I remove altogether.

(W-C 86)
I always thought your eye's pupil was after the blood of my heart,
But it reminds of your dark mole, so now I find it good for my part.

It's thanks to the kindness of the breeze the beloved's scent I get,
Otherwise each morning, what hint of your passing by would I get.

(W-C 88)
O puritan, of that place of solitude you stand ever in need,
To the lover perpetual ease has been divinely decreed.

Fortune is that, which, without blood, the heart gets by grace,
The paradise garden, relying on effort, is a valueless place.

Live not in fear of dishonour, but like the rose in happiness;
Because to please this passing world is really valueless.

(W-C 89)
This is a place of ambush, Hafiz, and you travel so rapidly;
Do not, for on this path to non existence dust rises easily.

(W-C 90)
From my embrace you swiftly departed and left my heart breaking,
In whose place I wonder, rest and sleep now are you finding?

(W-C 92)
In every city the eagle of violence its wings spread out it has got,
None bent the bow of seclusion, the arrow of a sigh no one shot.

(W-C 94)
Since grief for you has taken up residence in my heart,
Tumbling darkly, like the locks of your hair, is my heart.

Your fire coloured lip is really the Water of Life,
Water, that in us, a great fire has brought to life.

For a very long time, for the spirit within my soul,
That noble stature and high status has been the goal.

Indeed of *your* exalted, towering, stature I became a lover,
Since aspiring to such splendour is the work of a lover.

Since we shelter in the shade of that munificence,
Why is it you have withdrawn your beneficence.

This morning the scent of ambergris arrived on the breeze,
Perhaps to the desert that beloved of mine has gone for ease.

From my two eyes flow a river of purest pearls,
The whole world is encompassed by those jewels.

O cypress-like one, of flower covered chest, the verse of Hafiz,
Like the description of thy stature, attaining unto grandeur is.

(W-C 95)
O respected sir! For your fine movement, head to toe I die,
Bold Turk, move gracefully, before your great stature I die.

You asked when I would die before you, but why so hasty?
I died even before you made such a sweet demand of me.

This drunken seeking lover – (parted from that idol, Saki),
Says, "I die before your cypress-like stature, so move proudly"

That one's eyelashes, a life of love-sickness has given,
Say; "To die before your eye only one look need be given.

You spoke of ruby lip giving pain and also giving remedy,
But I die, sometimes before pain, sometimes before remedy.

Such a graceful mien you have, far from your face be the evil eye,
This thought I have conceived - that before your feet I will die.

Although Hafiz's place is not in the chamber of union with you,
Your every feature is fortunate, before each of them I die too.

(W-C 96)
Passion's fire for you, entered a long time ago into our soul,
On account of the void in our heart, into us, that desire stole.

In blood, flowing from the liver, the pupils of the eye drowned;
The fount of love for your face, in our sorrowing chest is found.

The water of life is but a drop from your lip, that sugar-sweet ruby,
The sun's disc but reflects our moon's face, shining so splendidly.

When I heard, "I blew into him My soul", it became a certainty,
That we are absolutely yours and that you are ours, absolutely.

Not made apparent to every heart, is love's great mystery,
The keeper of this secret, the owner of our very soul must be.

You, praising God; explaining faith! Going on and on. Silence!
In both the worlds our faith is being in the beloved's presence.

Until the Last Day be ever thankful for this great favour, Hafiz,
That our guest and comforter, from the First Day, that beauty is.

(W-C 98)
If a load, from one look of its owner, this heart must bear, so be it;
Whatever may have transpired between beloved and lover, so be it.

(W-C 99)
Happy the sight of the one, whose search for fortune led,
To the tavern's corner, and into the house of desire passed.

In a weighty goblet the traveller on the Way found,
The secret of mysteries that the passing world does confound.

Come; hear my words express divine knowledge, implicitly,
For subtleties from the Divine Spirit's bounty passed into me.

From my birth-star look for nothing but profligacy,
Because this deal my birth-star made and passed to me.

You awoke this morning and got out from the wrong side of bed,
Maybe your promise to give last night's wine from your mind fled.

A miracle from a doctor with Jesus breath is all that I am hoping,
I am so shattered this work won't be done just by worshipping.

A thousand thanks that last night from the tavern corner,
Hafiz has passed on to the place of devotion and prayer.

(W-C 101)
O dear, in grief and anguish for me, my beloved has left;
As smoke departs from a fire, so, of my love I was bereft.

Not a cup of joy-exciting love-wine, this drunkard got,
He was just made to taste, in full, harsh separation's lot.

When I became the prey, broken and shattered I was left
In an ocean of grief; that one on a horse just urgently left.

When I said, 'Maybe I will devise a means, the *beloved* to snare.'
That one scared my good-luck steed in eagerness to leave there.

When the blood of my heart found in the heart a deserted place,
My eyes shed rose-coloured tears that in that desert left no trace.

When the slave didn't get the happiness of serving he expected,
He served by just kissing the door step, and then he departed.

When the early morning bird came to the garden of Hafiz,
He cried out to see this rose still in the bud; now gone he is.

(W-C 102)
The narcissus tries to emulate your eye, an excellent eye!
But has no notion of the head's mystery or light in its eye.

You who claw for blood from the open heart of Hafiz,
Do not realise, maybe, that in it God's holy Qur'an is.

(W-C 104)
From seeing the Pir of the Magians, pleasure and joy came,
In the garden of the tavern so splendid the weather became.

At the beloved's feet, heads of the great and generous should be.
Understand this well for to give up this respect is sheer temerity.

Descriptions of paradise and the fame of the house of heaven,
Are just the tavern's menu that the daughter of the grape has given.

Our grace filled heart is trying to find the ruby wine and the cup,
Whilst the miser's search for gold and silver he will not give up.

Before time began a decree on everyone's neck fell,

Either the Kaaba or idol temple; either paradise or hell.

There is no treasure without a snake there, truth to tell,
Mustafa's ministry had the fire and the son of fire [1] as well.

Work! For though pure essence is the jewel of grandeur,
It cannot be inherited, that kind of style and splendour.

In just the same way, by the grace of God, the heart of Hafiz,
Engaged in constant work and effort, day and night always is.

W-C 106
Hafiz drink up! Give up this rationalizing of 'how' and 'why',
When He decreed a thing, what power is in 'how' and 'why'.

(W-C 107)
My heart is tired of the world and all that is therein,
In my heart is only the Friend who dwells within

If your perfume from the rose-bed of union reaches out to me,
Contained by skin, the rose-bud of my heart, for joy cannot be.

The counsel of one who, like me, became crazed in love's way,
Is told in the tale of the simpleton, the stone and the jug of clay.

Tell that pompous puritan, sitting alone, to make less fuss,
Because the curve of the eyebrow is the Mihrab for us.

[1] *Abu Lahab – the enemy of the holy Prophet was known as the 'son of fire'. See Qur'an 111.*

Between the Kaaba and the idol temple the difference is none,
However you turn, whichever way you look, He is there, One.

Being shorn of beard, hair and eyebrow does not a Kalander make,
The Kalander's way is, hair by hair by hair, a careful account to take.

To look like a Kalandar by shaving one's head so easy that is,
The true Kalander, parts with his whole head just like Hafiz.

(W-C 108)
Who speaks of the cypress' form in front of the Friend,
For who lends uprightness to the cypress in the end?

I can form no image of the Friend's cypress-like stature,
For, though splendidly erect, see the cypress' wayward nature.

The image of that cypress stature flows into my crying eye,
Because the cypress stands tall, the flowing river is nearby.

Of that hair, down and mole, the east wind to musk hinted,
It is due to this that musk became so very sweetly scented

One the shining face of that moon, a curved line it does display,
But if it is the crescent moon or eyebrow's curve - who can say.

A thousand precious lives are ransom for the head of that one,
That's a ball in the mallet-sweep of the hair of the beloved one.

From the beloved's mouth seek your heart's desire if you will,
Like Hafiz go not in pursuit of that one's eye with its combat skill.

(W-C 109)
From the moment the call of the beloved reached out to Hafiz,
The mountain of his heart, resonating with it, in desire he is.

(W-C 110)
Every moment a new pain comes to keep us company,
Heartless and soulless companions – justice let there be!

Ghazal 100 (W-C 111)
It is right that to you the country's beauties tribute pay,
For over all those lovely ones your crown holds sway.

Your drunken eyes disturbed both Khataa and Habash[1] alike,
Your locks of hair get tribute from friend and enemy alike.

The whiteness of your face is the daylight's brightness,
The blackness of your hair is deepest night's darkness.

Truly, respite from this love-disease, I can't find;
From you, for my heartache, no remedy do I find.

To the water of Khizr your mouth has given currency;
Over Egypt's sugar your sweet lip gained ascendency.

O my soul! Why do you shatter with hard-heartedness,
A heart that is as fragile as a crystal from feebleness?

Your lip fresh like Khizr; your mouth the water of life in eternity,
Upright cypress stature; hair-thin waist; your chest shining ivory.

In the heart of Hafiz desire has come for a sovereign - *you*,
O heaven grant he be a humble slave of your door's dust too.

Ghazal 101 (W-C 112)
If your religion's law, the taking of a lover's blood is allowing,
Between your law and our law then no difference is showing.

Your black hair - 'the bringer of darkness' it reveals;
Your white face - 'the breaking of the morn' reveals.

No one can escape the noose of your curling lock of hair,
Nor the eye-brow's bow and the arrow that flies from there.


[1]*Khataa – a town in China, and Habash in Saudi Arabia*

From your eye, into the heart, a river of tears is pouring,
So fiercely that, in it, no seasoned sailor can be swimming.
Your lip is the very water of life, the soul's very essence it is,
Wine, for the dust of our existence, its nightly remembrance is.

From your ruby lip a myriad devices barely gained a kiss,
With a hundred thousand pleas my heart's desire was this.

What cup! Your remembrance we drink!
From such a comprehensive cup we drink.

From the lover's tongue prayer for the soul every dawn is,
For as surely as evening follows morning, thus it ever is.

O Hafiz, seek not from me piety, penitence and morality,
In the crazy, wild and profligate lover how could these be?

Ghazal 102 (W-C 113)
See the new moon of Muharram[1]! Ask for a cup wine!
Of the month of peace and the year of security, the sign.

The beggar will not pick a fight with the meanness of the worldly;
Light of my eye! This is the king's war; his salvation, his victory.

Cherish the time of union, blessed that moment surely is,
Like the Night of Power and the Day of Victory[2] it is.

Bring wine, for a prosperous day there is for that one,
Whose morning drink is given by that great lamp, the sun.

How can there be suitable devotions from a drunken one like me,
The evening call and the 'dawn splitter of the sun' are one to me.

[1] *Muharram – the first month of the Muslim calendar, the first ten days are also a time of mourning for the martyrdom of the son of Hazrat Ali. In this month fighting was forbidden (W-C).*
[2] *Day of Victory – the first day after the fasting month of Ramadan.*

O heart, sadly, so careless you are of the work you do,
Lose the key and no one will open that door again to you.

It's the age of Shah Shuja[1], wisdom and law bringing,
Strive for ease of heart and soul, morning and evening.

Extend night into day, in hope of union, just like Hafiz;
For the rose of good fortune blooms where the 'Opener' is.

(W-C 118)
Gaze at the face of the beloved but feel obliged to your eye,
In the work of gazing it does - insight is the intent of the eye.

(W-C 119)
The venerable Imam whose desire was for the long prayer,
Cleaned the religious robe in the blood of the grape's daughter.

Come to the tavern and see how high my station really is,
Though the puritan is always making derisory glances.

(W-C 121)
Hafiz, in that one's fortune seek ease that lasts perpetually,
May the shadow of that one's grace lasting unto eternity.

Bring wine for ever imploring help is Hafiz,
And will do so from the Merciful's bounty.

(W-C 123)
With the absorbed lover God is present in every condition,
But seeing Him as if afar, he cries for help for his situation.

All those clever tricks that reason still employs, Samiri had used,
In spite of the white-hand and rod (of Moses) they were used.


[1]*Shah Shuja – the Sultan of Shiraz.*

(W-C 132)
Powerful deceivers, ignorant of the pearl's worth, pitying we are!
Making the shell equal to the precious pearl persistently they are.

(W-C 133)
Nothing is gained really, except the base metal of money,
The kind of alchemy they try to practice is merely a vanity.

(W-C 134)
Pass on, into the street of the tavern, where is a gathering,
Of those, who, only for you, in their own time, are praying.

In secrecy from unknown enviers, me to you be calling,
Those are wealthy, whose good works they are hiding.

(W-C 135)
Yes, the sun of your good fortune rising you will see,
If the heart's mirror, morning-bright they make it to be.

One flash of your two dark eyes and enough it will be,
To bring death swiftly to broken hearts wherever they be.

(W-C 137)
O watcher pass; and no further arrogance display,
At the Friend's door the dwellers there in dust they lay.

From the expression drawn on Hafiz face, you can see,
That at the door of the Friend, dust covered one must be.

(W-C 142)
Clean deceit from this coat! Where one hue alone is traded,
As worth less than red wine its coloured patchwork is treated.

(W-C 143)
To take one's eyes off the beloved's head and eye you call goodness,
Be gone! To Rends advice like this is completely pointless.

Come rosy cheeked Saki bring wine that's coloured,
For within us no other thought can be preferred.

(W-C 144)
In this Way, what has happened, that every king of spiritual reality,
On the threshold of this court has pressed the head of his royalty.

(W-C 149)
A 'breaker of the covenant' you call me, but you should know,
I fear that title will be yours when for Judgement you depart.
(W-C 150)
It shared my hardships; help and advice it supplied,
And every tender-hearted one for its help applied.

I searched, with tears of pearl trickling from the eye,
In vain they were! To be united was not given to me.
 (W-C 152)
If, in seeking the desired, one is not quick as lightening,
It's no surprise if life's harvest one is quickly consuming.

That bird, who gained affection by heart grieving,
On the branch of its life, joy's leaf never was growing.

In the workshop of love, infidelity finds not any remedy,
Fire consumes no one that is not an Abu Lahab already.

In the religion of soul dealers, refined etiquette is not wanted,
Here, one's breeding counts not; there, no accounting is needed.

In that gathering, in which even the sun is an atom merely,
Do you think one's social airs and graces matter really?

Drink wine! For if, in this world, eternal life is to be found,
Other than in the wine of paradise, nowhere is it to be found.

With heart-hurt Hafiz the beloved may only be united,
On the eternal day that by a night will not be ended.

(W-C 153)
O Hafiz with thy cup come from the quarter of the sun,
If the roll of the dice is cast and that full moon is won.

(W-C 156)
My heart was reminded of a corner of your royal headdress,
When the wind crowned the head of the royal narcissus,

Heart's ease came the night you came to be with me,
With memories of youthful days and friend's company.

(W-C 157)
Every clime has declared and each quarter released the news,
Of your excellent nature, from this may it be your security ensues.

Hafiz speaks words of praise about you with no lack of sincerity,
The universal grace, give you health and your praise speak freely.

(W-C 158)
Don't follow the Samiri, who gold turned into a braying ass,
Left hold of Musa and gone off in search of the calf he has.
(W-C 159)
Let it pass by; this poisonous time that's become so bitter,
And on its return the time of sugar will seem even sweeter.

Patience and Victory are age old friends, you see,
After patience surely comes the time of Victory.

(W-C 164)
Once your look-out shot an arrow into my chest,
In grief for you many arrows hit my unguarded chest.